LEAP

LEAP

A MEMOIR

BRENT LOVE

MANUSCRIPTS
PRESS

LEAP
A Memoir

ISBN   979-8-88926-020-2 *Paperback*
         979-8-88504-362-5 *Hardcover*
         978-1-63676-000-1 *Ebook*

For my family,
Whether brought together by blood, by time, or both, this book is for you.

And for the kid I was once who needed to live and to write this book.

CONTENTS

Not I, not any one else can travel that road for you,
You must travel it for yourself.
It is not far, it is within reach,
Perhaps you have been on it since you
were born and did not know…

—WALT WHITMAN
"SONG OF MYSELF"
Leaves of Grass

"Don't worry about me. Tell your story."

—MOM

AUTHOR'S NOTE

I am no expert on the institution of the Peace Corps. Nor am I an expert on Armenia. There are plenty of experts on both for you to find, listen to, and learn from. What I can offer you here is a taste of what it was like to serve in the Peace Corps and live in Armenia for a brief time. I can give you the glimpse of Armenia that I was given beginning in 2009. I can tell you what it was like to walk the streets of the small, charming towns and villages I lived in, to smell the wind that traveled from snow-capped mountains, to taste herbal tea made from a handful of wild thyme, to feel the warmth of the hot spring in the canyon, to hear the sound of my host family's daughters playing under cherry trees outside my window.

I can also tell you what it was like to come out and, afterward what it felt like for my sense of home to break. I never imagined I would come out and join the Peace Corps at the same time. But I did.

Finally, you should know that I've changed some names of people and places to protect identities. And, in very few cases, scenes were combined for clarity. The stories in this book come from my journals, some research, conversations with experts and old friends, and what I carry with me in my memory. Also, all Armenian spoken and translated for this book is Eastern Armenian, not Western.

PART 1

1

Peace Corps bought me a plane ticket for May 27—a Thursday at 5:30 a.m. I came out three days before I left.

For weeks up to that night, my family and I went through our normal motions. How wild everyday tasks seemed to me in light of the secret I wanted to tell them, a secret I feared would destroy us. Each day, I took a shower. I dressed. I loaded and unloaded the dishwasher. I cleared the kitchen counters. I went to the grocery store by our house to get Blue Bell ice cream and ingredients for my favorite meal, tostadas, which my parents had been sweetly eating almost daily with me without complaint, knowing I was coping with change but without knowing how much.

I walked around the house, my childhood home, over and over, alone. I stood in our home's only hallway, slowly moving between one framed photo and the next. I remembered the day we took the preschool photo, the way it felt to put my arm around my smiling oldest sister, her a toddler with a top ponytail. There was my brother's wedding photo on a day I'd never seen him happier. And the photo of me pushing my youngest sister on a swing, her soft baby hair catching the wind, how it tickled my lips when I kissed the top of her head.

This wall of photos captured years of us. I looked into them as if I could walk through them back into rooms full of our favorite ways of being together. I was struck then by the earnestness of my parents, the pride that propelled them to Olan Mills portrait studios. They wanted to carry that pride with them as if our house was a time machine. As though by looking at the photos they could bring the happiest days of our lives with us into our darkest ones.

I hugged my parents each afternoon when they returned home from work. "I love you," I said. "I'm hugging you every chance I get."

"Oh, Brent," Mom would say and then utter a small gasp that betrayed her leaping heart, which moved in her as if it could jump out of time, out of this time, away from my leaving.

When my parents and sister weren't home, I ran my hand along the walls again, walking through the hallway, through the living room, into the kitchen. Often, I laid my full weight into my dad's armchair and covered hours of anxiety with the balm of mindless television. In the afternoons, I floated in our neighbors' pool with a bowl of frozen grapes and a boombox my parents bought me when I was ten. From it, NPR broadcast stories of the recession. As soon as my mom got off from work each day, she changed into her swimsuit and came to our neighbors' yard. She held her breath and jumped into the deep end. She swam to me, put her arms on a pool noodle and talked to me as if we had nothing but time.

Three nights before I left for Armenia, I cooked dinner, raking refried beans over a hot skillet. I sliced tomatoes. I chopped cilantro. I put tostada shells into the oven to brown.

We ate. We watched something from the DVR. After tostadas, I dipped myself out a bowl with five scoops of cookies-and-cream ice cream.

"Dip me up some, too," my mom said on her way to her room. "I'll be right back."

When my mom came back to the table, she asked about my packing. "Do you think you have enough stuff? Do you have everything you need?"

"I do," I said. "Honestly, I'll be able to buy a lot of things in Armenia. There's a Facebook group with a bunch of volunteers who are currently serving, and they've talked a lot about stuff you can buy and stuff you can't. Sounds like tostadas will be pretty impossible." I lifted a bite of ice cream to my mouth.

She laughed. "You don't have to take it all. If you leave some things, we can mail them to you." Together, we made a list of my favorite foods and favorite things for my parents to send.

"But we may have to choose," Mom said, laughing. "Book or bean dip? Which one?"

I laughed, too, before I answered, "Bean dip!"

This was a sound barely anyone on earth knew, and no one loved as deeply as us—the sound of our laughter mixing in the air.

As she laughed, her mind moved from joy to thoughts of my leaving, and the corners of her mouth turned down, her eyes softening. She pushed ice cream around in the bowl, the rings on her fingers glistening in the dining room light. "I don't want you to go," she said.

"I know, Mom." I held an old spoon, one with tiny leaves that curled into roses at the end of the handle, the texture so familiar to my fingertips.

"You could stay here," she proposed, lifting her voice in the tone I knew meant a joke and a truth at the same time. "You've got a bedroom. You could get a job at the grocery store. You love that place. You can figure out something new. You don't have to work at all! Stay! Write your book!"

"Mom," I pressed. "I have to go... I have to..."

"No, you don't." Her voice became suddenly stern. Demanding even. "That's just not true. No one is making you. You're choosing to go."

"Mom." I used a tone grown from years of both of us letting go of each other. It dropped with exasperation and disappointment but rose with love and gratitude. "I don't want to wake up twenty years from now and wish I'd done it, Mom." I ate another bite of ice cream. I was concentrating now on not crying, concentrating so hard that I forgot to taste the sweet vanilla and the crunchy sugar cookies.

Mom pushed another bite of ice cream into her mouth.

We'd lost the will for dessert at this point. In the bowl was just a frozen reason to stay seated. Together.

"I know," she started again. "But please don't stay there if you're miserable. Please come home." How many times had she said this before?

My dad walked into the living room from the back of the house.

"Is Macey in bed?" I asked, thinking of my twelve-year-old sister in another room.

"Yeah." His eyes darted to my ice cream, and he leaned forward with an exaggerated finger pointed like an old vaudeville actor. "Did you dip any up for me?"

"No." And then, with Macey in bed and both my parents at the table, a weight in my gut seemed to press toward the ground. "But I can."

"Wait for a second," Dad said. "I'm going to take the trash out."

A flash of heat filled my body—a realization. Now. Tonight. My body knew before my mind did. Like a divine bell had just tolled. A signal leaped from my fingers and toes to my ears and eyes, like my cells were delivering the message to each other, all talking at once. My heart rate tripled. My skin flushed with blood.

Suddenly, I knew. We were still here together, and in three days, we wouldn't be. I wanted them to know. When my dad came in from outside, I would tell them I'm gay.

~ ~ ~

I knew I wanted to jump long before I leaped into the canyon. Four years before I left for Peace Corps, I applied for an internship in New Zealand. I hadn't known it was the birthplace of bungee jumping, though gravity pulled me to it. The rush of falling was already part of my dreams.

My parents hadn't wanted me to go, which I understood. No one in my family traveled. I had never traveled. How could I afford it?

"We won't be able to help you," my mom said softly over the phone when I told her my plan to intern at Auckland Church of Christ after my first year at Abilene Christian University. "Financially, I mean. You'll have to go on your own."

I raised the money, sending out letters and preaching at churches.

My mother didn't stay true to her word. She and my father sent the biggest check. Together, we asked everyone we knew if they would send money to help me teach others to love God.

In the end, I'm not sure I taught anyone anything. But I did jump off a cliff.

~ ~ ~

My dad walked out the side door with the white plastic bag about to burst from the weight of garbage left to pile up for too long.

I took another bite of ice cream. Tasteless.

I watched my mom, lost in her own thoughts or simply her own fatigue at the end of what she thought was a fairly normal day. Then, she looked up at me, offering a resigned half-smile before she said, "I better go to bed. I've got drop-off duty at school in the morning." I knew her call time was 6:30 a.m. She'd be getting up at 4:30 a.m. for that.

"Okay," I said. Suddenly, a wave crashed in my head, and I felt the whole of me turn over in the sea. She was getting up to go to bed. I could retreat. I could hide. I could put out the fuse on the bomb in my chest and go deep, deep underground with it. I could skip this night of truth-telling and fling it out into the future, two years away. Hell, I could send this day so far into the future it might never come. I could feel the creaking door open in my heart, and now that Mom was about to leave the room for the night, I could slam my heart shut again. Never tell. Never tell. Never tell. Never tell. Like a pulse running through my veins. Just as quickly as I knew this was the moment to tell them, I knew I didn't have to. This pain was about to come outside for the first time in my life, and I could shove it back in. They didn't know. I could decide to never tell them.

My mom stood up to leave, and then my dad walked back in.

In that brief second of time, I saw them—my mom, my dad, standing there side by side. Just like that, they stood over my bassinet, cooing to me, quieting the panic of my littlest self. Just like that, they stood at the bottom of a white sand dune on a family vacation, waiting for me to slide down so they could catch me. My mom and my dad who planned all the birthday parties of my life, who bought every book I read for eighteen years, who built their lives around me and my sisters and brother. I crawled into their laps after every nightmare. They kissed my cheek when they took me back to bed. And in the days leading up to this moment, I held on to their hugs for so long, so much longer than before, again and again and again and again and again.

"We're so proud of you," they said after every report card.

"We're so proud of who you've become," they said when I graduated from high school with honors and when I graduated from college summa cum laude with honors.

"We're so proud of who you are," they said when I landed at the airport after months in Kolkata, where the money they'd sent with me had built a family a house.

"We're so proud of you," they said when I was thirteen, and I reported two of my middle school bullies who taunted me daily while the band warmed up, cornering me behind the marimbas, the bass, and snare drums, jeering at me, "Are you gay, faggot? Do I make you horny?" Again and again until every kid in earshot was laughing.

These same parents stood in front of me, and for this last second, everything was still the same. And then, it wasn't.

"Dad, Mom, can you hang on for a second? I need to tell you something."

"What?" Mom turned. "Now?"

"Yeah." My chest tightened.

"Wait, is it serious?" My mom shifted forward. My dad tilted his head a bit, his brow furrowing just slightly.

"Yeah."

"Well, okay," Mom said. She moved to sit back in the chair she'd just stood up from. Dad followed her and sat at the end of the table.

I hesitated.

"Come on, Brent." Mom's voice dropped. "Tell us. You've got us sitting here now. Tell us."

And then, what had been my own secret became ours. "I've been attracted to men my whole life."

My mom's hands gripped each other. "What?" she said, her voice sharp and low.

"I've always been attracted to men."

~ ~ ~

Past a sign for Taupo Bungee, I arrived at the railing where suddenly the ground dropped away over a cliffside to a river 165 feet below.

I felt a tap on my shoulder. "Have you signed up yet?" Steve asked, looking up at me through thin gold-framed glasses. Steve, a kind older man from the Auckland church, had driven me here from a men's prayer retreat the church was hosting.

He gestured to an attendant under a sign that read, "Register Here," and as I approached, the attendant asked, "You wanna jump?"

"I think so," I said. I was only nineteen. What did I know?

"Great!" He asked me to fill out a form with my name and vital statistics. "Sign here."

On the form, I caught the words "potentially fatal." And "maimed."

"Okay, now walk over there." He pointed at a wooden walkway. "They'll hook you up to jump."

I handed Steve my camera. Steve told me he remembered a place on the other side of the canyon and left down a trail to a cliff edge where he could take pictures of me falling.

I walked along the wooden deck to the walkway that led to nowhere. I had expected a line of people before me whose jumps would give me belief that this business's equipment did, in fact, work. Instead, no one was there jumping but me.

I turned around to see a young man, blond and handsome, coming up the walkway.

"Okay then," he said. "Let's get you tied in."

~ ~ ~

"How do you know?" my mom said.

"I just do, Mom. I just do." I paused and tried to find her thoughts in her eyes as she stared at me. I went on, "I've prayed a lot. I've read the Bible a lot. And nothing anyone at church says about it makes sense to me."

"But you've dated women. What about Jenny?" she asked.

I sighed. I pressed my hands together and slid them between my knees, my shoulders curling in. "The whole time I was with Jenny, I felt like I was lying to her, that I had a secret that would ruin us, you know." I felt feverish, a heat coming into the room with every breath, filling my chest, warming the backs of my eyes, and pushing to the ends of my limbs.

This is a mistake. I was speaking to my parents now, and simultaneously, I began thinking, *This is a mistake. This is a huge mistake. This is an incredible, huge mistake. What have I done? What have I done? What have I done?*

"Were you being dishonest the whole time?" Mom asked. "You weren't lying?"

"No, Mom. I just wasn't telling the whole truth," I returned.

And she said, "That sounds a lot like lying."

~ ~ ~

When they tie up your feet for bungee jumping, you soon realize you will not be able to do anything to keep from dying. There is no bar to hold, no belt around your waist to keep you from flying out, no button to push to bring you back to safety. There is nothing to hold on to. A stranger is simply tying your feet together and then fixing them to a massive, heavy, elastic cord. And he tells you everything will be fine. Fun, even.

The man stood at the hut's doorway that opened to nothing but air. A small rope at waist level stretched across the opening, not to stop you from falling but simply to remind you that falling was very possible. The young man pushed a button on the wall, which signaled a machine to begin slowly pulling the bungee cord out the door and into the air above the canyon floor.

~ ~ ~

"I guess I just have to figure it out," I said. "I don't really think I'm a Christian anymore. I've always believed God would take it away, but he didn't. And now I don't believe he will take it away. So, I just have to accept it, I think."

"Accept it? Like, be gay?" my mom asked.

"Yeah."

~ ~ ~

The extreme weight of the bungee cord pulled at my feet as if it wanted me to join it in the canyon air. When the full length of the cord was finally dangling below the hut, the young man said to me, "Okay, then. Walk up to the door and put your feet on the white markers."

My breath left me and then returned enough so I could say, "I'm waiting for my friend." Sweat was gathering now under my T-shirt.

The young man looked out through the hut window to the ledge on the other side of the canyon's curve. "Is that him?"

"No," I said without looking. "He just left. He's going to take pictures."

"Are you sure? Is he wearing a red sweater?"

I turned and pretended to look. Yes. Steve was in a red sweater. Frankly, I was not ready to see him there, not ready to jump.

I should take these off, I thought, looking down at my ankle straps. *What am I doing?*

I'd made this decision on a whim. I'd discussed it with no one. I'd asked Steve to drive. No one in my whole life but Steve knew I was jumping. If I died, only Steve would know.

"We can wait," the attendant said and leaned against the opposite wall, putting one foot up on the bench.

~ ~ ~

My parents sat in silence.

"I don't think it's going to change," I said. "I think I just like guys. That's it."

I saw my mom's eyes glisten, the beginning of tears. After a few seconds, she said, "Brent. You know we love you."

"I know," I said. I'd said it quickly, almost to block what she would say next. Her next sentence would be the beginning. The beginning of a time I'd feared my whole life. Into this moment, I carried fear like a stone made by years of tectonic pressure. Everything anyone at church had ever said about homosexuality. Every time the word had been used in a list of damning sins. Every time someone hit me, shoved me, jeered at me for being gay or a faggot or queer. Every adult who let them.

Mom spoke. "You also know what we believe about homosexuality. It's a sin. It's a sin against God."

Her next words came like icy air on my skin, as if the beginning of great wind.

"And…" Her voice was steely now, her eyes wet with held-back tears. "If you choose to live this way, we will have to love you from afar."

And then the cold air rushed, my ears full of the roaring sound of it, my body seizing in fear.

~ ~ ~

Then, as I did every time, I felt afraid but not ready to give up. I threw myself forward in time to the end of my life and thought, *What will I want to say I did right now? When I tell this story, what will I tell them I did?*

And to answer myself, as if I didn't already know he was there, I turned to look out the little hut's window across the ravine to Steve and his bright red sweatshirt.

"Oh." I faked, willing myself to be ready. "I think that's my friend there."

The handsome man at the hut's door to nowhere breathed deeply to keep from rolling his eyes. "Okay," he said, "then stand up and walk to the door. Put your feet on these white markers there."

I stood up. I could only take the tiniest steps with my feet bound, but I was in no hurry. I prayed for good shoe traction because the cord, I guessed, must have weighed hundreds of pounds. With each step, it pulled me closer to the ledge, so far away from a river of some depth I didn't know. I held on to the wall until I could finally put my feet on the two white, sole-shaped markers by the door. I gripped the doorframe, planting my feet firmly on the floor.

"All right," the young man instructed. "There's no rush, but when you're ready, I want you to lean forward and let yourself fall."

I looked out into the void of the canyon, and my head spun. I let go of the doorframe and leaned forward into the air.

There is a point when you can't come back. You've leaned out so far from the edge that there is no clutching again to the frame you were standing in just a breath ago. There is no way to turn around and put your feet on solid ground. You are leaning so far out now that you cannot will yourself back. In that moment, you have an incredible feeling that you've made a huge mistake.

What have I done? That thought unwinds you. *Why would I do this? Everything was fine. What did I come out here for? I was fine. Now, there's nothing. Nothing.*

I could die because of this. And I was fine. I was just fine. A breath ago.

And then, with one more breath, you make a sudden pivot, a negotiation with your own soul.

I can remember the exact moment, the exact view of the cliff and the river unfathomably far below. The tilt of my body away from the door. The feeling of my toes still on the platform. The doorframe too far back to grasp.

And I can remember just a degree of tilt later, thinking, *If this is how I'm going to die, I ought to try to enjoy it.*

With my toes still on the platform, I made a final push away from the edge.

~ ~ ~

Mom and Dad and I sat there in silence for a moment, the three of us not knowing what to say next. My mom kept her eyes on me, rubbed her hands together, and then looked at my dad, whose eyes were turned down to the table. Then she turned back to me.

"Do you still believe in God? Or were you faking it this whole time?"

"No, Mom." My voice was rising now. "I was never faking it. I've never believed anything more. But it just stopped making sense. With all the suffering and all the ways it's so hard for people to be Christian, it just doesn't make sense to me. I mean, I studied theology at a university for four years, for crying out loud. And if being a Christian doesn't make sense to me, I can't continue believing that homosexuality is a sin or that God is going to take it away."

She was wringing her hands in her lap. "This is poison, Brent. Don't let Satan get a hold of you. Satan is trying to poison your heart. If you don't try to stop it, it will destroy your life. And it will hurt the people around you. Like it's hurting us now."

Any brave composure I'd maintained crumbled then, and I doubled over. All the air in my body left me in a deep, painful moan. I brought my hands to my face. Tears pushed themselves suddenly out onto my palms and down my cheeks. I fell over until I was bent in half, my palms still on my eyes, the back of my hands on my knees.

"Brent," Mom demanded. "Brent, sit up."

I sat up. She had suddenly stopped crying. She looked at me, cold. "This is what you wanted. You brought this up."

I stared at her, my insides twisting and twisting.

My dad spoke at last and said, "Brent, I believe in God. I believe in God's son, Jesus, and I believe he died for our sins so that our sins would be atoned for and we can have eternal life with him. And I believe in the Bible. I believe the answer to your problem is biblical.

"I'm not smart enough to know everything there is to know about the Bible," he kept going. "I haven't even read the Bible as much as you have. I've always admired that about you. But I believe in the Bible. And that's it. It says it in the Bible. I don't remember exactly where. But I know it does. Homosexuality is a sin. It says it in the Bible. And that's where we stand."

This was a mistake, I thought. *You idiot. You stupid fucking idiot.*

My mom looked at me. "Brent, I need you to know that if you decide to pursue this lifestyle, we can't let you spend time with your sister." I thought of my nearly teenage sister, asleep just down the hall in her room. "We will have to love you from afar."

My tears flowed now slow and steady.

"I have to go to bed," my mom said. She got up and quickly walked away from me toward her room.

My dad and I looked at each other from across the table. "We love you," he said. As he got up to walk out of the room, he put his hand on my shoulder and squeezed. "We'll get through this."

He walked to his bedroom.

I sat alone in the dining room, the light gone from my body. I walked to the bedroom that would only be mine for two more nights. I lay on the bed, face into the pillow, exhaling slowly into the fibers and inhaling my own breath back in until my head began to spin.

~ ~ ~

There are not many ways to experience falling. If you trip and fall, you are on the ground before you realize what's happening.

I'd heard that the bungee cord saves you, but you can't really know that until you feel it. When you're free-falling, you can do nothing to save your own life.

You can only fall. You can only feel the air rushing over your face and neck and arms and belly, between your legs, over your back, tossing your hair wildly. You can only see impressions of the ground, the walls of the cliffside around you, the water below, and perhaps the sky above. And you do consider the horrible truth that you might have been wrong all along, that, despite what you wished for, you might smash into smithereens.

I remember, even now, the rush of air and color. I remember, even now, the bright happiness that filled my body, the total release of myself. My cells lit up like stars.

I also learned that when you bungee jump, you don't fall just once. You fall over and over again. You experience the ripping away of the ground from your feet only once, but when the cord stretches out, it does so slowly, tension building until it finally pulls you back up into the air to nearly the same height as when you left the ledge. You fall again, and then you're pulled up again. Then you fall again, then back up again, over and over until finally you hang there by your feet, hands over your head.

A small raft putted along the river, and I was lowered head first into it. Attendants unhooked my feet and unbound them before bringing me to shore.

Steve and I walked up the cliff-face's snaking path to the stand where I'd signed up to jump. When I'd first arrived, I'd barely registered that after you bungee, you could buy a recording of your jump. I walked up to a wall of TVs next to the registration stand, and people were already laughing.

"We watched you jump," one boy said, fingering the end of his sweatshirt sleeve. "We wanted to come watch the video." The teenagers all looked around with shy grins while the video reloaded to start again.

On the TV, I saw myself fall, heard my scream, saw the cord stretch out, and pull me back up again. After a few more bounces, I was hanging upside down with my hands in the air and my shirt gathered at my chin, white belly exposed.

The jump had only been minutes ago. I didn't remember myself laughing, but there in the video, I was laughing from my gut. I was laughing in a way I'd never heard myself laugh before.

The small crowd around my video giggled at my hysterical laugh. I did, too, and so did Steve.

I sounded like a wild man.

2

I missed my connecting flight to Philadelphia, eating a personal pan pizza and staring at the wrong gate.

I hadn't slept the night before leaving, and with no phone and only a paper ticket to guide me, I'd missed the fact that the flight had moved to another gate. After sorting it out with the airline, I arrived so late to Philadelphia that I'd missed all but the last hour of our first group meeting as Peace Corps volunteers. I sat down at a table in a hotel conference room full of forty or so strangers just in time to hear one official say, "Tomorrow, you'll receive your tickets from here to Vienna and then to Yerevan. If you don't make your connecting flights, we will assume you are not fit to manage yourself in a foreign country, and we will terminate your service."

The next morning, on the flight to Vienna, my mind paced. I ate breakfast on my seatback tray, my arms folded like a velociraptor. I picked at my food, anxious about what I'd just left behind, running the days in my mind over and over. After a flight attendant picked up my meal, I took out my journal and wrote about what happened at home and what happened next.

After I came out, we had two days together before I left, and in those two days, my parents made space between us.

They went to bed early to avoid talking. They walked almost silently through the house in the morning. One day, I took lunch to my mom's third-grade classroom at school, and she cringed and pulled away when I tried to hug her.

I worried I would break more things, so I didn't tell anyone else. Not my friends who called to wish me well. Not my older brother in West Texas. Not my oldest sister, who lived across town. Not my youngest sister, who was still home with us, attending junior high school during the day and navigating a strangely quiet house at night.

The night before I left, I packed my bags, stuffing hot clothes from the dryer into a hiking backpack. I stacked books on top of the clothes and then toiletries. I slid family photos I'd printed at Walmart next to my computer and then jammed in a small collection of wall outlet converters, the prongs stabbing at the walls of the bag.

I walked to the bathroom and could see that a light was still on in my parents' room. I could hear them talking softly. I brushed my teeth, thinking that our last real conversation had been a mistake.

I'd felt a roiling in my chest, an anxiety that hardened into an immovable lump in my throat. I wanted to do something, anything, to feel better and calm myself.

What I chose to do next was something my mom would have done.

Throughout my childhood, Mom left notes for me. She hid them in lunchboxes, in books she knew I'd later read, in my top drawer when I moved into my freshman college dorm.

I went to the kitchen, found a stack of pink Post-it Notes and a pen, and put notes everywhere.

"I love you. Love, Brent" in the silverware drawer.

"Are you thinking of me?" in the refrigerator's vegetable crisper.

"I miss you so much!" rolled up and tucked into the bottle of ibuprofen.

"You are so, so special!" wrapped around the base of my sister's toothbrush.

"Pick up the phone and call me!" into the inside pocket of my mother's purse.

Close to 4 a.m., I heard my dad's radio alarm blare suddenly. He got out of bed and found me in the living room. In the dark, we quietly took my bags to the back of his truck.

I hesitated in the driveway.

"We got them all," my dad said, pointing to my bags.

"I know," I said. "I just want to check one more time."

Looking back at the house, every wall, every texture and color and contour of the house became electric with memory.

I walked and then nearly ran to my parents' bedroom. I stopped, eased open the door, and walked into the darkness.

"Mama," I whispered. I looked at her, asleep on the bed under a thin blanket.

"Mama," I whispered again, softly touching her shoulder.

She shuddered and then opened her eyes.

I looked down at her, but instead of leaning in for a hug, like any other time in our lives, I waited for an invitation, tears filling my eyes.

"Oh, honey," she said. "Come here."

I leaned into her, her arms around me, my oldest memory.

"Oh, Mama, I'm sorry." Tears left my eyes, slid down my cheeks and onto the shoulder of her nightshirt.

"I know," she said, the covers still drawn up. "You don't have to go. You can stay. You don't have to leave."

"I have to go." I leaned down to hug her then. "I have to go now."

She stroked my hair. "I know." Her voice shuddered in a cry. She pulled back, sitting up now, looking at me with the smile I recognized—a smile not fully realized, a veneer over pain.

"I've known for a while you'd leave," she said. "But Brent, if you're miserable, promise me you'll come home. I can't stand the idea of you miserable and trying to stay anyway."

"Okay, Mom. I promise. I love you."

"I love you, too, Brent. So very, very much. Now go."

On the flight from Vienna to Yerevan, I couldn't sleep. I checked the flight path simulator on the seatback screen in front of me and watched a digital plane trace a line from Austria to Armenia. The unknown scared me, even more so now, feeling that I'd broken something by coming out before I left. Was this a mistake now, leaving home and trying to live for two years in a place I didn't know?

Ever since its founding in 1961, Peace Corps has asked volunteers to serve two-year terms of service in countries all over the world. My two-year term of service in Armenia would start after ten weeks of language and skills training. On the plane, I couldn't stop my thoughts from racing between an idea that the next two years would heal something in me and another idea that spending two years in Armenia after coming out would be a huge mistake.

I ran through reasons to stay anyway.

Because I didn't have another place to go.

Because even though I'd given up on my ministry degree at Abilene Christian University, even though being Christian no longer made sense to me, I still wanted to do something good in the world and make something good out of my life.

Because I didn't give up on things that mattered to me.

On the plane I thought of the nonprofits and schools and other groups who applied to have Peace Corps volunteers come work in their organizations. I'd signed up to help. I would stay, I told myself, until I felt like I had nothing left to give.

In a sleepy stupor, under the fluorescent light of the Zvartnots International Airport, I staggered to the customs desk, where a man spoke to me in words I didn't understand. He grimaced at my grimy appearance and stamped my passport.

Exiting with my bags down a final long hallway into the dark morning, I heard shouting, cowbells, and clapping.

Voices bounced up the long ramp to a parking lot, yelling, "Welcome! Welcome! Welcome to Peace Corps!"

One woman's sign read "Welcome to Peace Corps" with the dove from the Peace Corps logo flapping with the posterboard. Another sign said, "Welcome, A-17s!" and had a mountain drawn onto it in crayon.

I boarded the charter bus last and took the only seat left in the back. A frenzy of chatter took over, but I stayed quiet. A world I'd never seen before passed by in the window as we drove. New sights—styles of buildings, signs in the Armenian alphabet, a dusty sunrise light passing through boulevard trees—all tickled a part of me that saw in them a hope to discover a new place in the world and a new way to be myself in it.

The bus drove us to ruins of an old cathedral. Still exhausted, we followed the current Peace Corps volunteers off the bus, where stray dogs greeted us in the early morning light.

"This is Zvartnots," an Armenian man in a suit told us. He wore a badge that identified him as Peace Corps staff. "And you're lucky today. The sky is clear, and you can see Ararat."

A few people turned around. Fewer people let out an audible gasp of delighted surprise. I squinted into the distance, ignorant as to why we should care about this mountain.

"Welcome to Armenia!" he said. Everyone cheered. We took a group picture on the stairs.

And that was it. The leaving was over. I was simply here now. Here in Armenia. I wasn't leaving home anymore. From this moment on, I'd already left.

3

We spent our first days in a hotel outside a town called Charentsavan. As A-17s, the seventeenth group of Peace Corps volunteers in Armenia, we attended orientation sessions and ate meals together.

In that time, I had one crush—the first of my life that I tried to enjoy instead of deny. He was a young Armenian named Tigran who played volleyball with us in the afternoons. He singled me out, called out to me in the few Armenian words I had picked up in my first days, words like "Barev" and "Vonc es?" Each day, we'd shake hands, and he'd put his strong arm around me while we strolled the hotel grounds.

During our last game of volleyball, he accidentally spiked the ball into my face. He ran to me and put his arm on my shoulder. He spoke words I couldn't understand. He looked to me from below his unified brow, his big brown eyes wet with concern. After he returned to the game, I sat on the edge of the sand, embarrassed. The last time I saw Tigran was at the end of that game, him walking off with the other Americans to get sodas from a nearby shop.

As new volunteers, we were told we'd spend the summer in villages surrounding Charentsavan, learning Armenian and attending training courses in our assigned sectors. English teacher volunteers would be given pedagogy. Environmental protection volunteers would study Armenian geography, natural resources, and environmental threats. As community and business development volunteers, we'd learn engagement strategies and Armenian culture.

Peace Corps staff led sessions on the operations of the organization. How we would be placed with host families during summer training. How, after summer training, we would be assigned to a permanent site with a permanent job and required to live with a new host family for ten weeks. After that, we could find our own places or stick it out with the families we'd been assigned. How Peace Corps compensated our host families in an amount I never learned, and how we would receive a stipend for food, water, shelter—bills of any kind—in an Armenian bank account in Armenian dram that totaled about three hundred US dollars per month.

We were told that we weren't allowed to travel outside of our town without permission from the Peace Corps office in Yerevan. That meant some of us would be the only Americans we saw for long stretches of time while others who were placed in towns with a few other volunteers would have the comfort of American camaraderie. We learned how to contact the Peace Corps doctors in case of illness or injury, and we learned that certain conduct would get us removed from Peace Corps after an assessment of Peace Corps staff, though what acts fell into "certain conduct" would remain, for the most part, unclear.

After our final morning of sessions, all volunteers and Peace Corps staff dressed in the best outfits we'd brought and went outside into a warm midday, sweating in our suits and dresses. Garine, the Peace Corps training manager, asked all the volunteers to line up in front of the crowd of Armenian families who were each selected to host one of us for the summer. She called our names one by one.

"Brent Love," Garine pronounced my name loudly over the crowd. "You'll be living with Mikayel and Talin in the village of Teghenik."

Teghenik. The name had a letter in it that we don't have in English, ŋ written in roman characters as gh. I remembered our language teacher just yesterday telling us to roll it up to the roof of our mouths like the French.

A couple stepped forward, a man and woman in their forties. Talin wore a maroon blouse. Her curled bangs leaned over her eyes as if to shade them. Mikayel looked older, but his athletic windbreaker and casual, "Barev," gave me the suspicion that he carried a perennial youthfulness.

Peace Corps staff gave us carnations to give to our host parents, and I walked up to them both with the bundle. I said, "Barev dzez." *Hello*. I handed Talin the flowers.

"Shnorhakalutyun!" Talin said, deliberately slowly, with a wide smile and bright eyes. She nodded, looking at me to see if I even understood her "*Thank you*."

I clasped my hands together and smiled, trying to nod back to her in a way that said, *I'm delighted. I'm nervous.*

After every volunteer name had been called, Garine dismissed us, speaking first to the Armenian families and then speaking to volunteers in English saying, "You are now free to leave with your host families. They will take you to their houses and help you to settle in. Good luck, and we wish you a great summer."

Garine clapped, which signaled more clapping from other staff and rippled out to the crowd of strangers who would now live together for months.

Talin spoke to Mikayel in words I didn't understand, no smile in her eyes, seriousness, a job before them.

She said something to me in Armenian and mimed a person carrying a suitcase. She looked to me with kind eyes, like those meant to reassure children.

"Ah," I said. I held up one finger, a gesture I hoped would say, *One minute, please,* and went to gather my luggage.

Talin continued to try speaking to me, her voice ringing with a code I couldn't decipher but with music I could feel.

I smiled in the sun that came through their Lada window, the white SUV taking the three of us out of Charentsavan and down a road into a valley shaped like a bowl with golden grass waving in the afternoon sun. We turned right after a church and passed a sign with the village name, driving up a slope so steep it threw me to the back of my seat.

Mikayel parked the car at a building in the fork in the road. Talin climbed out and then waved to me while calling into the building.

A large bubble-lettered sign hung above the door with the word—KHANUT. *Store.* Underneath it, a teenager emerged, a young man in skinny black jeans and a black T-shirt that slimmed his already slim frame. He stepped out proudly in pointy black shoes.

Talin spoke again in words I didn't understand. She pointed to the store and then to herself. Then she pointed to Mikayel and back to the store. She raised her eyes to me expectantly. She didn't speak English. It seemed no one in her family did. So, she was trying another way to communicate because I didn't speak Armenian.

I understood. This was their store. I repeated the sequence, pointing to her, to Mikayel, and then to the store. "Ayo," she said, delight in her voice. "Ayo!"

She repeated the same pointing pattern between herself and Mikayel and pointed to the young man. This was her son.

"Aaaaaaah," I said. I shook his hand.

"Hakob," Talin said

"Barev, barev," Hakob said in a low tone that betrayed his effort to sound older than he was. When we shook hands, he broke character, smiling as brightly as his mother.

They spoke to each other again, and then Talin went into the store. She came out with potatoes, tomatoes, and cucumbers.

We climbed back in the car and took the road that continued up the mountainside.

In just a few minutes, we stopped at a gate made of two giant sheets of metal lined along the top with tiny prongs shaped like sword tips. Talin got out of the car and swung the gate open. We parked, and as I pulled my bags from the car, I looked up to the porch, where a girl, maybe thirteen, stood on the steps. Talin yelled to her, gesturing sharply up the stairs. The girl smiled an embarrassed smile and turned, walking quickly out of sight.

The house had the quality of something handcrafted, stones mortared together one at a time, steps made of concrete with large pebbles and rocks visible in the hard mix. A rail made of wrought iron and rebar ran up the staircase and around the porch. Above the rail clothes hung to dry, pinned up and heavy with water.

A woman older than Talin walked out, drying her hands with a dishtowel.

"Barev dzez," she said to me, so nervous she nearly shouted her greeting. *Dzez* I knew was an addition to hello that, when used to address just one person, meant deference or respect for you as an elder, a boss, a superior. My language teacher at the hotel told me that word was reserved for elders or powerful community members.

I shrank, curled my shoulders in embarrassment. *I'm younger than her*, I thought. *Why was she saying "dzez" to me?*

I offered it back. "Barev dzez."

I extended my hand and took hers, which was wet with dishwater. She grinned in a way that felt clumsy with an effort of kindness. Her shoulders were broad under her red sweater thanks to shoulder pads. I could feel the strong muscles of her hands, the skin on them thick, the joints knobby.

"Anun?" I asked her. *Name?*

"Lala."

I turned from her and met the girl, Sona, Talin and Mikayel's other child. Sona approached my handshake with a shy smile, her shoulders curling in.

Carrying my bags, Talin and Mikayel walked me through a doorway with two skinny French doors that were paneled in glass.

Talin waved as she entered the room, speaking Armenian and pointing to a wardrobe with a dingy mirror in the center. She opened its doors to an empty shell with hangers on a pole at the top. She pointed to my bags.

"Ayo?" she asked.

"Ayo," I smiled. I could tell she wanted me to unpack my things and store them there.

"Shnorhakalutyun," I said. *Thank you.*

Talin gestured in turn to the bed and then to the one electric socket under the one window.

"Lav?" she said, bracing herself for my response. *Good?*

"Lav," I said. "Lav. Lav. Lav." I didn't know yet the words for "very" or for "I'm so grateful."

The rest of the family had been watching us from the doorway, and Talin shooed them out of sight. She closed the two skinny French doors behind her and left me alone in the room.

I stood for a few minutes, taking in the cement walls, the tangy smell of grass and earth, the silky comforter on the bed, which bowed in the middle, and my wavy reflection in the cloudy wardrobe mirror.

I walked up to my reflection and scanned stickers that had been stuck to the glass. This was Hakob's room, I guessed. I saw bare-chested men wearing leather underwear and wide leather cuffs. The WWF symbol was in the corner of nearly all of them. In another sticker, a bare-chested cyborg, Arnold Schwarzenegger, stared with a bright red laser eye, his bottom half ripped off by someone trying to remove his image from the mirror.

I could never, I thought. Not with stickers of muscle men in leather underwear. Not Arnold. My interest in them would have gone farther than idolization to lust. I couldn't have handled the pressure of hiding my sexual interest in them and never would have allowed myself to put pictures of men like this up in my room. Yet here I was, in a room where someone had already put these images up. I chuckled to myself at the irony of it.

I fell onto the bed and stared out the window. The air of the room, which smelled of an overripe mixture of sweet grass, laundry, and wet fur, fell cool on my bare arms, my neck, and face. I was caught suddenly, overwhelmed by the sense that I'd passed through a threshold and arrived at a moment I'd dreamed of.

I'd wanted to live somewhere far away, in a place utterly foreign to me. And I'd done it. I'd gone to a country I didn't even know existed until I received my Peace Corps invitation letter.

Months ago, on the day after Christmas, my family went to our cars to drive to Barnes & Noble. On a whim I went to the mailbox and found, with some surprise, my Peace Corps invitation packet with my country assignment inside. I pulled open the envelope and read the welcome letter.

"I don't know where Armenia is," I'd said. I was shocked. This was before anyone had smartphones and could simply google it. We all still had flip phones or tiny handsets.

My mom could hear the panic in my voice, the fear of the unknown. "Well, we're going to the bookstore," she said. "We can find it!"

When we arrived, my sisters, my brother and his wife, and my parents threw themselves into searching the bookshelves. They shouted out to each other, "Did you find it?" and then, "Not yet!"

"I found it." I heard my mother's voice and ran around a shelf. I found her with arms at her side, shoulders low, a frown, and eyes wet with a well of tears.

"You aren't going. You aren't going, Brent. I won't let you."

"Mom, what are you talking about."

"Brent... it's next to Iran."

She held out a book to me with a map. I'd studied international politics in college. I had just finished a BA in political science in 2007, just two years before. I'd taken an entire semester to study terrorism, and still, the only thing on my mind was the impression of the Middle East I knew many of my friends and family held in their hearts—a fear of Muslims, a fear of terrorists, a fear of being attacked by a foreign power you couldn't understand. And I knew my mom was afraid that the rumors were true and that I'd move to the Middle East where something bad could happen.

Mom put her head in her hands and walked away.

"I just don't know anything about it," I said.

I looked up at my sister, Lisa, with tears in my eyes.

"Oh, brother," she said. She hugged me. "It will be okay."

"I know," I lied. "It's just crazy. Like, I'm about to move to a country that I didn't even know existed until right now."

She was still there, my sister. She was less than twenty minutes away from that Barnes & Noble while I lay on my bed in Armenia and stared out the window at golden grass waving at the summer sky. I was on the other side of the planet.

I went to my suitcase and took out a vacuum-sealed bag of Puppy Chow my aunt sent with me. She made this snack for me every holiday—Rice Chex cereal covered in peanut butter, chocolate, and powdered sugar. Before I left, she handed me two bags to pack in my suitcase.

I took a pair of scissors and cut it open, immediately filling the air with sweet powder. This was the smell of every family holiday. It was the smell of the ride home from Lometa, Texas, where my aunt and uncle lived next door to my Grandmom. It was the smell of packages sent for my birthday or packages sent as a surprise during college in Abilene.

I walked out of my room and into the kitchen, where Lala stood over a sizzling pan and Sona sat idly at the table.

Sona saw me, stood up straight, and patiently said a few words to me I couldn't understand. "Inch es uzum?"

I shrugged, smiled, and made a sign with my hands, hoping to convey a bowl, and then pointed to the snack my aunt made.

"Aah," Sona said with a finger raised into the air and went to the kitchen. She came back with an ornate bowl with a filigreed rim and a pedestal at the bottom. Inside it, painted pastel people sat among yellow and green trees. Sona set the bowl down on the coffee table and held out her hand for the food I'd brought. She poured the contents into the bowl, making a little sugar cloud puff up between us.

"Surj es uzum?" she said. "Surj?"

Coffee. I knew this word. "Voch." *No.* And then I asked, "Talin? Lala? Hakob?"

"Mi rope," Sona said. She left the couch, calling out to her family. Talin and Hakob walked into the living room and sat down. Lala followed, wiping her wet hands on the apron tied to her waist.

"Mikayel?" I asked.

"Voch," Talin said, smiling. She pointed at the wall toward the center of town. "Khanut," she said.

Store, I thought. And then wondered if every night someone was missing from home to sit at the store.

With everyone else seated, I gestured to the bowl of Puppy Chow. I wanted them to taste a flavor that felt like a piece of my life—a piece I'd carried from Texas.

Now, in Teghenik, this was the first bridge I tried to build. I pointed again to the bowl.

Talin picked a piece up between her fingers. She looked to her daughter and then to her son. She smiled and put it in her mouth.

"Oooooh," she said, her smile growing.

"Lavn e?" I said. *Is it good?*

"Ayo, ayo," she said, nodding and exaggerating her enthusiasm to help me understand.

All of us put our hands in the bowl then. Everyone smiled as they ate. Hakob began miming ecstasy with each bite, performing a simple comedy for us. After all the coming out, the flights across the planet, the days among strangers, Hakob's miming, and the family giggles felt like a kindness to me, a welcome, a joy.

As we ate, just like every holiday with my family at home, tiny snow drifts of powdered sugar began to form under our chins on our shirts.

4

Talin and Mikayel's house seemed to hang on the eastern slope of Teghenik. A dirt road passed their property and evaporated into the grassy hillside.

The seven other volunteers assigned to Teghenik were sprinkled through the community with other families. Shannon lived next door with Talin's nieces, who shyly smirked during our nearly daily nardi (*backgammon*) games while they absolutely crushed me. Aaron from Chicago had already started dating a young woman from Yerevan before we arrived. Sarah and I bonded over growing up in Texas, and Amanda offered TV shows she'd saved on her hard drive before coming. I hardly ever talked to Landon because he rarely said anything kind about Armenia. And Hayley whom I'd become friends with online before arriving and who eventually came over to Talin and Mikayel's house attempting to train their dog with a clicker she used with her mutt at home.

And then there was Zoe.

Zoe shared a Snickers with me before language class and told me that while growing up in Maine, the parents of another kid at school called her parents to accuse her of being a witch and putting a curse on their daughter.

"It just wasn't true," she told me. "I'd never have cared enough to put a curse on her."

The eight of us went everywhere together. We walked to our daily language classes and rode in vans together to our twice weekly training days in Charentsavan. We called each other in the afternoons and met at each other's houses in our free time. Our new relationships took on a kind of fervor, and we talked for hours about each other's families and how hard it was to leave them, though I kept my coming out story to myself.

We rode into training days in Charentsavan together, and on one day, the Peace Corps Armenia assistant director opened the floor for any comments before we went back to our villages.

Kevin, who lived in another village in the valley stood and walked to the front of the room where thirty or so of his fellow PCVs stared back at him. His hand passed over his mustache and mouth before falling into his other hand, where he held them and began to speak.

"I just want to talk about this now so everyone knows," Kevin said. "I'm gay. I don't mind you guys knowing, but I plan on keeping this a secret from my host family and my village. I would really appreciate you keeping this to yourselves. I've heard that it's not really well-received in Armenia, and honestly, I think it'll be easier and maybe even safer for me to be in the closet around Armenians. So, please help me do that."

The assistant director stepped next to him and patted Kevin on the shoulder. "Thank you for sharing that, Kevin."

In the front row, another volunteer, Peter, rose slightly from his chair and looked over his shoulder to speak to the group. "I'm also gay, and I would appreciate your help in keeping that part of my life hidden. I really don't want it to affect my service. Thanks."

Zoe stood up next. "So, hi, everyone." She smiled. "I'm also part of the LGBTQ community, and I think I speak for all of us in the group when I say that it isn't easy to be queer in Armenia." She laughed. Everyone comfort-laughed with her. "We're all here together to help the communities we live in, and it really means a lot to have your support. And if you have any questions on how to do that, I'm happy to talk."

A couple of people stood up to say they were straight but also committed to supporting the LGBTQ volunteers in our group.

I did not stand up. I didn't have words to share yet.

Telling my parents had gone so much worse than I thought it would, and I wasn't ready to process the reactions from this entirely new group of people.

But that afternoon, I considered telling Zoe. I needed someone around me to know. I'd held the truth in for so many years until just a few weeks ago. I needed the truth to stay outside my body.

The next morning, during our language class break, Zoe was in the yard of the schoolhouse eating sunflower seeds. I asked if I could eat lunch with her after classes finished.

"Oh, sure," she said, flicking away an empty seed shell. "I'm on my own today. My host family is in Yerevan, so I'm just making lunch for myself. You can come over and eat whatever I throw together."

I walked to the khanut and told Talin that I'd be eating lunch with Zoe, saying clumsily in Armenian, *"I eat now with friend. Zoe."*

When I arrived at Zoe's host family's house, Zoe was cooking an egg in a pan on the stove in the kitchen. She sliced tomato and cheese. She'd taken off her blazer and stood cooking in an aquamarine tank top. Her tattooed arms swung over the stove and countertop, her movements wide and fast. The low cut of the tank top revealed part of an eye tattoo on her chest.

While she cooked, she told me about her home in Maine, her dad's farm, her mom's house in the Sufi commune, and their family cabin on the coast.

I told her about Texas, about my small town, about my Christian college in the dusty plains.

"Well, that sounds… very interesting!" She tilted her head and laughed. "Sorry, I just know so little about that part of the country, but I hear there are a lot of guns and not a lot of gays."

I laughed.

"So, I actually wanted to talk to you about something," I said.

"Oh," she said. "You have an agenda."

"I do." I thought, *a gay agenda*. But I couldn't brave the joke. "You said you're bisexual. Right?"

"Yeah," she said. "At least last time I checked."

I took a breath. "Well, I came out to my parents three days before I left to come here."

Zoe looked at me. Her eyes went wide. She smiled and stopped moving for a moment. She let the air fill with my remark.

"Wow," she finally said. "Just, wow." She leaned toward me in her chair.

"Yeah," I said, "and it did not go well."

When I told her my parents' reaction, Zoe came around the table. "Okay, can I give you a hug?" she asked. She held me in her arms in the first hug I'd had since I left home.

We talked for the rest of the afternoon. Zoe ate her eggs and listened to all of it, her eyes on mine, pausing her eating when it looked like I might cry. At the end of my telling, she said I would be all right. She said I had a friend now. She said I'd make a lot of friends who would love me.

"You aren't alone," she said. And together we finished lunch.

~ ~ ~

At the next training day in Charentsavan, the grey-suited Peace Corps assistant director advised us that now was the time to quit.

"If you're going to quit," he said, "the summer is the time to figure that out before you move to your permanent site. We want what's best for you, and we also don't want you to waste the American investment and disappoint our Armenian partners."

Some volunteers did quit, most making an announcement of it during a training day.

No volunteers living in Teghenik quit. We'd been put in the training village together because we'd all been recruited as community and business development volunteers. Stubbornness and a sense of American boot-strapping were strong within our group. I felt I didn't belong among a group that confident, but I couldn't consider quitting on a dream I'd had since childhood.

In my earliest days, I assumed the whole world was just like my small Texas town. For most of my childhood, I would have told you that everywhere on earth was covered in oak trees with wiggly trunks like those I lay under in the summer, stretched out in the front yard on an old quilt with a book and a large glass of ice water. I would have said that every child goes to school with libraries and PE and bologna sandwich lunches packed in a plastic box with their favorite cartoon on the front and very often a note from their mom inside. I assumed kids everywhere ate Taco Bell and goulash and sandwiches, their dads taking them for donuts on Saturday morning. I thought every other kid in the whole world put on stiff clothes on Sundays and sat in between their parents on a bouncy church pew, falling asleep while their mother rubbed their hair.

This changed during a summer trip to the library before the painful years of middle school when I checked out *The Voyages of Doctor Dolittle*. After a few chapters, I began whispering to crows, to roly-polies, or to lightning bugs I caught in cupped hands at dusk. Had any adult caught me, I would have told that adult I was just pretending. Really, though, I was experimenting with the world because if a person really could talk to animals, you wouldn't want to miss out simply because you didn't try.

And then, at the end, Doctor Dolittle and his animal gang of jibber-jabberers crawled inside a giant snail and traveled under the ocean to a land of people that lived in utterly different ways than either the Doctor or I had imagined was possible. And suddenly, I understood travel.

The snail trip activated a flood of insight, and I immediately began to wonder what was in the world that I didn't know existed. And did some people live in ways I couldn't imagine?

When I read my Peace Corps invitation letter, I had never considered that my assignment could be a post in Armenia solely because I didn't know the country existed. And now, I was living my childhood dream in one of Armenia's smallest villages, walking its sloping dirt roads that clung to a mountainside above a golden valley.

Teghenik was hundreds of people living on a slope so steep it was nearly a cliff. My time in Teghenik was mostly spent in one of two places—the school, vacant for summer, where we had our five-hour language classes or my host family's khanut. I learned the Armenian word for shop, "khanut," early, and my host family's khanut became the center of my life in Teghenik.

When language class ended at midday, I would finish lunch at the house and then follow Hakob down the sloping road to his afternoon shift with my Armenian study packets in my cross-body messenger bag.

Hakob would take a seat behind the cash register, and I would sit next to him, pulling out workbooks full of verb tenses and noun declensions, balancing the work on my lap. When a customer entered the store, I listened to Hakob speak to them. I tried to pick up words. I waited anxiously for attention to turn to me and for Hakob to introduce me.

"*Hello*," I'd say in Armenian.

"Barev," a customer would say back, eggs or butter or beer in hand. Or, if empty-handed, I'd hear words I didn't understand as a customer asked for groceries. Hakob would then often reach behind and scoop out sunflower seeds or sugar or something else, weighing a bag on a scale next to the register.

"*Where are you from?*" the customer might say to me in Armenian.

"Amerikatsi em," I'd return.

"*Oh, America?*" they'd reply. And then, "*What are you doing here?*" or "*You speak Armenian?*" or, perhaps referencing the city with the highest Armenian population outside Armenia, "*My family member is in America. In Glendale. Do you know it?*"

Eventually, orange light from the setting sun would ease in through the khanut door, and a cow would walk into the view, followed by another and another. I'd walk outside, lean on the khanut's stucco wall, and stand on the porch to watch the cows come down from the mountain and turn onto one street or another on their way home to eat hay and sleep in a barn and be milked in the morning.

Often, an owner would wait outside the khanut, watching for their particular cow so they could escort her home. Eventually, my family's cow, brown with black eyes, would saunter in front of the khanut porch, and Hakob or Sona or Talin would be there to walk the cow up the mountain to its stall in the basement under my room.

I'd never seen cows come home and had never understood the idiom said most often in my home about love. "I'll love you 'til the cows come home," my mom would say, which I perceived to mean forever.

In Charentsavan, during a training day break, I emailed my parents about these cows and the pleasure of watching them during each sunset. Weeks later, I received a letter from Grammi, my mother's mother. From Louisiana, she sent an old black and white photograph of her aunt and her aunt's cow, its udder swollen so large the skin was taut.

"We used to wait for the cows to come home every night," Grammi wrote. "And the cow would be moaning to be milked!"

"She loved that you got to see the cows come home," my mother wrote later in an email. "She remembered her childhood. She was so excited to share that photo with you."

I thought about Grammi most nights after that. As the cows came home each night and the sun set, we would close up the khanut and make our own walk up the mountain slope. The walk winded me at first but became easier with time.

On the walk, I often missed home. A cow would pass, and I'd think of Grammi. I might even let myself imagine coming out to her.

Grammi had taken up Greek Orthodox Christianity despite having no Greek heritage. I fantasized that she might visit Teghenik, that we'd go pray in the village church, light candles, and breathe deeply the air full of frankincense before walking home with the cows and tapping their behinds with a stick to guide them.

Sometimes, walking home, I'd think of my mother. Stones littered the dirt road, so many of them black and glassy. Obsidian gleamed, catching the light from the sun or from house lights shining from windows. I never heard anyone from Teghenik mention the stones, but I knew my mother would think they were remarkable.

For most of my teens, my mom was a part-time jeweler. After her day teaching school, she'd set up shop on the kitchen table, covering it with trays of beads and spools of jewelry wire. She sold necklaces, bracelets, and earrings up and down the I-35 corridor. I wished I could send her a box full of the stones. I pictured myself showing up on my parents' front porch to offer them a suitcase full of volcanic glass.

I missed them. I played the night of the coming-out conversation over and over again in my head as days continued to pass, and like walking up the mountain, it became easier. I couldn't speak Armenian yet, but I wouldn't have talked to my host family about coming out if I could have. Before arriving, someone in the Armenia Peace Corps group on Facebook had asked about coming out, and multiple current volunteers said it was a terrible idea with varying degrees of vehemence.

I didn't want to come out to other American volunteers, either. I just wanted to be.

But the night I came out to my parents played over and over in my mind. I kept thinking of conversations I wished I could have with them. I wanted to tell them I was sorry I ruined our last days together. I wanted to tell them I thought there was a chance they'd be okay with it and that if I'd known they weren't, I would have kept it to myself. I lay in bed at night, riddled with guilt that I'd done something that ruined the safest place I had in the world. I wanted to find a way to put things back just like they were. I felt unmoored.

And then, days into my life with Talin, Mikayel, Hakob, Sona, and Lala, I began to feel something new.

It started in the khanut, actually, when I noticed Hakob introducing me to customers in Armenian as, "mer Khaghaghutsyan Corpusi kamavory." *Our Peace Corps volunteer.*

I felt it when I told Talin and Lala how much I loved mashed potatoes, and then mashed potatoes began showing up at our meals together.

I felt it again in the way Lala called to me from the kitchen when I was putting my things away in my room.

"Surj uzum es?" She'd cry, almost like a melody.

I'd pop out of the thin French doors and sing back, "Ayo, surj em uzum!" *Yes, I want coffee.*

Our intonation became the same every time, almost musical, so much so that Sona would sing the words out after I said them as a sort of song, giggling at my accent and my musical tone. I could tell what she was doing, and we laughed together each time, so pleased to share something, even if it was so simple.

I couldn't put my finger on this blossoming new feeling until one morning when Talin started playing a game at the breakfast table.

On this morning, when I reached for my egg, Talin called out to me.

"Brent jan," she said. She pointed to the bowl of eggs. I pulled my arm back, and she said, "Ed inch e?"

These words I recognized. *What is it?* she was saying.

She looked at me, her eyebrows raised under her curled bangs, her mouth open in an expectant smile. She'd sat with me in the khanut. She knew how much time I spent studying Armenian. She wanted to know if I knew the Armenian word for "egg."

I did. "Dzu," I said.

"Ayo!" She drew out the long O in celebration.

She held up a fork, looking into my eyes, challenging me.

"Patarrakakh," I said.

"Ayo," she cheered.

Sona joined in and pointed to the shallow bowl of fried potatoes. "Brent," Sona said, testing me. "Ed inch e?"

"Kartofil."

"Ayo!" She clapped with glee, looking to her mom. The three women laughed. Mikayel laughed. Hakob smiled, thinking.

Lala was beginning to overexcite. She made like she wanted to stand up with glee. "Brent," Lala said, eyes scanning the kitchen counter for something to point at.

Hakob interrupted her. "Che, che, che."

He stood up and walked to the kitchen counter and picked up a bottle.

"Brent, ed inch e?"

"Vodka," I said.

"Ayooooo!" he nearly screamed. The entire table laughed. I was laughing and nearly crying, not so much from the laughter itself but from the sheer happiness of human connection.

They'd welcomed me into their home. And now, I realized, they were rooting for me.

5

Midway through the summer, after language class, Amanda stood on the gravel road outside the school and lifted up a small rectangle into the air so we could see it over her shoulder.

"I can actually get emails in my house," Amanda told us, and a glint of light from the sun flashed off the device and stung my eyes.

I hadn't seen an iPhone before. Behind the rounded rectangular glass, she said we were looking at a map. She told us that the blue dot on a wordless grey screen was us. She pinched at the glass, unable to reach through it, but nevertheless, white lines began to appear, and finally, the word "Charentsavan" came into view.

Amanda seemed delighted and a little embarrassed by the privilege this thing afforded her. She told us she could use it to navigate. She said she could send emails to her family from her room while the rest of us waited for the training day break in Charentsavan to visit an internet café. She could send text messages with a little keyboard that popped up on the screen. She could download emails using internet data she loaded with scratch-off cards from the khanut. She could carry it around in her pocket.

It seemed expensive, not terribly useful, and easy to drop and break. I was happy enough with my iPod and my little Nokia phone I'd bought while traveling a bit after college. The numbers were wearing off the keys, but I could use the flashlight to walk outside at night and find the bathroom door on the side of the house.

As far as emails from home, I sat in the internet café in Charentsavan once a week surrounded by teenage boys playing video games on large PCs, all of us sweating from the rising temps of summer in a town without air conditioning. I checked messages from friends on my Facebook Wall and read emails from home.

In my mom's first email to me since I arrived, she updated me on the latest episodes of *The Young and the Restless* she and Dad saved on the DVR. She told me that my oldest sister, Lisa, adopted a cat that had been dumped at the vet office where she worked. She named it Tweezer, which I knew was connected to a conversation she and I had about how much we love when people name pets after weird objects.

Mom told me she wanted to see the family I lived with. "We want to see who's so lucky to be with you," she wrote.

"The internet at this café isn't strong enough to upload photos," I wrote back, but I told her that I loved my Teghenik family, that my Armenian vocabulary was growing, and that I'd learned to make surj. "That's *coffee*," I translated and told her I'd started drinking it every morning from tiny cups the size of shot glasses.

We carried on like this for the first weeks, trading small details while avoiding the biggest topic on both our minds.

"They still aren't letting Macey pitch," she wrote in one reply. This devastated me and sent me railing over email.

The week before I'd left, Macey, my twelve-year-old sister, had pitched for the first time, putting to use years of private lessons my parents paid for.

For years, my parents had cheered her on from outside the pitching cage in a big pitching complex built inside a barn. They'd grumbled but accepted the nepotism when Macey was sent to the outfield while the coach's daughter took to the pitcher's mound.

And then, in the last game, I got to watch before I left, Macey had pitched for the first time when the coach's daughter was sick. And she pitched a no-hitter.

My entire family had screamed in the stands, whooping and hollering so loudly and for so long, it felt like the whole stadium was ours, built just for us to watch this miracle happen right before our eyes. We transcended together. We rose up in the stands and nearly floated away on the pure energy made from watching someone you love become themselves so boldly.

And then, after pitching a no-hitter, my mom wrote that Macey had been sent back to the outfield and the coach's daughter back on the mound after recovering from strep.

"Excuse me," I wrote, "but that coach can suck it."

Sometimes, in other emails, we toe-dipped toward the elephant in the digital room. In one email, I wrote, "I'm wishing I hadn't told you and then left." In some ways, this was true, but in other ways, it wasn't. I looked over my shoulder to make sure no one could see my emails, though, of course, none of the gaming Armenian teenagers cared to look.

What I actually wished for, more than anything, was that after I told them, she and my dad had simply wrapped their arms around me, understood instantly that I'd carried this around with me my whole life—alone without them. I wished they'd said to me right then, "You'll never have to do this alone again."

They hadn't said that. They'd said something so different from that. Now, I simply wished for a way back to being together.

In an email reply, Mom wrote, "We're afraid... but if telling us helped you in some way, we needed to be told. We're scared. We love you."

Returning to a Peace Corps training session after I'd taken an internet café break, Garine, the training director, called out my name among a list of those who'd received mail. Before we left home, we received orientation packets, and in them was the address to this school in Charentsavan.

On a table on one side of the classroom, a box stood with corners gone soft from a trip around the planet, my name scrawled across the top in black sharpie.

My mother's handwriting, my name. Seeing them together plucked a string in my heart connected both to love and to fear.

I carried the box with me unopened all afternoon, and when I was dropped off by the Peace Corps van at my host family's khanut, Talin asked, "*What is that?*"

"*Family. From Texas.*" I scrambled to get the dictionary from my pocket to look up a word while still holding the box under one arm. "*Send. My family sends this.*"

"*Oh, how wonderful,*" Talin said, and she watched me walk up the hill toward the house.

In my room, I set the box on the end of the bed and went into the kitchen to ask Lala for a knife. She handed me one and asked what I was doing. I tried unsuccessfully to explain, and when she followed me into my room, I didn't know how to ask for privacy.

I wasn't sure what was in the box, and I didn't want to open it in front of her. So, I set the knife on the windowsill, the box on the end of the bed, and then excused myself to the bathroom by pointing to the door and saying, "Zugaran."

When I returned, I was alone with the box on the bed next to me. I pulled open the cardboard flaps and pulled out the envelope on top.

I read the letter first in which my mom gave another update from *The Young and the Restless* because she knew I'd love the quirk of an update on so-and-so's misplaced revenge.

"You are so loved!" she wrote and then more updates, including my grandmother's brief hospital stay after a fall. A soft guilt swelled.

From the box, I pulled out Fritos, cans of bean dip, packets of Hidden Valley Ranch seasoning, gummy worms, and Oreos. Then an empty leather-bound journal and a copy of *The Fellowship of the Ring*. All my books were stored in a cabinet in her living room, and I'd marked some with a red line on the spine and asked her to grab one or two if she ever sent a care package. She also sent a Sesame Street coloring book, which I recognized as a gesture meant to charm me and induce a wave of nostalgia. Then a pair of blue jeans that I lifted up, thinking then of my mom and my dad at a small department store trying to decide whether the jeans would fit, if they were my kind of "cool," and if they would last through two years of being apart. I pulled the denim to my face and wept.

I felt swept out to a far side of the world, away from the most stable source of love in my life. I felt like I'd had to leave and should have stayed, like it was right to leave them and wrong to leave them, like it was right to come out and wrong to come out, and I picked at these feelings until none of them seemed whole or complete at all.

Gravity now held us down on opposite sides of the planet. I pulled at the blue jeans as if I could rip them apart, which of course, I couldn't. I pulled and twisted them and cried and lifted the jeans to my face, balling them up to my open mouth. I let out a wail, which I wanted to scream up into the clouds and stuff back into my gut at the same time.

I held myself down to the bed until the crying stopped. I looked back into the box. Underneath the jeans were two more bags of Puppy Chow from my Aunt Susan. Next to those, a blue Post-it Note had been placed on a Bicycle deck of playing cards with the words "Our Cards" and "Love Vibes" written in my grandmother's handwriting.

Fanning them out, I noticed a very small, irregular triangle cut out of one of the cards. I picked it up to examine the tear and realized quickly that a beak had punctured it. Her canary.

These really were "our cards." We were playing with this very deck the last time I saw my grandmother, and I'd watched her tiny yellow bird climb from her shoulder to her hand and then lean over and bite the eight of diamonds.

Pain and worry and love and longing ballooned. I couldn't imagine my parents had told my grandmother about my coming out. I'd learn later my hunch was right. She had no idea. And what would she have thought? And could we have sat and played again?

When my tears were dry, I packed away everything from the care package into the wardrobe. Only Lala and I were home, and I could hear her moving quietly through the house on the other side of my door. Rain pattered on the window, making the glass waver and the scene outside more blurred into simply an impression of the hill and the dark grey sky lit up by the falling sun.

I heard knuckles rapping at my door. "Ayo?" I said.

The door opened, and Lala leaned in, her large brunette curls moving slightly around her small face, her awkward smile. The shoulders of her bright red dress puffed out, and those large shirt sleeves leaned with her as if they could wave hello.

She said something I could not understand. She lifted a square book into view.

With still no idea what I wanted to do next, I waved her in. She walked over and sat uncomfortably close to me on the bed, the sides of our legs pressed together. Then she brought the square book to her lap.

"Ynteniks." She said it with a slight hiss on the S and pressed her finger to the square book's grey, wordless cover.

"Oh," I said back in Armenian. "*Family.*"

"Ayo," she said, her voice rising with glee.

"*Your family?*" I said.

"Ayo! Im yntenky." And she pulled back the grey cover, her big sleeve brushing my shoulder. There on the first page was one small black-and-white photo of a man dressed in a black suit with a thick beard and hair that seemed to be receding, though still rendering jet-black in the print. Next to him, a woman in a black dress with a wide, soft collar, her hips turned as she sat on a bench, her arm around the child that stood on the bench next to her. Four children were in the photo. All young. All dressed in white. No one in the photo smiled.

Lala pressed her finger on the chest of one of the children and then said in Armenian, "*Me.*"

"*You?*" I asked.

"*Yes*," she said. Her responses lagged, and I thought perhaps she was traveling between a memory and this moment with me.

"*Your family?*" I asked.

"*Yes*," she responded, still smiling.

"Oh," I said and deliberately moved in closer as if to see them all more clearly, intent on gesturing to her that I was taking this seriously. She wanted me to see her family. I wanted her to know that I was seeing them.

She turned the page. A collection of photos this time.

Two men standing together with stern faces. A large group of new people, all adults, the women sitting in front of a row of standing men, everyone in dark clothing. A girl on a small tricycle.

"*You?*" I asked, pointing to the girl.

"*Yes*," she said. Then she said a long sentence of words I didn't know.

"*I don't understand*," I said in Armenian.

She spoke again, though I heard only sounds as beautiful but untranslatable to me as river water splashing over stones.

She thought, her finger now pressed on the girl on the tricycle.

"*Me*," she said and then slowly articulated another word.

I smiled and nodded without understanding.

She flipped the page and then another, pointing at images. Some words I knew.

"*My brother.*"

"*My sister.*"

"*My grandmother.*"

When she saw I didn't understand other words, she changed the way she said them to me.

"*Mother's brother*," when I didn't know the word for uncle.

"*Mother's brother's daughter,*" when I didn't know the word for cousin.

She explained something, but I only caught a few words of it— "*Mother brother... living... Talin... mother... now.*"

"Talin?" I asked, grasping a bit to catch up to her. "*Mother, sister?*"

"*No. Talin...*" and then more words I couldn't catch, like fireflies that light up and disappear though you know they are simply flying next to you, unseeable.

Finally, I asked clumsily, "*Talin is inside your family?*"

"*Yes,*" she said, and her grin widened, her eyes fixed to a photo in the book on her lap.

Then gradually, she stopped explaining, and as she grew quiet, I maintained body language that expressed a deep interest in her album. I'd spent weeks with her in this village, and I was surprised that I recognized not a single face in any photo. Where were all these people now? As she continued to turn page after page, I occasionally looked up to her face and saw her eyes glistening.

How deeply I felt her own heart being moved by the images of her family. I thought for a moment of walking to the windowsill and opening the copy of *Matilda* in which I'd stored a few photos I'd printed at Walgreens before leaving Texas. Macey and I with puppets from a show about our family that we'd put on for them before I'd left. A photo of my brother and his wife at their wedding. Our family at my oldest sister Lisa's graduation. A photo of my grandmother and me playing cards in her kitchen.

But I didn't get my photos. I didn't want to change this moment for her. Lala's welling eyes produced a tear that I saw on her face, a small, still river that shone in the yellow bedroom light.

I looked up a word in my dictionary to make sure I remembered it correctly. I ran the sentence in my head a couple of times to check the verb conjugation. Then I said, *"Your family is beautiful."*

She smiled at me. And she said, *"Yes."*

6

Our summer days blew past in the wind over the golden hills outside my window.

As days wore on, a foreigner crept into my own body—some germ that brought on a cold that swelled my tonsils and kept me up at night and in bed during the day.

While other Peace Corps volunteers attended their classes and trainings, I stayed in my room, my eyes closed and my mind wandering. My body ached, and I writhed under the thin blanket and pink satin bed cover. Rain pelted the window. Cold air crept in through the cracks between the wall and window frame, sliding over my sick body and over the copy of *Leaves of Grass* in which I'd been pressing poppies and daisies and any other flower I found in Teghenik.

In the last few days, I'd seen only Lala and Talin, who came in with broths and teas and lavash and to check on me. After I'd missed a couple of days of language class, Zoe offered to come visit. She'd brought me M&Ms and a Sprite.

She sat on the floor against the wall.

"It's the last week, dude," she said.

"I know," I said. "Already the end of summer. It sucks."

"And the rain. That sucks."

I looked at my wardrobe. "I still have Puppy Chow. My aunt sent it. Should we eat some?"

It had been over a month since the Puppy Chow had arrived, and as my mother would have said, it had a wang.

While we snacked, we circled things we'd grown to love talking about with each other. All summer long, we shared our histories. I told her about the traditions and requirements of my Christian college. She found mandatory worship services and the amount of prayer circles otherworldly. Zoe told me about living in Indonesia, about some of the loves she met while traveling, and about her family in the woods of Maine.

We talked some about the Peace Corps volunteers who had started dating each other and a couple who found a way to date Armenians even though we weren't technically allowed to leave our villages.

After treading this familiar territory, we landed on the current most-important topic among volunteers, our looming site assignments.

Zoe placed a few pieces of Puppy Chow in her mouth, a little sugar wafting into the air. "Yeah, in just a couple of weeks, we'll be moving to our sites."

"And then, it's two years," I noted.

"Two years." Zoe paused at this, grabbing another handful of Puppy Chow.

"What are the odds you and I will be on total opposite sides of the country?" I asked her. Since I'd come out to her, we did nearly everything together. We hiked with other volunteers in the mountains. We ate ice cream in the afternoon in front of the khanut. And when my parents and I broached the subject of my being gay over email when they dug their feet into their Central Texas Christian ground and told me they'd never be okay with it, Zoe was the one I called, the one I asked if I could walk to her host family's house just for a hug.

"I don't know," Zoe considered. "I've heard so many volunteers who have other volunteers within a few minutes' drive or even in town with them."

"So, it could happen," I said while chewing. I wanted it to happen. I wanted to look out at the next two years and know Zoe was there, that I could still walk to her any time I needed comfort. That my first queer friend would be the same friend I'd see for weeknight movie nights and Saturday morning coffee.

"Maybe we will be," she said. " Or at least being on the same side of the country is pretty likely."

"Yeah. Or... maybe this is it, and I'll never see you again." I laughed, which made me cough, compelling me to cover my face with a pillow.

I placed my sugar-dusted bowl on the bed stand, laid myself down and turned onto my side. "You'll probably be so far away that I only see you once a year. You'll forget me."

"Jesus H Christmas, dude. I'll see you. No matter what, we'll meet in Yerevan."

I giggled—a response meant to indicate that I was joking—but I wasn't. From a young age, my fear of being alone had been a constant companion, like a ghost that settled on me as soon as I'd heard that being gay could ruin your life and separate you from your family. That fear had never been heavier, and the thought of my new, safe friend being far away made my current body aches sink deeper toward my bones.

I spent the entirety of the next day, a Saturday, in bed reading and half-sleeping. My tonsils hurt, and my lymph nodes were swollen, and I ached. I wanted to call my mother.

I hadn't called her much since I arrived. I was scared to call her, but I was sick. I always called my mom when I was sick.

I'd called her when a virus kept me in bed for days in Kolkata. There, the family hosting me gave me steam baths every night to break up my congestion, covering me in a bed sheet and then sliding a pot of boiling water under the edge of it while we sat and talked. I breathed deeply and then deeply again.

"Shaji and Beena," I'd told her when my mom emailed me to ask the names of the couple taking care of me. She'd remembered those names, and when I returned to Kolkata years later, she told me at the airport in Austin to "thank them for taking care of my baby."

In Antigua, Guatemala, the summer before my senior year of college, I'd gotten dengue fever, known by another name as "bone-break fever." I broke and cried in bed, sobbing into my Nokia, and Mom spoke softly to me over the phone, "It will be okay, Brent. It will be okay. It will be okay." She listened to me cry in the darkness of my room, where I lay alone and waited and waited for my body to win.

I wanted to tell her now that I wished I was home. I wished I was on her couch, my eyes closed, the TV on softly, my parents and my sister quietly walking around the house, their mere presence a comfort. But I wouldn't tell her that. Not now. I still didn't want her to have any idea that I might be considering that coming here was a mistake. And I was. Lying there alone in my room after days of aching, a thought swept in like a cold tickle of wind through the crack in the windowsill. *I've made a mistake.*

I've made a huge mistake, I thought again. *This is too hard. I miss home. Maybe I shouldn't have left.*

Site assignments meant Zoe might be far away. My Armenian host family had been so gracious to me all summer, but I couldn't talk to them, mostly because of language but also because I wouldn't know how to tell them about the thoughts I had. I needed words not on the vocabulary list we were learning—lists of food words, family members, types of transportation, how to ask for help at a grocery store. I needed the Armenian word for pain. For gay. For family. For fear. For broken. I was too afraid in this small Armenian town to talk to them about how I'd just come out, how I didn't know how to be gay at all, and that there seemed no way to learn.

I'd dreamed of living abroad like this since I was a kid, of living in a place so foreign to me that the challenge of finding my way—learning a new language, a new culture, a way to work and add value—would all change me in some way, like discovering myself and a view of the world that would be truer than the one I had before. I didn't want how hard it was to be gay to take that away from me. I didn't want to leave saying, "This is too hard."

I wanted to be out and to be loved. But here I was in Armenia surrounded by people who had been so kind, so welcoming, but who barely knew me. I didn't have the language skills to speak to most people around me. I ached in bed. And I wondered if this was a mistake.

I wanted to call my mom, but I couldn't. And then, a spark of memory revealed what she would have told me to do.

It was late now, and I walked out of my room and found most of my Teghenik family settled on the couch to watch a Russian-dubbed Rambo movie.

In the kitchen, I found Lala washing dishes and said, *"Excuse me. Please. Cup?"*

"Of course," she said smiling widely. She lifted her hands from a dish she was scrubbing in the sink and handed me a glass. Suds from her fingers dripped onto my hands, which still ached with illness.

"Water, please?" I continued. *"Hot."*

Keeping her grin, Lala turned to the stove and put her hand close to, but not on, a thin-metal kettle. With a box of Gorilla brand matches in her hand, she turned on the gas stove and lit it. Soon steam rose from the teapot's spout.

She poured me water and gave me salt and a spoon after I requested both. I didn't have the words to explain or to ask if gargling salt water was something she would do or is done in Armenia. I simply expressed gratitude, saying, "Shnorhakalutyun," and scooped salt, stirring it into the water.

I had intended to go to the bathroom on the side of the house and stand over the sink so I could spit into it. But I stopped myself in the cool air that moved over the porch.

Clothes hung on the line, heavy and wet, but not dripping. There was no wind, and they did not sway. I stood at the end of the line of clothes, pulled a mouthful of salt water over my lips and looked up into the cloudless night sky.

I gargled, humming so that the water bubbled and splashed in my open mouth.

I leaned forward, cold wet clothes grazing my shoulder, and I spat over the railing, the water plopping onto the grass below.

I did this again and again. I could hear no sounds from this perch on the porch and had no view of any other houses. Just the view out into my host family's cherry tree orchard where the trees appeared as dark silhouettes on the long grass below, which shone silvery blueish-white in the moonlight.

I put notes to my humming, and rhythm, and my gargle became a song. With each mouthful of saltwater, I began humming the song "I'd Like to Teach the World to Sing (In Perfect Harmony)." The water splashed, and the tiniest droplets sprang over my lips and landed on my cheeks and my chin like kisses. I took in the sky full of stars and the nearly full moon.

I thought of my mother and then of her mother and this home remedy they'd passed down to me. As I hummed, I looked at the moon, the same one my mother would see soon. I hadn't needed to call her. The love had traveled from my grandmother to my mother to me and had arrived on this night, when I needed it, when I could feel it working its way through time and distance to this spot on the porch where that love arrived like healing.

7

During the final week of summer training, Garine gathered us outside the Charentsavan school, where Peace Corps staff had spray-painted a map of Armenia on the parking lot with names of Armenian towns and villages written in Armenian letters.

"We'll start in the south," Garine announced, walking to the narrowest part of the map, "When I call the name of your site, please go stand near it on the map."

The first name called was Danya's, the only black American in our group of new volunteers. Before we knew it was hers, we'd talked about the site at the farthest end of the map. Meghri would be three hours from any other volunteer and ten hours from the capital, Yerevan. When Danya's name was called, I shuddered with worry.

A few volunteers were called to live in or near the next southernmost city, Kapan. Then, slightly farther north, Goris. Two volunteers were called out and assigned there together—Chris. Then Zoe.

Zoe stood next to Chris on the southern part of Armenia, wrapped her arm into his, and started whispering to him and then laughing about something. I wanted to catch her eyes, send a look of worry, but couldn't.

Garine continued north, exhausting sites closest to Zoe and then those closest to Yerevan. As she walked further up the map, I felt in her steps the hours of travel between the places that held my new friends and the hours I'd have to travel to see them again. Then, as far north as any site left, Garine called my name and told me I'd be living in a town called Stepanavan.

Three days later, on the morning I left Teghenik, my host family surprised me, their eyes tearing up as they helped me carry bags to the car sent to fetch me for the last time from their gate. I walked back inside, pretending to check whether I left something, only to take a picture of my empty bedroom. Then I took quick snaps of the empty living room and then the kitchen. While my summer host family waited outside, I imagined seeing these pictures again, trying to recreate my memories of our time together in the photos of empty rooms.

I hugged each of them and then turned my digital camera around to try and take a group photo with us all one last time. I knew my aim would probably be off, but I'd be glad I'd tried to capture this last moment together.

In Charentsavan, near the spray-painted map of Armenia, volunteers from Teghenik and the neighboring villages found Peace Corps vans headed toward their assigned part of the country. They threw their bags in and meandered around the parking lot of the school saying goodbye.

The day before, we'd all been sworn into service by the US Ambassador to Armenia, Marie Yovanovitch, who spoke from the podium about the importance of our work with our assigned Armenian organizations throughout the country. Now, we were heading to our permanent sites for two years.

I hugged Zoe before she climbed into the van heading south. She promised to call. It didn't seem enough, but what else could I have asked of her when her new home would be ten hours away?

Eventually, I climbed into a van headed north. I stopped thinking of Zoe, her van headed in the opposite direction and instead thought of my host family in Teghenik, buoyed by the gratitude and joy I felt in thinking about them. I was hopeful I'd find some similar joyful rhythm with the family I headed to now.

Peace Corps had given me details about my new host family before I arrived, and when the Peace Corps van dropped me off at my new host family's home, Hovsep, the father of the family, met me at the top of a flight of stairs. The front door, like my bedroom door in Teghenik, opened in the middle like skinny French doors. Through it, Hovsep reached out a small hand for my rolling suitcase, which he pulled in with a scrape over the wooden lip of the threshold.

Hot August air swept gently through open windows. Lace curtains billowed, waving as I passed, and a smell of grass and old furniture traveled on the warm air, which mixed with the cold air inside, both temperatures hitting me at once.

The sound of rolling luggage wheels filled the hallway. In the back of the house, Hovsep opened the door of my new room, sliding my bag inside.

"*Thank you,*" I said in Armenian.

He responded, "*Welcome,* Brent jan."

His gaze followed me, his close-set eyes tracking as I walked carefully in the narrow spaces between the bed, the armchair, and the coffee table. A wardrobe towered over the room, and without floor space for luggage, I heaved my suitcases onto the bed.

Arevik, Hovsep's wife and my other host, stepped into the room next to her husband, both of them the same, short stature.

Arevik asked, "Josh kutek?" *Would you like to eat?*

I assumed that the name "Arevik" came from the Armenian word I'd learned for sun— "arev," But when Arevik asked, her tone was sharp, tactical, almost frigid. I told myself that tone of voice is cultural, but I felt myself wondering immediately if they wanted me in their home, even though they'd signed up for the task.

"*I will wait until the time… all of us will be eating,*" I answered. "*It's okay?*"

"*Of course,*" she said, and without any more words, they both left me in the room to put away my things.

The lacquer on the wardrobe gleamed. The doors wouldn't swing open past the coffee table, so I bent awkwardly, passing my clothes and shoes through a six-inch opening. While I unpacked, I thought of my Teghenik family. A feeling of loss crept in—loss of the ease we'd had with each other and the comfort I'd found in their home.

When I'd unpacked my bags in my new room, I wandered into the living room where Hovsep was watching TV. Not eager to sit with him and try to understand the Russian show, I walked further into the house hoping to find Arevik, or their daughter Gohar engaged in an activity I could join.

Gohar had gone out, it seemed. Arevik was watching another smaller TV in her room, and when she saw me wandering, she came into the hallway and asked, "Brent jan, lav es?"

"*Yes,*" I said and then lied about the intent of my wandering. "Zugaran?"

Arevik pointed, and I went through the motions of entering the water closet and then entering the bathroom next door to wash my hands.

In my room again, I lay down on my bed, which was short enough that the crown of my head pressed uncomfortably against the headboard while the bottoms of my feet pushed against the footboard.

I let my thoughts wander, mapping out my first walk to work at the World Vision office the next day. When I'd exhausted that line of thinking, I played Snake on my Nokia until I heard a knock at the bedroom door.

Arevik's voice penetrated. "Ari, Brent. Josh kutenk."

Over time in their home, this knock and call through the door became the only time I was certain I'd see them, the only time I really felt part of their daily lives. I longed for lazy afternoons getting to know each other over cups of surj. I wished for the kind of long talks I had with Talin or Mikayel or Hakob at their khanut as they waited for me to find words in the dictionary to describe my family, my work, my hopes, my observations.

While most days and evenings were spent in my room reading or journaling or watching TV, after a knock on my new bedroom door, I would obediently walk to the dining table while Arevik brought out dish after dish for dinner, setting them over a white tablecloth. Many of the dishes would be leftovers, and each night Arevik added a freshly cooked dish to the rotation. Maybe a beef pilaf. Perhaps fried noodles. On some nights, there were dolmas wrapped in grape or cabbage leaves, savory steam rising and filling my nose.

Often, Gohar joined her, the sound of plates and utensils clanging down the hall until Gohar or Arevik arrived with a dish or perhaps a garnish like sour cream, stringy cheese, pickles, or lavash. Hovsep started filling his plate as soon as the first items arrived. I followed suit, trying to settle into expectations and avoid questions like, "Why aren't you eating yet?"

I looked forward to weekends when Arevik made pelmeni. She stuffed two circles of pasta with a soft cheese and served them in a white dish in a bit of pasta water. I followed the family's lead each pelmeni night, watching them pull the cheesy little UFOs onto their plates, adorning them with fat dollops of sour cream sprinkled with black pepper. The tang of the cream and cheese and the kick of pepper made my nose itch and my throat sting in a way I loved.

After we'd all slurped them down and sopped up the pasta water and sour cream with fat chunks of bread, Hovsep would look up at me with eager eyes, smiling with deep creases in his cheeks and invite me to play backgammon. "Nardi khaghank?"

In the first weeks of my time in Stepanavan, nardi games with Hovsep felt like a feast for my heart, hungry for companionship. Hovsep was vicious. Ruthless. The bone-white dice, a quarter of the size of dice at home, were wielded by Hovsep like swords. He raised them high in a hand that sliced the air. Then he released the dice into a spin, the cubes clattering against the board. Whatever the combination of numbers, he moved quickly.

He raised a draught, lifting it six to twelve inches high, and smacked it hard against the wood, sliding quickly and perfectly into place. On my turn, he usually told me my best move before I could see it. When he didn't, I knew he was hoping I'd do something wrong that he could take advantage of. After my error, he chuckled, smiled at me, and took every advantage. He won every time. I never won. Not once.

I savored these games, the only moments of connection in our daily lives together. Otherwise, each evening, I sat alone in my room.

In the first days, connection to people in Stepanavan felt like my primary goal. As a community and business development volunteer, I reported to the Peace Corps manager of that sector, Stepan, who had told us during a training session in the summer that no one expected big projects or accomplishments in the first weeks. "Meet people," he said. "Make connections. Learn about your organization. Learn about the town."

Previously called Jalaloghli, my new town, Stepanavan was renamed in 1923 for the Bolshevik leader Stepan Shaumian. Every day, I walked blocks and blocks down Stepanavan's main street on the way to my Peace Corps assignment. In the center of town, I passed a statue of Shaumian that towered before the main town buildings behind him, a bridge north before him.

There Shaumian stood, his sharp broad shoulders casting a long shadow, his form angular and Brutalist. Sharp shoulders. Sharp elbows. Sharp chin. He was looking up. His long coat covered the ground around his feet and his legs. Behind him, the rest of the haraparak, the *town square*, stretched out, the surface covered with large cement tiles and regular flower beds full of cosmos still in bloom in the late summer. White, pink, purple, and maroon flowers danced in the wind and bobbed as I passed my fingers over them, walking alone toward the Stepan Shaumian Museum in front of which streams of a fountain splashed.

On the northwest side of the haraparak, my assignment sat quietly in the museum's cool shadow. I'd been assigned to a World Vision office, a field-level operation that was part of the largest nonprofit organization on the planet. The Stepanavan office managed the funds collected through their child-sponsorship program. The office and the team inside it facilitated letter writing between children and their sponsors, and they managed the programs those sponsorships funded in twenty villages surrounding the town.

Liana, my official Peace Corps counterpart and manager of Stepanavan's World Vision office, looked out for me from the moment her application for a Peace Corps volunteer had been accepted. She'd tell me later she had thought of applying for a long time.

As a child who looked up eagerly in class through dark curly hair, she'd been singled out for a special award from a volunteer who had been placed in Stepanavan as part of the very first Peace Corps group to arrive in 1992.

"That changed my life," she'd tell me during one of our first meetings, talking about how that award and the tutoring that came with it had emboldened her efforts at school. She continued to seek out tutoring and work with Peace Corps volunteers who stayed present in Stepanavan, year after year, including my arrival in 2009. Now, her fluency in English and work with nonprofits had landed her in the director position of the largest nonprofit in the region.

On my first day, she walked me around the World Vision building. We started upstairs with the translation office, where five women sat surrounded by children's handwritten letters, which they transcribed from Armenian to English to send to child sponsors in England.

Downstairs, I met the finance officers, and then we stepped outside to meet TDFs. "Transformational development coordinators," Liana explained, pulling her dark curls behind her ears. "They do the work in the villages we support. There are twenty villages and five TDFs, so each of them works in four villages.

"This is Melik, Vigen, and Tirayr. Artavan and Petros are in the field." Three men turned to me, each with a firm handshake and a buoyant, "Barev, Brent jan."

Walking in the front door, Liana gestured with one long, elegant arm toward an empty grey desk with a black chair behind. "We moved it down here for you so it would be easier to meet people. And next to you is Yeraz."

At that, a small woman with hair pinned off her face stood from her desk and came over to shake my hand. "Is this my new harevan?" she joked, mixing English and Armenian in a musical, songbird voice. She looked up at Liana. Their height difference shocked me a bit.

"Harevans?"

"My neighbor," she translated with surprising warmth.

"Do you want to settle in?" Liana asked, mirroring Yeraz's warmth. When I said yes, she walked with clicking heels back to her office.

After my first day at the World Vision office, my final weeks of summer passed by in a flash. Beyond the museum, in what I found to be a kind of old amusement park, I made friends with another young man in his twenties who sold ice cream and managed a number of ping-pong tables he rented to kids in the afternoons. After a couple of weeks, he wouldn't take my hundred-dram coins and stood shoulder to shoulder with me licking cones of ice cream made with farm-fresh milk. We talked in what few Armenian words I knew about our lives, limiting us to understanding each other by the makeup of our families, our jobs, and foods we liked.

Sometimes, we played each other in ping-pong when the tables weren't full, and my body buzzed with electricity when he looked into my eyes smiling, his dark eyebrows raised in delight after a point. Once, he took me to an old carnival ride, one unlike any other I'd ever seen with rust exposed by crumbling paint.

With great effort, he explained to me that Stepanavan used to be a Soviet resort town where people came for "*good air.*"

Together, we climbed into a cage suspended between two heavy legs of metal. The ride had no engine but instead was powered by us using our own bodies to sway the cage. I leaned toward him. Then, as the cage swung the other way, he leaned at and then away from me, his chest heaving in tandem with mine.

To keep the cage moving, we forced our bodies toward each other in a rhythm of effort and breath, the two of us smiling at each other as the swings of the cage took us higher and higher. Finally, we were flying in circles, around and around, sweating and laughing and hollering together until we decided to stop thrusting our bodies back and forth, letting the cage come to a quiet stop near the ground while we caught our breath.

We ate ice cream together every day, played games, and talked. Then, one afternoon, his stand simply wasn't there. I stood in the park and looked in every direction. I knew only his name, and I was afraid to ask anyone about him in case people became curious about my interest in him. I never saw him again.

As the weather grew colder, I tried to make other friends but couldn't understand who was there to befriend. I learned from colleagues at the office that most people in their twenties, like me, moved out of the country for jobs or school or simply moved to Yerevan to try and make it in the city. Everyone else was married with children, so my social life happened at work.

Yeraz, always in her black shirts, black pants, and black shoes, greeted me every day with, "Bari aravot, harevans," which I would return with the same, *Good morning, my neighbor.*

I sat next to her checking emails and my Facebook Wall while adding pieces to grant proposals Liana sent my way. I asked Yeraz for translation help daily, and she never, not once, looked anything but pleased to help me with a word or phrase. Certain that I interrupted her work too much, I took her buoyant responses as a kindness to me and used that kindness like a life raft for days when connection seemed hard to find.

Others tried to help me integrate into the World Vision community as well. Ayda cleaned and managed office upkeep. She welcomed me each morning to the team's morning meeting with confident eyes and a proud smile, saying, "Surj uzum es, Brent jan?"

And when I said yes, she always followed with, "Shakaravas?" *Sugar?*

She knew the answer after two days. She knew I'd say, "Kes gdal." *Half a spoon.* But she asked anyway, just to offer me a pleasant exchange. She stood behind the kitchen stove, holding the black-handled jazzve over the flame as the rest of the team moseyed in each morning to the kitchen table, the women saying hello, the men cheering, "Akhbers!" before grabbing my hand to shake it.

Liana asked each of us to talk about our work and what each person wanted to focus on during the day. We all listened, steam from our small cups of coffee rising gently to our noses. I couldn't understand most of what was being said, but I kept my eyes on anyone speaking, trying to communicate my intent to support, to stay engaged, and to learn and listen.

On my best days, I sometimes thought of my memories of childhood.

As a small boy, when my parents had friends over, the kids were all sent away to play. I never wanted to leave, and sometimes, the parents let me stay sitting next to them on the couch or in their lap at the dinner table. I loved listening. I tried to understand them, to see them, to have their world blend with my internal one.

On worse days with my World Vision coworkers, I sat unable to follow anything, every minute of my misunderstanding plucking a string to a place in my heart that felt isolated, like an outsider. A place in my heart had always known I was different from people around me, and I feared my difference would eventually doom me to a life lived alone.

Every morning, I felt either more connected to my new coworkers or more isolated. Sometimes, I felt both in the same morning.

Nearly every day, at the end of the meeting, Liana asked one of the TDFs to take me with them to appointments in their assigned villages and to introduce me to people with whom the World Vision team worked. I rode with Vigen or Tirayr or Artavan or Petros or Melik, spending most of my workday in one of the World Vision Ladas, watching the Northern Armenian landscape pass me by like a breeze.

Then, at each village stop, walking through schools World Vision had renovated or playgrounds the team had installed, I looked for clues, any small morsel of inspiration for how I might be helpful. In those first days, they were incredibly hard to find.

One morning, I sat by Vigen for nearly two hours driving out to one of the villages he served. Vigen was slick. He was charming—the kind of guy who laughed at everyone's jokes, so, of course, everyone came to him when they had a story to tell. I saw strangers-to-me come into the office foyer just to greet him. He gave the most high fives of anyone on the team, and though he never went out of his way to make me feel welcome, when I was around, he always made me part of what was going on.

In his Lada, we sat quietly, listening to the Armenian pop artist Tata playing from Vigen's flash drive, which was plugged into the car stereo. We passed mountains, fields of sunflowers, and then fields of wheat. We arrived at a kindergarten with a community garden planted outside the playground fence. Liana explained to me before we left that the gardens were funded by World Vision to supplement child nutrition. The teachers and parents harvested the vegetables and prepared meals for kindergarteners.

Getting out of the car, we greeted the mayor and walked together to the garden past a brand-new swing set and slide, which Vigen tried to explain in simple words that World Vision had provided to the kindergarten.

In the garden, Vigen stopped between rows of vegetables.

"*Are you good*, Brent jan?" he asked.

"Ayo." *Yes*, I said, and I wished I could ask anything relevant. I wished I knew enough Armenian to ask when the garden was funded. Who planted the seeds? Who cared for it? How much food did the kids eat from this garden?

Was any of it preserved and pickled for winter? Were they keeping any seeds for next spring?

I only managed to point to tomatoes, which I knew were tomatoes, and say, "Ed inch e?" *What is it?*

"Lolik," Vigen said.

"Ah," I said. "Amerikayum asum enk, 'toh-may-toh.' *In America, we say "tomato.*"

The ride home, like all rides home from village visits, became my favorite part of the day. With Vigen or any of the TDFs, the ride back was simple. At other times of my daily routine—every meal, every walk to the grocery store, every meeting at World Vision, every time I showed up in a village mayor's office or a school principal's office or a women's co-op office—I pushed myself to be valuable, to have purpose. I squeezed every bit of Armenian I'd learned out of me and into conversation. I looked for any way to be relevant, to connect.

But on the ride home from a village visit—and I especially liked the hour or two-hour rides home—I just listened to music, looked out the window at mountains, gorges, rolling hills, pastures, and rows of crops. I didn't have to try to be anything to anyone. Just myself in a seat, wordless and wondering.

We saw no signs of humanity on many of these drives, just the barren hills. They hadn't always been barren, I'd been told. The earthquake of the late eighties and the fall of the Soviet Union in the early nineties brought such scarcity that the trees had to be cut down so babies could be kept warm through awful winters. I looked out at the tree-barren hills and imagined what it would be like to walk to the top of one and look at everything at once.

8

During the final warm days of summer, all the puppies at my new home died.

Hovsep and Arevik's dog, a rat-faced Manila-paper colored mutt, wagged the ash-black end of her tail when I came home from the World Vision office, and often I sat at the top of the stairs to pet her for a while before going inside. When her white belly grew larger than her head, I announced at the office that I might be getting a puppy, which only some of my colleagues cheered for.

"I've never really had a dog," I told Zoe once on the phone, "but it could be great, you know, to have a someone. A pal."

By the end of August, I could hear the tapping of their little claws on the metal porch as I made my way up the circular staircase at the end of the day. I sat at my spot at the top of the stairs and let them jump into my lap. I stroked behind their ears until they fell asleep, lifting them gently from my lap when Arevik called to me to join the family for dinner.

At the office, I shared pictures of the puppies with Ayda and Liana, who craned over the tiny screen on the back of my camera, cooing at their little faces pointed toward the lens. Despite Liana and Ayda's eager encouragement of my puppy adoption, the rest of the office was divided, speaking about disease, noise, and money. One coworker told me the idea was dangerous. He said his wife had a miscarriage, and the doctor blamed the hair of their household cat. He said that breathing in the hair had caused them to lose the baby. I stopped bringing up the puppies at work after that.

Still, on my porch perch, I spent my evenings cuddling. One little girl, almost completely ash-black, rested each evening in the crook of my knee, her baby eyes closing as the sun set. I thought of her as the furry companion I'd been waiting for, the two of us alone to listen to the leaves rattle in the wind.

A few weeks after they were born, I stepped onto the porch on a particularly cool September morning, and the little girl who slept in my knee limped to see me. Her paw had turned under, and she walked quickly and clumsily on the joint. She couldn't climb into my lap, so I lifted her.

The next morning, she crawled on the joints of both front legs, and in the afternoon, she dragged herself to see me, unable to stand on any legs at all.

In the evening of the next day, I found my little girl lifeless in the long shadows of the vines that grew on the side of the porch.

When I heard Hovsep climbing the metal steps to the front door, I called to him in Armenian, *"Did you see? Small dog. Outside from the door. Dead."*

I didn't understand his Armenian response, except for the part where he said, *"Gone."*

Unsure of what to do, if I should even try to save the rest of the litter in a land where so few people kept pets, I sat with each of the other three puppies in the morning and evenings until quickly, they'd all folded themselves completely, lying lifeless on the porch like crumpled paper.

The well of sadness I felt for their passing surprised me. I'd never had a dog. But I'd seen in the puppies the promise of an unconditional friendship, a wordless bond needing no moral judgment, built simply on the fact that we belonged together.

"How are the puppies?" Liana asked me over morning coffee at the end of the week. The whole team entered the office break room, shaking hands and patting shoulders. Ayda stood at the stove making coffee in a jazzve.

"*The puppies have all left now. All dead. Sad. Many days... sad*," I told them in Armenian.

"*That is very sad*," Ayda returned. "*And now, you won't have a dog.*"

Wishing I had more vocabulary to tell them how much I'd longed for a pet, I shrugged and said, "Inch anum?" *What can I do?*

Ayda lifted her jazzve from the flame and gently swirled its contents.

I'd never seen or certainly used a jazzve before coming to Armenia, but they were now in every house and office I entered, as ubiquitous as salt and pepper. Ayda's jazzve was large enough for a dozen cups. The metal pot's wide base sat against the stove flames, and its shape narrowed toward the top with a handle usually rising out at an angle or straight up.

Each morning, she asked the room if they wanted coffee, and for each *ayo*, she filled a tiny coffee cup with water and dumped the water into the jazzve. Then, for every *ayo*, she spooned a teaspoon of very finely ground coffee into the water. She turned on the gas under the burner.

I watched Ayda after telling her about the dead puppies as the coffee gurgled and threatened to climb over the lip of the jazzve. Ayda lifted it off the flame. I recognized the move, able now to anticipate her lowering it again to the flame, watching the coffee bubbles crawl again to the lip until she removed it again and set it on a flameless stovetop grate.

"Surjd, Brent jan," Ayda said and then placed a small cup on a small saucer before me.

Wanting to leave thoughts of the dead dogs behind, I noticed that Ayda rarely sat to drink with us. I asked her in Armenian, "*When will you drink? Sit with me?*"

She chortled and let a smile creep. She put the jazzve back on the stove and brought a small cup for herself to the place at the table next to Liana, both of them across from me.

I lifted my cup and pulled coffee through my pursed lips to keep it from burning my mouth, the heat of it racing over my tongue, into my throat, and down to my chest.

"Shnorhakalutyun," I said to Ayda. *Thank you.*

She smiled her charming smile, her endearing gap in her front teeth peeking through barely parted lips. She said, "*You're welcome.*"

I'd acquired a taste for this thick, grounds-in coffee. I'd heard that there was a tradition in Armenia of reading coffee grounds, but I'd not seen anyone do it. At the end of sipping all of mine, my lips met the collection of fine grounds that had settled at the bottom.

I looked to Liana. "Can someone read my grounds?"

She looked up at me and laughed. "Okay," she said. "You really want this? Ayda can read coffee grounds."

Liana turned to Ayda and said things in Armenian. Ayda visibly blushed, leaned back from the table smiling, and waved her palm at me. "Che, che, che," Ayda protested.

"*Please,*" I begged in Armenian. "*Very, very please?*"

Ayda laughed. "Lav, Brent jan," she said, and then she gestured for my cup. "Ari." *Come.*

I slid my saucer and my cup across the table to her with its sludge of grounds settled at the bottom.

She pushed it back, again saying, "Che, Brent jan," before lifting her own coffee cup into the air. "Like this," she said. Teaching me, she tilted her cup away from her. The thick coffee creeped slowly out over the edge and onto the plate.

Looking into her eyes and then back to my cup, I mimicked her movement, watching wet, syrupy grounds drip to the plate.

Ayda said something, and Liana translated. "That's for the future, Brent jan."

Then Ayda tilted her cup toward her, and more coffee slipped to the plate. I followed.

Liana translated again, "That is for the past."

Ayda then gestured with her pinky finger as if it was diving into her cup. She spoke again. Liana translated, "Now, your finger."

"My finger?"

"Yes," Liana said. "Swipe the bottom of the cup with your finger. Make a mark."

Doubting myself, I pressed my finger gingerly into the thick grounds.

Ayda and Liana giggled at my approach. Liana told me to try again, to really go for it, so I pressed until I felt the porcelain and smeared.

"Lav," Ayda said, lifting my small cup from my hands. Her gaze moved to the coffee as she twisted the cup in the air before her, looking down past her nose at the grounds.

"*I see a flower,*" she said.

"*Flower?*" I looked at Liana, not sure I was translating for myself correctly.

"Yes," Liana said. "A flower."

Ayda continued manipulating the angle of the cup. She spoke.

"The flower is in your past," Liana translated. "It means you had fertile ground to grow in your past."

"Oh, how nice." I smiled. I thought of my childhood, me under the oak trees reading in my parents' front yard, that enduring memory of a time in which I felt so grounded while looking out into the world through books.

"And a moon with bright rays," Liana translated.

"*Look*," Ayda said. She tried to point at the sludge in the back of my cup where the past was laid out in bits of wet bean from some other part of the world.

Liana translated again, "There is a light in your past now, though still hidden in some ways."

"I don't see the moon or rays," I said. "But I'm new at this." I laughed and shrugged like a puppet, which made Liana laugh. I made a conscious effort not to let them see on my face my surprise and immediate skepticism of a reading so close to the truth.

Liana continued translating and sipping on her own coffee. "There's an ostrich in your past, for luck."

Then, after a pause, Ayda looked into the bottom of the cup. The present. Liana translated, "She said there is a rabbit. That is a symbol of a personal fear or doubt." I cringed and then stayed motionless.

Ayda finally turned the cup all the way around to look into my future.

"But," she said through Liana, "an eagle is flying, saying you will have a good fruition for that which you have doubts."

In my heart, I ripped a little as two parts of me diverged for a few seconds.

One part of me wanted to keep this exercise light, to laugh and shrug for Ayda, Liana, and me to keep a comical demeanor.

To that end, I said, "Well, that seems on the nose. Doesn't it? I have been hoping this whole Peace Corps thing works out!"

Liana waved her hand at my joke, rolling her eyes sarcastically before translating for Ayda.

The other part of me leaned forward to look into the cup, which Ayda opened toward me. This part I hid from Ayda and Liana using my look-over-there joke—the part that feared losing everything—crawled out to see if, in the cup, an eagle truly flew. All I saw were ground beans.

"And a cat leg," Ayda said through Liana. "A cat leg. Do you see it?"

I looked in earnest, though predictably, I could not find a stray cat leg.

"That means you will have a problem leaving something."

"Leaving what?" I asked.

Ayda put the cup down and smiled at me. "She doesn't know," Liana said. "She is just telling you what she sees."

9

The first snow drifted down on a September morning. I'd been watching the snow caps grow on the mountains around Stepanavan every day since I arrived, watching the white creep closer and closer to us. As the first snow fell outside the office, my coworkers, all over thirty years old, went outside to celebrate with a snowball fight. I joined them, taking more hits than I felt comfortable delivering back. I'd worked up a sweat before Karine, who worked in the translation office, insisted we all stand together for a photo.

That day, I bought sweaters on the way home from work. I'd only packed a hoodie and a ski jacket my parents bought me for one church sponsored ski-trip. My Texas upbringing had not prepared me for the cold. There, if snow stuck to the ground up to a quarter inch, my entire town would just shut down. And the next week, it could be back to shorts-wearing weather.

I'd been fearing the cold for weeks. The temperature had already started dropping at night, and when my Peace Corps program manager Stepan called for our regular check-in, he asked me where the heater was in the house.

Hearing that there wasn't one near my room, he asked, "Brent jan, how are you staying warm?" I told him I took my thick duvet from the bed and wrapped up in it like a cocoon.

Stepan insisted on sending a Peace Corps Lada to my host family's house carrying an electric radiator and a small space heater. I continued wrapping myself like a cocoon but tucked the small space heater into the cocoon at my feet. The electric radiator confounded me, and I could not figure out how to coax a single degree out of the thing. But when Arevik came to my room to call for dinner and saw it plugged into the wall, she exclaimed a string of words.

When I told her I couldn't understand, she loudly chirped, "Tsk, tsk, tsk," and then said, "Brent jan... Pogh... pogh..." (*"Money... money..."*) while rubbing her fingers together in the air.

The snow came and chilled me so deeply that eventually, I accepted the fact that my toes would be cold nearly all day, every day. Making connections became harder because everything needed to happen indoors. I kept my routine of walking home in the evenings, stopping each night for comfort snacks at the same khanut along the way.

The young woman behind the counter began to anticipate my requests and would place a bag of M&Ms, which she called "Em Em Dems," and a liter bottle of Coca-Cola on the counter when it was my turn in line.

After dinner and nardi with Hovsep, I took to staying up past midnight watching TV, consuming both the bag of candy and the liter of soda in their entirety. As the evenings grew colder, I peered through cold puffs of my own breath, crunching and sipping away, losing myself in shows I'd downloaded from other volunteers' hard drives during the summer of training.

I watched all four seasons of *Grey's Anatomy* twice. When the friendship of the four twenty-something surgical interns coalesced in the orange light of a post-all-nighter morning, I ached to ride off to breakfast with them. When one of their patients died, I wept. When an intern's friend walked into the rain to hug them, I pulled the duvet around me and wished for a friend who understood me, who knew what I needed when I couldn't even say it for myself.

"I want friends," I told Zoe one night on the phone. "That's all I can think about watching this TV show."

On so many nights before, Zoe had told me about the friends she was getting to know in the far southern town of Goris.

"I'm sorry, boo. I don't know what it's like," Zoe told me. "I have Chris and Patrick and Meghan. I'm lucky."

She'd already told me about their movie nights, their game nights, the weekend afternoons sitting together and quietly reading, the evenings spent talking for hours about anything at all.

"You're lucky," I said back. "I'm not sure I can do this, Z. I don't know. I mean, I just came out." I thought of home, of my family who I wasn't sure I could return to, of a life I could see like a mirage in my mind in Austin, where I'd heard gay people were at least somewhat safe to dance and go out and get jobs and make friends.

"I've always wanted to do this," I said to Zoe. "But I just don't know."

"Me, too," she said. "I mean, I always thought joining Peace Corps, I'd be in Papua New Guinea or something. You know, somewhere with palm trees."

"Yeah," I said, looking at my dark bedroom window and knowing snow was already on the ground. "There are no palm trees here."

She laughed. "No shit."

"And there are no gays. I mean, like, no gays." Then, feeling cheeky, I said, "I haven't seen a single limp wrist."

Her laugh at that made me brave. "I'm serious, Zoe. I haven't seen a single curious glance my way. I've got my eyes peeled for any Armenian man to even just glance toward my crotch or look at another man's butt. Is that too much to ask?"

I heard her peel back from her phone in an uproarious giggle. "You need to get laid," she said.

"Well, yes. And how? It snowed, Zoe. It snowed already. The people in this town are wonderful. They are gloriously wonderful. I'm just lonely as hell. The only people I have to hang out with are imaginary ones who live on my computer and do surgery, and even they don't know I exist."

She paused. "Dude. You will be okay. We're going to get to Yerevan soon. There are gays in Yerevan. I've already found out about a gay bar."

"That. I want to do that," I said, my voice bright all of a sudden with a flash of hope.

When Zoe hung up the phone, I missed her. My jealousy writhed around like an earthworm in a mud puddle, unable to get out and unable to dig in. I knew if I quit, I'd be starting over again. And right now, I could barely have a conversation with the people around me because I didn't speak Armenian.

The women who did speak English in Stepanavan were kind and welcoming and so friendly, but I didn't think any of them would have felt comfortable hanging out with me one-on-one because, as I understood it, women and men didn't hang out together alone unless there was romantic interest. And I couldn't tell them that, in my case, they were totally safe from my romantic interest.

I felt a pilot-light-sized bit of excitement about my trip to Yerevan. If we found the gay bar, it would be the first gay bar of my life. Maybe I'd make gay friends in the city. *God,* I thought, *maybe I'll meet a man.*

But I wanted what Zoe had. I wanted to talk about being gay with friends I lived near. And I wanted to talk about home. I wanted pats on the back, encouraging words, and to feel understood in a way I couldn't seem to find.

After nearly two months in Stepanavan, Peace Corps allowed us to travel to Yerevan. So, at the end of September, I took a marshutni south.

The Peace Corps home office in Yerevan hosted volunteers in the capital who wanted to participate in interest committees—volunteer-led committees centered around topics like gender equity or youth engagement or environmental awareness. The committees were meant to organize mutual support in the form of resource sharing and idea generation. The meetings took place on a Friday, and no matter how serious any of us were about the work of these committees, all of us were excited to be in Yerevan, especially the A-17s. For us, this was the first unchaperoned weekend to stay in hostels, eat in restaurants, and party in the city's bars and clubs.

In all corners of Armenia, we found schedules for marshutnis, the vans that served as public transportation, and crammed ourselves into the small seats to make our way to the capital.

My marshutni from Stepanavan pulled into a Yerevan bus station, and I took a taxi from there to Envoy Hostel. Zoe was already there walking up the steps into the reception area.

"Zoe!" I screamed out of the window. She turned and dropped her bags, throwing her hands into the air. I stumbled through an exchange with the driver, giving him whatever he asked so I could run to my friend and wrap her in a hug like I hadn't been hugged in so many, many weeks.

"Zoe!" I screamed again. "We're here! We're here!"

"We're here!" she screamed back, and we jumped like children, our fingers intertwined in front of us.

My eyes welled up.

"I needed that hug," I told her.

"I know." She grabbed my hand and squeezed it. "Let's check in."

After registering at the reception desk, we walked into the largest sleeping area. I threw my bag onto a bunk, sat down, and leaned over to rest my greasy, unwashed hair on the white pillow. I watched Zoe nest, a ritual I'd never seen before and observed with admiration. Though we were the only people currently in the communal room, the beds above and around us were clearly claimed by strangers, the sheets mussed, bags or clothes strewn lazily on bed corners and laid against walls.

Zoe lit incense, waving the stick up and down the length of her bottom-bunk bed. Then she took her things out one by one. Her shirts and pants, she laid folded on the shelf built into the wall. She took out a book and her journal, laying them on the shelf with a pen placed on top. Her toiletry bag she left on the sheets, which I understood meant she was about to take a shower. She was wearing sandals and placed tennis shoes neatly under the bunk.

We both showered and then taxied to the Peace Corps office with wet hair. There, we saw other volunteers neither of us had seen since our summer training. We met volunteers from the A-16 cohort who'd already been in Armenia for a year and who began immediately sharing knowledge of an incredibly niche subject—how to enjoy Yerevan as a PCV, which included names of the best restaurants that served international fare and the best shaurma stands to grab snacks late at night when you're happy and drunk and stupid with hunger. Other kinds of advice came from older volunteers who partied less and delighted more in tactical fair—where to find the best vanilla for baking or where to find great wool yarn for all the knitting one might do over winter.

I sat in on the youth engagement committee meeting and the media and communications meeting. At lunch, the assistant director of Peace Corps found Zoe and me and invited us to a dinner.

"I have a friend, Garen," he told us. "He's lived here for many years, and he's gay and Armenian. He's agreed to host some of the A-16 and A-17 gay volunteers tonight for dinner."

A chill swept over me while he talked. Zoe was my first queer friend. And then there was John, an A-16 who lived an hour away from Stepanavan. He'd come once when I first arrived to Stepanavan to hike with me. I'd tried to come on to him and had desperately failed while we walked in chest-high grass in the mountains behind Stepanavan. My sweater became so embarrassingly matted with spiderwebs that I nearly decided to throw it away rather than give it to Arevik, who insisted on doing all my laundry, which I knew she did by hand.

John, with his easy smile and thick arms, and Zoe, with her bright queer confidence along with others I barely knew—Alisha, Kevin, and Peter—would all be at this dinner. I'd never been in a room with only gay people. I hadn't even actually made any kind of announcement to other volunteers that I was gay, and I knew that going with Zoe to Garen's house would officially put me in the Peace Corps queer sub-group. It felt to me like the last plunge into strange, gay waters.

I went to dinner.

Garen lived in a building that appeared new to me. The cement still had sharp corners, each brick and each stair a clean uniform grey.

John, Zoe, Alisha, Kevin, Peter, and I walked up the stairs together. Before we could knock, Garen opened the door halfway and said with enthusiasm, though not loudly, "Welcome. Welcome."

"Hello," John said. They hugged. Garen rubbed John's back with his hand in a familiar way, his smile shining through his black stubble, which connected at his temples with a head full of thick, black hair cut into a fade.

Garen shook my hands with his, which were thick and firm, with dark, soft hair on the back. My eyes traveled up his thick arms to his thick shoulders and his eyes, which because he was so tall, looked down on me with kindness.

Garen had ordered takeout, presenting on his table a spread of lavash, skewers of ground meat, a bowl of tabouleh, another of hummus, and another of olives. He lived alone, his apartment clean, cool, and well-adorned with comfortable seating and modern Armenian art.

"Wine, anyone?" Garen asked, and when we all said yes, he poured for each of us in handblown, tall glasses before handing them out, looking each of us kindly in the eyes. His welcome filled me with a sense of ease. We were safe here. I was safe here.

"Okay," he said, looking at the A-16s. "Let's tell them what it's like."

And so, they did. Alisha told us what it was like to be bisexual, to have her body touched in ways she didn't want on buses or in crowded grocery stores. She talked of catcalls thrown at her while knowing the callers had no idea she'd more easily fall in love with an Armenian woman than some man calling to her from the street.

Garen talked about his decades of traveling between Armenia and America, his family in California but his heart in Yerevan. He revealed that he'd just ended a long-term relationship with a Yerevantsi man whose family never knew they were together. He talked about how painful it was to have reached the age his grandfather had been when Garen first came out years ago, yet still in Yerevan he couldn't walk down the street holding hands with the man he loved.

"But you can dance with him," John said.

Garen laughed. "Yes," he said and then waved his hand in a gesture to all of us. "We're all going out dancing. Tonight. At Cocoon."

"Oh really," Zoe said. She leaned over the table, swirling her wine glass in front of her in a caricature of intrigue.

"Cocoon is the only gay club in Yerevan," Alisha said.

Another chill moved so fast through my body that I worried I'd knock over my own wine glass as I reached for it, desperate to drink and hide what I was sure was visible fear on my face. I'd never even seen a gay club from the outside.

"It's in a basement," Alisha continued. "It's not an official gay club, but all the queers find their way there. Mostly men, though."

The conversation eventually moved on, and when I told everyone at the table the secret that only Zoe knew, that I'd come out only a few days before arriving in Armenia, some of them quietly gasped.

"Congratulations," Kevin said.

"Oh my god," John said. "Cheers to that."

"Cheers to that," Garen repeated but with less exuberance, a hint of sympathy and understanding in his eyes.

The table raised their glasses to me, and we all drank together.

After dinner, out in the summer night air, I breathed deeply as we walked back toward the center of the city. All of us were giddy with wine and the confidence that comes from looking into someone else's eyes and feeling seen in some way most everyone else doesn't see you. We were queer, all of us. And here, in the low land of Yerevan, we were somehow younger with a night of promise ahead of us.

Garen didn't come with us but said he might come out later. When he offered a taxi, all of us gracefully declined the generosity in favor of taking in a warm night in the city.

A gay bar. Cocoon. I wanted to go there straight away, but I could tell John and Alisha were texting friends and guiding us to where they were. Perhaps we'd make it to Cocoon later. I didn't want to press it.

"Zoe." I ran up to her where she walked next to Alisha and wrapped my arm in hers.

She squeezed my hand. "I need to dance," she said.

"I need to dance," I said back.

We ended up at an outdoor café near the Opera, a giant circular building where actual operas were performed, another thing that had seemed so left of masculine to me that I would never have dared show interest lest someone see beneath that interest and find my gayness.

Zoe and I ordered ice cream and shots with funny names. Mine came out with a turquoise liquid floating above a yellow liquid. Combined, it tasted like dried pineapple and cotton candy.

Other volunteers joined us—Amanda and Hayley, who had spent the summer with us in Teghenik, and A-16 volunteers I didn't recognize, except for Scott, whose square shoulders and calm eyes snagged my drunk and swirling heart like a fishhook. At every other time of my life, I would have seen him, felt my interest come up as a wave, and then immediately banged my inner gavel so hard that instant quiet took over. I would never have let myself think of him, would have gotten up and left if I needed to.

I had such control over my desire. And while I did not, in that moment, apologize to myself for years of internal self-flogging meant to subdue my longings, there in that café by the Opera, I saw another volunteer. Scott's dark blue T-shirt lay over his chest, holding his biceps, his snug blue jeans hugging his legs and rubbing them as he walked from table to table, saying hello to each volunteer. I let my desire move through my body, not out of it, not in any kind of expression of want that anyone could perceive. But a warm feeling traveled through me, a feeling I let myself perceive and even enjoy.

Eventually, this group of volunteers grew to more than twenty, and all of them wanted to go to a bar that was not Cocoon.

"Zoe," I said, quietly grabbing her arm. "Cocoon. I have to go."

"I know," she said, putting her empty ice cream dish back on the table. "We're going."

We got directions from Alisha, and together Zoe and I walked down Sayat Nova and then Teryan Street past the small man-made pond with a statue of a musician with exaggerated features stretching his skinny fingers over a piano. We walked past Yum-Yum Donuts and then a grocery store. Then, finally, across the street from a billboard that hung on a fence displaying a very large portrait of Kim Kardashian, we arrived. The neon sign for

Cocoon glowed above a cement staircase that led to a big black basement door. A few men stood at the top of the staircase smoking. Zoe grabbed my hand and pulled me down the steps with her.

The walls, the floor, the ceiling, the bar, and the built-in benches and small tables were all painted the same shiny black with a few recessed lights that cast a yellow sheen on everyone. Behind the bar a woman with naturally red hair slung drinks. She twirled bottles, her thin frame and broad shoulders creating a silhouette in front of a wall of booze lit by blue lights in a plastic tube that snaked around the bottles. Small groups of men sat at tables or stood on the floor sipping drinks and talking over music so loud they had to lean in to hear each other.

My nerves took over, and I couldn't look at anyone, afraid I might make eye contact with a stranger and not know what to do.

"We're getting shots," Zoe said. We'd had a handful of drinks over the past five hours, and I somehow still needed more courage. I stood barely a few steps inside the door and watched Zoe move her way through a crowd of men across the small room that made up the whole establishment. I watched Zoe order drinks and then lean over the bar, invite the bartender in for a whisper, and then gently place her hand on the back of the bartender's neck while she spoke into her ear. The bartender smiled and then slid two clear shots to her, followed by two vodka sodas.

"She's so fucking hot," Zoe said, handing me the shots.

"Voghch," I said.

"What?" Zoe said.

"Voghch," I said louder. "It's a toast. I think it means health in Armenian."

We found a table, and I tried to take in the room. Most of the men wore softer variations of what I'd seen men wearing all night. The typical Armenian male uniform I'd seen was a black shirt, usually a T-shirt, and slim-fitting black pants with black leather shoes, the toes of which reached out in front of them to a point. In Cocoon, men still wore a lot of black shirts and pants, and everyone wore pointy shoes. But those who wore black added jewelry, maybe a necklace or a silver ring. I saw a few black scarves, and one man wore a black newsboy cap.

Some of the men wore the same kind of uniform but white. A few threw in a colorful scarf or a necklace with a colorful stone. These were all clothes they could wear anywhere on the street without drawing attention, or so I guessed.

When I was five years old, I made my first friend, a girl named Katy, who told me she liked a boy and then chased him. She was my first friend, and her game seemed fun. It even made my heart flutter. So, I picked a boy, one in a black T-shirt with a gold necklace. I chased him around the playground, which he didn't like. He ran away from the playground to the group of teachers keeping watch.

My kindergarten teacher asked me why I was chasing him.

"I like his necklace," I spluttered, searching for a reason but unable to explain.

She told me, "Boys don't chase other boys." She sat me out of recess while the boy I chased went back.

Fear settled into my chest. He'd tell everyone I'd done something wrong, something classified as wrong based on the fact that we were both boys.

And then she'd told my mother when Mom came to pick me up that I had been chasing another boy, and she needed to watch my behavior. This was the first time I felt I could be separated from her based on how I interacted with other boys.

From that moment, I watched my behavior, trying desperately to catch any fairness, weakness, flounce, or misplaced smile that would invite scrutiny and then discovery that I was different, that my body was pulled by a gravity that pulled no one else I knew. And I was constantly vigilant of the world around me. I could detect the slightest curl of the lip, the slightest glance that indicated what a person might be thinking. The smallest signs of danger, maybe a question about who I liked from a school mate, or a grin when I said I'd enjoyed a musical, and I would figure out how to correct the perception or imperceptibly run away as fast as I could. And if ever any boy around me showed a sign they might be gay, I fled.

Now, here they were—Armenian men looking at each other with longing, intent, flirtation, and proximity. At a table, one man's hand rested on top of another man's hand. At another table, a man with the sweetest expression in his eyes looked up from where he rested his head on another man's shoulder. A group at a third table burst into laughter with high pitches and flailing hands. In the center of the small room, men danced to Nelly Furtado and Timbaland's "Promiscuous," and two of them wrapped their arms around each other, their hips grinding softly in rhythm with the drums.

I fled.

"I need to use the restroom," I told Zoe, and I climbed stairs to a black door. Inside, the fluorescent light caught every bit of dirt on the white walls. I looked into the mirror. I splashed water on my face. I turned to the toilet and lifted a flimsy plastic seat to pee. Someone knocked on the door, and a scene flashed in my eyes that a man could be behind it, could push his way in after seeing me, pursuing me up the stairs, thrusting open the door, and pinning me against the wall to kiss me and touch me and take me.

"Jesus," I told myself out loud. "Calm down and wash your hands."

When I came back into the room, Zoe was leaning over the bar again, talking to the bartender, who listened and washed glasses, half-smiling.

I sat down at a table, unsure of what to do. Over an amped-up bass thud, Nicki Minaj sang "Starships" as a few men laughed and jumped in the air. I watched them, imagining that they must know each other well. I wondered how they met each other in a world that forced them to assimilate, to put their heads down and blend into a crowd of Armenian men on the streets of Yerevan. How would a young gay man know there were other gay men in the city? How would they find each other? And how would a young gay man on his own know there was a place like this to find the smallest crowd of people throwing their arms around each other or hip-thrusting to top forty American hits?

A tall man walked over to me in black boots with tall heels and a steel ring strapped to the side of each. He wore long black jeans over long legs, a black T-shirt, and a black leather vest. His thick, black hair was swept away from his face and ran down the back of his neck. His black mustache curled when he looked at me and smiled.

I didn't stand.

"Hi," he said to me in English.

"Hi," I replied.

He knelt and put one knee on the ground.

"I'm Hayk," he told me.

His smile was kind, his eyes staring at mine, steady and half-closed. He asked if I was American.

I took a swig of my vodka soda. "I am." I had no idea how to have this conversation, my first in a gay bar with a gay man, who I was pretty sure was coming onto me. I felt like an old door without a key, and he was trying out magic words to unlock it.

"I'm Iranian," he said. "And Armenian. I come from Iran. Tehran."

"That's great," I said.

He reached up to my face, covered in stubble, and stroked my cheek with his hand. "You're cute," he said.

"Thanks," I said.

He brought his hands together to unbutton the top button of my Oxford shirt and then the button after that until a whisp of chest hair peeked out of the crevice.

"This is cuter," he said. He reached just barely inside my shirt, stroked my chest, and fingered wisps of my chest hair, grazing my skin with his finger tips in circular waves. He moved his hand out of my shirt and took my left hand in both of his, massaging my palm.

He asked me more questions, and to each, I gave short one-word answers, unsure how to return affection, unsure if I wanted to, unsure of what I would want on the other side of this moment. I was frozen, and his heat wasn't strong enough to melt me.

Suddenly, after so many one-word answers to his questions, he said, "It was nice to meet you. Have a great night," and let go of my hand. And with the abruptness of someone just drunk enough to be short without being mean, he turned and walked into a group of men on the other side of the room.

Minutes later, Zoe returned. "Siren gave these to us," she said, and she handed me another vodka shot.

"Who?" I asked, fatigue starting to settle in and mingling with disappointment that I had turned to stone in the first openly gay flirtation of my life. Why hadn't I said anything back? Why hadn't I raised my hand to meet his?

"Siren," Zoe repeated. "That's the bartender's name."

"Okay," I muttered. I threw my shot back, and in midwince, I squeezed out, "This is the last one."

Zoe threw hers back and then sat next to me.

"I saw that man coming onto you," she said. "Rawr." And she pawed at me with her hand like a claw.

"Yeah," I said. "Not my type."

She laughed and said, "If he's not your type, who is?"

I wondered if I was supposed to know. I surely didn't now. And would I ever?

Then, a familiar piano glissando broke my train of thought. A chorus of men and women from the sixties sang out from the speakers, a tune I remembered immediately from my father's record collection.

"Dancing Queen!" I shouted to Zoe, and she pulled me up to my feet. I tingled with sudden embarrassment, feeling unable to hide as the only non-Armenian man in the bar. I felt an impulse to run, but I stayed there in the center of the room, swaying and listening to Abba sing.

None of the men, in fact, were staring at me. The room was being swept up in music, and I was suddenly and completely being swept up with it. Men quickly joined us on the dance floor. Men started swaying around the perimeter. Some men climbed on top of their tables. And then shirts and scarves swirled in the air while they sang, keyboards and bass wrapping around us.

I gave myself to the moment then. I danced, spinning to see the room, to see every man's flame burning, a fire of joy made from pent-up energy releasing into the air and into each other.

I'd been embarrassed at my failure to flirt with a stranger. I'd been embarrassed about my otherness in a room full of people who wore otherness like a hidden badge of courage. They'd found each other, these Armenian men. They weren't embarrassed. They were waving their shirts and scarves in the air, happy to have found each other, happy to be alive.

I carried that energy into the night. Zoe and I walked to a twenty-four-seven grocery store where I bought Pringles and water, and she bought Schweppes Bitter Lemon and a packet of gummy bears. Outside the store, next to a building being remodeled, Zoe found a flattened cardboard box and placed it on a dusty step, sitting there and snacking.

I felt a sudden welling up, a fullness. I had a queer friend I found charming, sitting now on a perch having her peculiar late-night snack. I had gone to my first gay bar, been the object of desire, felt myself in some way more desirable. I crossed over a threshold, and what I found on the other side was a garden where I could be planted, where love was water and our own eyes, our own witness of each other, warmed us like sunlight.

10

After the dinner at Garen's and my first night in Yerevan, John and I kept texting. Happy to have a gay friend, I texted questions about being gay in Armenia, what it was like to date, and how he met gay men. I thrilled less at his answers than I did envisioning his burly hands typing out responses to me on a tiny phone, me in my small town and him, an hour away in Vanadzor, the capital of the Lorri region and its biggest city. After a few weeks of our new friendship, he invited me to a Peace Corps volunteers' Halloween party hours away. When people asked about the snowflakes I'd cut from paper and draped all over me, I told them I dressed as the scariest thing I could think of—winter.

I danced with another volunteer, Vanessa, the sound of her crinkling corset made of beer cans mixing with "The Monster Mash." Both sounds drowned my longing to dance with John and Peter instead, the two men grinding and then making out on the dance floor until they took their kisses outside into the cold night.

When John invited me to his apartment in Vanadzor, I fantasized about holding his face in my hands, his chinstrap beard scratching my palms.

He showed no such intentions for any kind of intimacy. He'd invited me along with all the other volunteers in the area, a group designated by Peace Corps as a Warden Group—the volunteers we would gather with during an emergency like a major earthquake or political upheaval. Together in John's living room, we read about what we should do if we had to evacuate, just the six of us together, heading up to Georgia.

We unpacked a blue plastic emergency barrel, checking off a supply list that included an axe, toilet paper, and MREs. Then we made dinner and waited an entire evening for Lady Gaga's new video for "Bad Romance," to load on YouTube before watching it over and over for an hour. Afterward, I washed dishes with John in the kitchen and listened to him talk about growing up Mormon, comparing our stories.

"You'll get there," he told me when we talked about how I'd so recently come out. "You'll make friends. And we're going to be hanging out a lot in the Warden Group."

I swooned.

When we finally decided to turn in, most of our group unrolled their sleeping bags in the living room, but John invited me to sleep with him in his bed. In his bedroom.

Waiting until all his guests were done, John brushed his teeth last in his only bathroom, and by the time he came into his room, I'd already decided against crawling under his sheets. Could I have climbed under his sheets without that explicit invitation? I unrolled my sleeping bag on top of his duvet, the bright orange polyester nearly glowing in the dark room. We undressed on opposite sides of his full-size bed. I didn't look at him but wanted to. I stripped down to my boxer briefs, hoping he would turn and look. I couldn't, though, turn to see if he was looking, afraid of the connection I wanted but petrified to initiate.

He turned off the light.

From inside my sleeping bag, the hood of it pulled over my head, I said to John, "Good night."

"Good night, Brent," he replied.

"Thank you for having us here," I said.

"I'm glad you're here," he muttered and went quiet.

As the moonlight shone down on us. I imagined John turning to me, the light on his face, his hand on my shoulder, my chest, my belly. He didn't move.

Turn to me, I said to him inside my mind, my mouth soundless and dry. *Turn to me*, I thought.

My heart began to beat and then pound so hard I could hear blood rushing in my ears. From inside the sleeping bag, I could hear the friction of my skin against nylon as I breathed, which to me seemed so loud I was sure he could hear it. I was sure he could hear me.

My lust turned to panic, my panic to dread. I tried to comfort myself with thoughts like, *Any minute now*, and then, *not tonight. Your first kiss won't happen tonight.* Not the first kiss, the first touch, the first grope, the first man to hold me at night and breathe into the back of my neck and fall asleep feeling my heart beat against his hand.

He, of course, wouldn't have known I felt any of these things. John, the first out, gay friend of my life, wouldn't have known I wanted him to take me. I only ever returned his smiles with half-smiles, patting him on the back when he held me in a hug, draping my sleeping bag over his duvet so two thick layers of fabric lay between us.

What was I afraid of? I finally turned on my side to face him, hoping I would see his eyes looking for mine. Instead, I saw only the back of his neck, the hair on his nape curling away from me. I watched him breathe slowly and knew he was asleep.

When my heart finally calmed enough that I no longer heard the friction of my pulse against the sleeping bag, I tried to coax myself to sleep by playing the "Bad Romance" music video back again in my head. I wished myself away from this apartment. I wished myself into a fantasy where I was the one clad in white leather surrounded by other people in leather crawling out of plastic cocoons and then dancing unafraid into the light.

~ ~ ~

The following Monday morning, I returned to the office. I entered the break room to find Karine making the coffee and standing at the white stove by the back door, a hand on her hip as she waited for the water under the coffee grounds to boil.

Near the end of the daily morning meeting, Ayda finally entered, swinging herself through the doorway with half a dozen full-to-bursting cellophane bags in her hands and hanging from her wrists. Yeraz and an intern named Varhuni stood to help, removing the bags from her hands.

Next to me at the break room table, Liana turned to me. "Brent jan, I forgot to tell you yesterday. Everyone in the office decided that today we would eat khash. Do you know khash?"

"I think so," I said. I'd heard other volunteers speak of khash with the article "the." The khash—spoken of like a ghost that might visit you during service. Like a dish you'd have to brace yourself for.

"I don't really know how it's made," I told Liana, "but you don't eat it often. Right?"

"No, we don't. Once or twice a year, really. It is a stew made from the feet of a cow. Have you had that?"

"I haven't." I concentrated hard on not moving my face, not giving any sign of what I might think about eating the feet of a cow.

"Is it the whole foot?" I imagined that perhaps only the lower leg was cooked, the chef harvesting what little meat hid between ankle bones and then drinking the broth.

"Yes, the whole foot. The part at the end and the part they walk on."

"The hooves?"

"I don't know that word, Brent jan."

Liana continued, her hands on the table between us. "Everyone contributed to this meal. Two thousand drams. Do you want to contribute?"

"Of course," I said. I walked to my desk and fished my wallet from my backpack, returning with two thousand-dram bills. I hoped someone else on the team would see the American contributing, hoped they'd see my effort to belong. I wasn't surprised to see that no one lifted an eye.

The day passed with me at my desk, writing emails and looking at project plans. Yeraz asked for help writing a newsletter to donors in London, and I spent a couple of hours rewriting or trying to translate passages about kindergarten upgrades, clothes distributions, and winter concerns for kids in villages.

The office filled with wet air and the smell of stew. Though new to me, I heard my coworkers talk to each other with brightness, the way I talked about holiday food, with nostalgia and camaraderie.

"Lav hot a galis, che?" Vigen said as he passed my desk. *A good smell is coming, no?*

"*Yes*," I said, though I honestly had no opinion of it other than it was new.

"Khash kutenk! Khash kutenk!" Tirayr sang these words to Yeraz and me as he passed in front of our desks, dancing a bit with each step. When Hermine tried to pass him, he took her arm, singing his khash tune. As their feet shuffled, Hermine's giggles floated through the steam.

By lunchtime, condensation clung to the break room windows, filtering the light. On the stove, the lid of an enormous pot rested off center, tilted up on the knees of cows, the legs just barely too long to fit in fully, no brain to tell them to bend.

"Brent jan?" Yeraz called for my attention as I sat at the table for a light lunch of bread and homemade salty cheese. "Do you know why we eat khash?"

"Not really," I said and leaned in, starting to get caught up in some new holiday feeling.

"We always eat this at least once a year," Yeraz said, her voice bright and sparkling. "In winter. In the coldest months. For the... what do you say... for the inside of the bone?"

"The marrow?"

"Yes. The marrow. The marrow and the stew from the bones helps your bones in winter. And this soup makes you strong."

"Really?"

"Yes, Brent jan. Every winter, we eat the khash for strength, to build our bodies up for the rest of winter."

My imagination traveled then to what I knew of the earliest days of Peace Corps in Armenia, those years after the Spitak earthquake that killed tens of thousands and left half a million Armenians homeless. A few years later, the Soviet Union fell, leaving the country isolated and disconnected from food, supplies, and hope for many. For years, the hills were stripped bare to make fire for the long winters. When the hills ran out of trees, some families ripped up their own floorboards to give warmth to their children.

Then I thought back to my summer in Teghenik and an afternoon when I saw the cow I'd walked home with slaughtered, the meat sold to a butcher, the head and skin and hooves kept in pots in the cool bathroom until they could be taken to a relative's freezer.

Instead of the normal late afternoon departures home, everyone at the office stayed past sundown. Tirayr and Artavan left and returned with more cellophane bags, making trip after trip back to the car. In came soda bottles and bottles of vodka, bags of bread and lavash, and bags of herbs. Women came down from the translation office upstairs, and Yeraz stood to enter the break room while the TDFs left the last cellophane bags and went outside to smoke their thin cigarettes.

Finally, Liana called me to dinner. "Ari, Brent jan. Khash kutenk."

In the break room, places were set with wide bowls on plates, behind which stood water glasses and shot glasses. Small groups of soda, water, vodka, and wine bottles created centerpieces down the long table, in between which Ayda had piled plates with bread, herbs, and cheese.

Yeraz arrived to greet each team member, asking them something in Armenian I didn't quite understand. Each passed her and took a seat at the table. Ayda ladled the stew into wide bowls, which Yeraz then placed in front of each teammate. In each bowl of broth sat a piece of leg, some with a hoof on the end.

"Do you want a middle or an end?" Yeraz asked me.

"A middle is good, maybe?"

And quickly, with a light delivery, Yeraz presented me with a brothy soup and a cow ankle. From one joint burst what I assumed was cartilage, a yellowy mass of shiny, semitranslucent wiggling. The joint rested in a bowl full of clearish stock filled with pink-grey bits I couldn't identify.

Karine sat down across the table, and I asked her, "What are these?" pointing to the pink-grey pieces.

"That is…" She stopped, leaning back to catch Yeraz as she passed with another bowl. "How do you say this in English?"

Yeraz paused, and the broth in the bowl she held nearly sloshed over, another hoof waving as it rolled with the soup. "The intestine."

"Ah," I said over-quickly, battling my unwarranted fear of eating parts of an animal I had never considered eating. Without missing a breath, I said, "Where I'm from, we call this part 'chitlins.'" I'd only ever seen them eaten once when my university's dining hall hosted Black History Month options one Sunday at the cafeteria buffet.

I felt embarrassed. My head knew that food was food. That a cow ankle was not different from a cow shoulder or a turkey neck or the giblets my grandmother turned to gravy every Thanksgiving. But still, part of me was repelled by intestines. And Karine could see it. It made her laugh.

"Chitlins," Karine repeated, looking down at her bowl and listening to the sound of a new word in her own voice. Then she picked up her piece of leg and took a bite out of the hoof.

When everyone had a bowl of khash, Tirayr stood at the end of the table, raised his glass, and said loudly over all conversations, "Bolory… kenats!"

Kenats. *A toast.*

Now, months into my Armenian life, I'd eaten at enough birthdays and holiday celebrations to know that no alcohol could be nursed. You could drink only after a toast. Tirayr was here to begin the toasts and, therefore begin the drinking. I'd also picked up that the youngest man at the table should pour drinks, so I wrenched the lid off the nearest vodka bottle and offered it to everyone at the table.

"Kenats, khashi hamar," Tirayr said. *"We eat this meal for strength. Strength for our beautiful office friends."* Then he went on. *"To your health, we drink, my friends. For health for each of the beautiful women here. For the strength of my brothers. And for the beautiful women, that they will have more strength than ever before. And become more and more beautiful..."*

"Tirayr, lav eli," Liana said, prompting everyone to laugh together before we all cheered together, "Voghch!"

After the acidic shot burned my throat, I dipped my spoon into the broth, tasting the intestine and then suppressing a gag that induced guilt. *They are proud of this,* I thought. I wanted to be, too.

Without a shred of judgment in her voice, Hermine called to me from across the table. "Tes," she said. *Look.* Then she ripped lavash into small pieces, filling the bowl until all the broth had soaked into the bread.

After another toast from Tirayr, this time again *"for the beautiful women."* I threw back another vodka shot and picked up my joint.

I surprised myself, finding the bulging cartilage pleasant to chew on, like gummy bears flavored with salt and bone. I ate all the nearly fist-sized bulge, sipping on Coca-Cola between bites.

I will need to be drunk for the intestine part, I thought. I threw back full shots when Tirayr said a toast *"for the mothers,"* then another "*for the fathers*," and then "*for the family*." I started to sip half shots by the toast "*for Stepanavan*" and "*for World Vision*." I barely sipped all the others until Tirayr looked to me red in the face and said a charming but sloppy toast, "*for* our Brent," saying the last two words in English. To that, I drank a final full shot, letting tears well up while everyone looked at me, lifting their glasses toward my smile.

I left some edibles on the bone but cleaned most of my cow ankle, the meat tasting of earth and salt, the broth of ligament and gelatin and pepper and more salt. The bits of intestine delivered a foul effervescence, but I ate most of that, too, sliding down pieces with uncouth and sneaky off-toast swigs of more vodka.

I, of course, became completely toasted.

"*I love it here*," I proclaimed in sloppy Armenian to anyone who would listen. To Hermine. Then Aram. Then Artavan. Then Melik patted me on the shoulder and told me, "*We are glad you are here, Brent jan.*"

"Jan," I replied, beaming. "*What a nice word. We don't have a nice word when we talk to someone to tell them they are a good person to us. To tell them we love them without using this word, 'love.' No one says* 'jan' *in English. We don't have it.*"

Melik patted me on the shoulder again.

I rolled up lavash and nursed it for a while, nibbling and knowing I'd tied my stomach in knots turning from khash to vodka to lavash to khash to vodka in a circle I lost track of.

When I noticed Liana had left the party, I looked out the break room door past my desk to see Liana's office door open. Liana was typing at her desk, her face lit in the dark by her computer screen.

Soon, I was leaning on her doorframe asking, "Are you working?"

"Ayo, Brent jan. Just trying to get a few things done." I recognized the amused lift from her voice that let me know she knew I was drunk.

"I love it here," I told her. "I just love it."

"I'm glad," she teased. "I think you've really enjoyed the khash?"

"I did. I did. I didn't think I would. We don't eat cow hooves in Texas," I said.

"Ah, but you will be strong for all of winter now. The khash gives you strength. The marrow of the bones fortifies your bones."

"I hope so." I smiled and fell into a slump in her black office chair. I leaned my head on the wall behind me and closed my eyes.

"I wasn't sure," I told her. "I wasn't sure I would like it here."

She looked up again from her computer. "Really?"

"I just left home at such a weird time," I said. *I should tell her now*, I thought. *I should tell her I'm gay.*

"It was just a weird time," I went on. "There's so much you don't know." And, like some vaudevillian, I mimed being overwhelmed, slapping my hands on my face and planting my elbows on my knees. Then, immediately, I sat up. "There's just a lot happening."

"Like what."

I paused. *Tell her now*, I said to myself. And the three words played over and over again. I ignored the thought long enough that my pause had become too pregnant.

"Just family stuff. Family. And the way they understand me. Or don't understand me."

Liana shut her computer, leaving us both lit only by the light that bounced off the walls from the break room, where the rest of our team laughed together and drank and sipped broth.

"Family can be hard," Liana said. "Being away from family is the hardest part of the Peace Corps experience, I think. It is something every volunteer I've ever known in Stepanavan talks about."

"Yeah," I said quietly, hoping she would find a way to my secret without me.

"Is your family okay?"

"Yeah," I said, and then put my hands in my face again.

I didn't tell her at all. I couldn't let her in, couldn't tell her I'm gay. I was simply too afraid.

I thought, walking into that room, that maybe Liana would be okay with it. With my drunk head in my drunk hands, I still clearly felt the frozen river of fear in my veins. Liana could reject me the way my parents had. Liana could tell the rest of the office, and they could reject me. And I would have to go home to Texas alone, unable to return to the house I grew up in. No money. No job. No idea where I would go.

The voice that prompted me to tell her faded. I lifted my head from my hands.

"I'm just emotional. It's a big deal, you know, being away from family." This I said to a woman who lived through the fall of the Soviet Union, the Spitak earthquake, the days when some Armenian families were so poor they pulled up the floor from beneath their feet to burn the wood and warm their children in winter.

"It is," Liana said. "I know it is very hard."

11

The days grew colder in Stepanavan, and I moved from warm place to warm place. In the mornings, I walked to work in my ski jacket, knit hat, gloves, and scarf I wrapped and wrapped around my face until all but my glasses were gone.

I didn't know how to live here, to be cold and confident. I tried to follow my coworkers' examples. When I saw them typing in fingerless gloves, I kept mine on throughout the day. When I saw Yeraz walk to make tea, I followed her for a warm drink. I went through points of gratitude like a rosary. I was grateful to be given heaters without having to buy them. I was grateful for the radiator behind my desk at work. I was grateful Yeraz made me tea.

And then, at night, I rewatched *Grey's Anatomy* again. I continued chasing bags of M&Ms with liters of Coca-Cola each night until I was too tired to sit up in my duvet cocoon. Then I'd transfer to the bed.

One night, after I'd already constructed my cocoon and was two episodes of *Grey's Anatomy* deep into my night, I had to pee. I emerged and walked out of my room into the living room to find no one. Some of the furniture was gone, and the TV had been removed. I walked into the entry hallway and saw that my host family had installed one of the living room couches into the hallway next to a newly installed, small, rectangular metal stove on metal stilts with a hose running into it. At the end of the hose, a flame burned and lit up the box. Hovsep, Arevik, and Gohar were all in Gohar's bedroom watching the TV they'd moved there from the living room. The bedroom doors were open, I assumed, to let in heat from the stove. The entry hallway was warm, some ten to twenty degrees warmer than my room.

As I peed, my heart sank.

They left me, I thought. They left me in the farthest away, coldest room in the house, freezing every night without even an invitation to sit with them by the fire.

It didn't occur to me that by this time, they already knew my routine, that after dinner I retired for hours alone in my room. Why wouldn't they think I was self-sufficient?

I did not yet know that many Armenians move to one area of the house, heating only a small portion of their home to save money. I didn't think about the fact that in the layout of their home, their yearly tradition of moving all household activities to their bedrooms and kitchen would leave no room for an extra person. I did not consider that they did not know and had not been told that I had no idea how to make my plug-in radiator work. I didn't even know at the time that it was called a radiator. We didn't have them in Texas.

I went back into my room and rejoined Meredith Grey and friends and thought about how the characters on that show needed each other.

No one needs me here, I thought. No one called me. No one asked me to eat lunch with them at work. No one invited me for dinner or came to have a chat just to see what I was up to. No one seemed curious about me at all. I felt I could disappear from this town, and the very few people who knew me would shrug as if they'd smelled a curious waft of smoke.

I called Zoe. "They moved into the other side of the house." She understood my loneliness but couldn't get into the sunken place with me. Multiple nights a week, she was eating dinner with other American volunteers. On weekends, they watched movies together, cooked their favorite foods, and played board games. They traded books, and Meghan, an A-16, knitted a hat for everyone to keep their heads warm.

"No one cares that I'm here," I told her.

"I care," she said.

"I know. But you're a million miles away."

Arevik brought me dinner in my room now that half the house was too cold to sit in for very long. This nightly dinner delivery was not something we discussed. Arevik just showed up with a plate at my bedroom door. After a few nights of this dinner delivery, I understood that we would no longer be eating together.

After one dinner delivery, Arevik stood at the doorway and spoke with her sharp, high voice. "*Brent, jan. December is coming. Do you have a plan?*"

"*Yes,*" I said. I put my plate of chicken leg and vegetables on my small table next to my computer.

Peace Corps requirements for many things vary from country to country. In Armenia, one requirement for volunteers was that we stay with host families for ten weeks. After that point, we could decide to stay with our host families or move out on our own.

I was terrified of being on my own. The constant cold. My inability to heat even a single bedroom properly. With how little I could speak Armenian, how would I navigate bills with my landlord? And how sad would I be to simply go to a big cement-block building alone every night to see neighbors all around me who cared about my presence even less than it seemed Hovsep and Arevik did? Perhaps I could figure out how to get them to love me, stay in their house, and survive winter with this family. I knew at least at dinner time they would call for me.

"*I hope...*" I said in limited Armenian. "*I hope I stay here in your home. Maybe until spring?*"

Arevik pursed her lips and brought her eyes down. I assumed this meant she was concerned and disappointed. "*No.*"

I sucked the air out of my closed mouth so my cheeks and lips pressed hard against my teeth—a barely detectable way to brace myself.

She said something I couldn't discern. I heard the words, "*Your... ends.*"

"*I'm sorry,*" I said. "*I don't understand. My Armenian...*"

She breathed in thought for a minute and then tried again. "*You paper.*" She mimed showing me words on a page and then signing it.

I understood now. My contract.

"*Your paper. It says you stay in our home for ten weeks.*"

I wanted this to be a misunderstanding. I ignored the cues she was giving me and pressed on into my own hope. "Ah," I said. "*This paper. It can be...*" I couldn't find the words. "*I can stay. Peace Corps... they say I can stay until November, December, January, February, March, April... I can stay for a time that is good for me and good for you. And the family. Everyone.*"

She said immediately, "*No.*"

A shock ran up my spine.

"*In two weeks...*" And she said more words I didn't know.

"Chem haskanum," I said again. *I don't understand.*

"*In two weeks, you leave.*"

~ ~ ~

A few days before I left Hovsep and Arevik, I got sick. Maybe I ate something wrong. I noticed that my family started keeping food in the very cold living room, which I realized was likely the temperature of a refrigerator. On my way to work each morning, I passed by uncovered plates of food—meats, vegetables, sometimes yogurt or sour cream. In my mind I blamed the living room food for my somersaulting stomach.

Arevik brought me dinner, and when she saw that I was curled up in bed instead of wrapped in my cocoon in front of *Grey's*, she asked me, *"Are you all right?"*

I looked up and smiled weakly. *"No. I have bad... here is bad."* I pointed to my stomach.

"Come with me," she said.

I held my stomach and stood up while concentrating on keeping myself from vomiting. Arevik set my dinner, this time a bowl of borscht, on the table. She gathered my duvet and pillow. *"Go there,"* she said and pointed me to the living room.

I stepped into the room, and she came around me and into the warm entry hallway where the gas stove blazed. She put my pillow on the couch and laid my duvet out over the cushions. "Ari," she said, pointing to the couch. *Come.*

I lay down. The couch itself was warm enough to shock me with comfort, my cold skin responding so intensely that I felt overcome with gratitude.

"What happened?" Arevik asked. Hovsep was watching TV in Gohar's room, and Gohar was out. Arevik sat on the edge of a cushion near my feet.

"Maybe food? Now it hurts."

She put her hand on my leg near my ankle. "*Do you want…*" Another word I didn't know flew by me.

"Chem haskanum." *I don't understand.*

She mimed putting a handful of something in her mouth, drinking, swallowing.

"*Dictionary?*" I said. This trick I'd started when no amount of miming or talking around a word would help me and another person understand each other. I stood, my stomach churning, and walked softly to my room, bringing back my Armenian/English dictionary.

Arevik looked through the book, found the word and pointed to it on the page.

"Ah," I said. "*Medicine. Yes. Please. Thank you.*"

She made a sort of satisfied "hmmf" sound and stood up, walking to the kitchen. I felt tears in my eyes. This moment of mother and child, this care for my vulnerability, helped me relax, and the warmth of the fire and her invitation to stay warmed me.

"*Drink,*" Arevik said. And there she was, sitting again at the end of the couch, this time holding out a glass that held water still moving slightly in a circular motion after having been stirred. It was cloudy and slightly bubbly.

"*Thank you,*" I said and took the glass, tilting it against my lips.

"*Drink,*" she coached me. "*All of it. Drink all of it.*"

She watched me drink it. Curious to me, she continued sitting after I drank it. I felt she was watching me. She didn't move, her eyes on my face.

After a minute or two she asked me how I felt.

"*Good,*" I said. I didn't feel any different.

She didn't move.

Then, like a small flame at the bottom of a pile of sticks, I felt a flicker of something in my belly. It grew to a rumble and then a roil and then an overwhelming and complete urge to run to the water closet.

"*Excuse me*," I managed to say. As I got up, I caught Arevik's satisfied nod as she stood and followed my rush to the bathroom.

I threw open the toilet and lost everything inside of me in a series of terrible, gut-binding surges. I was bent at the hips with my hands pressed against the mustard-colored tile walls of the small closet, my insides turning outside. I felt the horror of the surge and the embarrassment of the splashing toilet.

And behind me, I felt Arevik right there. With her hand on my back, her voice was close enough that I could tell she was leaning forward over me. She yelled like a coach on a pro-team's sideline. "Tapir! Tapir! Ayo! Tapir! Tapir, Brent jan!"

I dry-heaved for many minutes, well after I had nothing left to leave behind. I stood up, and Arevik stepped back, folding her hands in front of her as I walked back and lay down on the couch next to the heater.

"*Do you feel better?*" she asked.

I lied. In that moment, I did not, but I was suddenly exhausted. "*Yes,*" I said.

"*Good.*" And with that, she went into her bedroom.

In the light of the stove's gas flames, I looked up the word. Tapel. To throw away.

The knots in my stomach began to untie themselves. My body relaxed, and in the warmth of the fire, I fell asleep.

12

"Talk to Aram," Liana told me. She'd listened while I'd panicked in her office about not knowing where I'd live. And then she calmly replied that Aram from the World Vision finance office knew everyone.

It took Aram just three days to find me a new place.

When we pulled up to the house, I could barely make out the home's brown stucco and white trimmed windows through the rain on the windshield. Aram honked his horn.

A tall, bald man opened a metal door in the large green metal gate and leaned out, looking with kind eyes beneath discerning brows. Seeing us, he waved, and we climbed out of the Lada.

Inside the gate, a staircase rose up to the left where a woman stood with two children at her feet, two girls. The younger wore a barrette. The older wore a braid. The mother had hands on her daughters' shoulders. I lifted my hand to wave and smiled. The mother returned my smile tentatively, and the smaller daughter giggled and turned inward, burying her face in her mother's legs.

The owner who'd opened the door in the gate walked ahead of Aram and me in single file. We walked on a dirt path between leafless, woody stalks of raspberry bushes underneath fruit trees wet and nearly leafless.

In the corner of the garden rose a grey stucco house. The building itself matched the height of a large stone wall, which encircled the entire property, and a brown tin roof rose to a central ridge in the sky.

The entire structure had two halves. One was the house, and then behind the house was an open shed with odd pieces of wood and mismatched tools piled inside. On the house were two windows and one door. The owner, who still hadn't spoken a word, unlocked the small cottage's front door and then walked inside.

My god, the pink, I thought.

When I'd imagined the house I might live in during Peace Corps, I'd imagined, perhaps too stereotypically, a mud hut with a thatched roof on a distant African plain. When I'd been assigned to my post in Eastern Europe I started dreaming of pastel A-frame houses with chickens roosting on a porch railing. After Arevik and Shiran asked me to leave their home, I'd resigned myself to the likelihood of an apartment in a grey block building in the center of town.

This was a box. A pink box. Low ceilings with white crown molding, tan tile, and walls painted with a pink so matte it was almost chalky.

I suddenly felt cramped with the other men in the small room. All of us began slowly shuffling around each other as I made moves to look at the house. This would be a short home tour.

"Brent jan? *What do you think? Do you like it?*" Aram asked.

I walked across the combination kitchen-living room in ten steps. "*It is good,*" I replied, walking the six steps it took to cross the single bedroom. I hid the slimy anxiety that crept up from my gut as the men stood watching me come back into the living room and run my hands over the tops of the two green chairs and then over the counter in the middle of the one wall of cabinets that made up the kitchen.

The owner crossed his arms. He spoke in Armenian to Aram. I reached down to the sink and raised the handle. No water came out.

"He says that maybe he cannot rent it," Aram said to me in English. "He built this for a vacation house. People come from Yerevan to stay here. I told him you can rent all year. This is true, no?"

"Yes," I confirmed. "I am looking for a place that I can rent for two years."

I opened the bathroom door, my steps echoing inside the windowless room tiled in bright blue. I tried flushing the toilet, which I could tell was new. No water rushed into the bowl. Typical of most Armenian homes I'd been inside, no shower curtain hung around the bathtub. I tried the water faucet, and again, nothing came out.

"Does water come?" I asked in Armenian.

"It comes," the owner said. *"Tuesday, Thursday, and Saturday."*

I looked at Aram. "Is there heat?" I didn't see a heater.

"Vararan?" Aram translated.

"No," the owner said.

"I would like a gas heater," I said to Armen.

He spoke with the owner. "He says he thinks he can get one. But, Brent jan, you will have to buy it."

"I can do that." I looked at the bedroom, which was devoid of other furniture. "I also need a wardrobe."

Aram spoke with the owner and then explained, "He says that's no problem. Wardrobe he has."

I walked into the bedroom and looked out. The two men watched me look at the empty rooms one by one, corner to corner, looking for cracks or mouse holes.

"Okay, I'm finished," I said. We all walked out into the drizzle where the sun was setting, and the porch light illuminated the haze.

Close to the gate, I called out, "Aram." I paused on the dirt path in the garden. "I didn't ask his name."

"Oh," Aram smiled. "His name is Vazgen."

I turned to Vazgen who was standing on the stairs now next to his wife.

"Vazgen." I smiled and held out my hand. Vazgen took my hand and shook it, smiling back.

"I'm Brent," I said. *"Thank you for showing me your house. It is very nice."*

His youngest daughter giggled at my Armenian, spoken with my American accent. The sound of her small laugh sparkled in the cold dusk air.

Vazgen replied, "Khndrem." *You're welcome.*

~ ~ ~

I moved into the pink house after Vazgen installed a heater and brought in the wardrobe he'd promised. On move-in day, Vazgen and his wife Naira and their two kids I'd seen on my first visit, Nazeli and Ani, followed me and Tirayr, who'd driven me from Hovsep and Arevik's house, as we carried my bags and my heaters into the tiny space.

They all left me to unpack. I'd been nervous about the space at first but hadn't wanted to end up in an apartment building with neighbors who didn't know me. Peace Corps provided me with a kind of agreement that stood in as a lease because Vazgen and Naira had never rented to anyone before.

My heart settled down once I unpacked, hanging my sweaters in the wardrobe and taping so many pictures on my bedroom door that I nearly covered the entirety of the door's glossy white paint.

In the house, I picked up new routines. Cleaning became a breeze with only the small bedroom, the combined kitchen and living room, and the bathroom to care for. Because water only ran on Tuesdays, Thursdays, and Saturdays from 10 a.m. to 1 p.m., I stayed home on those days to shower and then clean the house, washing dishes and doing laundry in the tub by hand. Then, I filled three large buckets with water that I'd use to clean, cook, and flush between water days.

Naira invited me to hang my laundry on their clotheslines, which stretched out over the cement patio they'd made over their cellar roof. On the first morning, I hung laundry, Naira came outside and walked over with a loud, "Che, che, che, che…" and showed me how to keep the laundry organized. I watched her, confused as she pulled my clothes from the line putting them into my basket.

"*Watch,*" she said to me in Armenian. She started with pants and then pulled long-sleeved shirts from my basket. Then, short sleeves, socks, and finally, underwear.

"*See,*" she said when she was finished. And I understood then that there was no reason to hang clothes without considering the most aesthetically pleasing way to do so.

"*Next time you call me,*" Naira said. "*We can do it together.*" Which we did after that. She helped me hang all my laundry.

In the evenings after work, partly because I wanted them to know I was home and partly because I wanted them to care that I was home, I took to knocking on their door. Naira always invited me in for coffee, which I drank while she patiently tried to talk to me despite my broken Armenian. Sometimes, the girls joined me at the table while Naira made coffee and snacks, and we colored together with their over-waxy crayons while Naira swirled her jazzve over the stove's flame. Some days, Naira sat down with me and her own cup to ask me about my family, about my work, about what I liked to eat or do, or where I liked to go in Stepanavan.

Often, I lingered at the table, savoring the attention and hoping I'd be there when Vazgen came home from his law office. I'd ask him to play nardi before he had even set down his briefcase, and most of the time, he acquiesced.

We got to know each other this way, and soon, I forgot that I was ever scared to move out on my own from Arevik and Hovsep's home.

I wasn't on my own. I lived with this family now, a tenant in their garden cottage. Our days began to pass in these rhythms that I savored. Evening coffee with Naira and the girls. Nardi with Vazgen. And then, after I finally retired to my cottage to cook myself dinner, the sounds of them playing or cooking or working in the yard.

Sometimes, they crept close to a secret they didn't know was there. They knew I wasn't married but would ask if I wanted to be.

I knew they assumed I'd marry a woman. Because they assumed it but didn't ask directly, I didn't have to lie. "*I want to be married one day,*" I'd say and then add an Armenian idiom I hoped would endear me to them. "Astvats giti," I said. *God knows.*

A kind of safety and even comfort began to bloom in their home. The girls wanted to play in the garden with me or color at the table. Naira stayed curious and seemed delighted to have me in her kitchen, bragging about her new tenant to the occasional visiting neighbor. And Vazgen joked with me and called out, "Akbers!" to me when he saw me coming up the garden stairs.

The first time I saw them almost frown at me came a couple of months later when I asked them if I could bring a kitten to live with me. They both nearly frowned, but then they looked at each other as if they could see what the other thought about it on each other's faces.

"*Will it be dirty?*" Naira asked.

"*I'll wash it every week,*" I promised. "*I will give it a bath.*"

Vazgen and Naira both nodded, half-smiling, which was enough for me to arrange a pickup.

Two of Liana's friends, a mother and daughter, had found kittens on the edge of the mountains outside of town. They'd given one away, and when I came to their house, they introduced me to a grey and white tabby cat. Nar, the daughter, scooped her up to me but then shouted, "Kittik! Kittik, no!" when the kitten scratched at her gripping hands.

I sat with Nar and had tea while I let the kitten rest on my lap, ignoring how she clawed at my hands while I petted her. Then, I carried the kitten home in a cardboard box.

My evenings quickly became filled with me trying to tame a wild animal.

The girls, Ani and Nazeli, loved seeing the cat but were thankfully afraid of it so much that they wouldn't come near my house unless the doors were closed, and they could watch it from the window. When Vazgen came to the door for his monthly water and gas meter check, he asked me to put the cat in the bathroom and shut the door.

I named the cat Sanity.

"*What does that mean?*" Ayda asked when I told my coworkers about my new pet over coffee break.

"Khelamtutyun," Karine translated.

"*What?*" Ayda tilted with an inquisitive look.

"Khelamtutyun," Karine said again before sipping her coffee.

Ayda looked at me puzzled.

"*Because*," I explained in Armenian, laughing to myself, "*maybe I will lose my head in the house alone. The cat will help me not lose my head. She will be my sanity.*"

Ayda slapped the table and laughed, rolling her eyes before taking up a dish towel to wipe the table.

In my cottage at night, I tried to pet the wildness out of my cat. This didn't work. While Sanity did curl up in my lap every night while I watched TV on my computer, the beginning of any petting threw her into a spasm. She would whip herself around and attack my hand, gnawing and clawing at it, sometimes so violently that I had to push her and then push her harder, and then when she still wouldn't stop attacking, push her so hard she'd fly from my lap.

When she wasn't with me in the chair, she prowled the small pink rooms, dashing under the bed in reaction to what I was sure was a hallucination. Sometimes, she'd hide at the top of the kitchen cabinets, waiting to pounce on me. One morning I woke up to find she'd eaten almost all a kitchen sponge. Another morning, a third of a kitchen towel was gone.

The one thing that felt like success in the world of taming my wild cat was the cat pan. I gave up one of my two baking sheets to this effort. Every couple of days, I filled the pan with dirt, bringing it into my kitchen-living room. There I slid it under the table that held my laptop and hard drives. While she never peed outside the cat pan, I was shocked every time I'd eat dinner in the green chair, watching TV, and then notice Sanity below the table, standing in the dirt, her back arched, making droppings, her eyes glued to mine as if at any moment she would either fight me or flee.

Weeks went on like this—enjoying the time with Vazgen, Naira, and the girls and then trying to tame Sanity in the cottage at night, often waking up to her dashing across the top of my head with her claws out. And each morning, I'd leave Sanity in the cottage and walk for twenty minutes to the World Vision office, making my way past the shops on the town's main road and past the giant statue of Stepan in the town square to the small yellow World Vision building in the center of town.

I marked my time with projects and holidays. I helped the TDFs translate their project plans into updates for Yeraz's newsletter to child sponsors in England. At the end of October, I threw my coworkers their first Halloween party, giving them the shivers when I showed up with a cemetery cake. Yeraz helped me hang tissue ghosts from the ceiling and offered a bunch of old-world Vision posters, which she helped turn into costumes for the kids.

After helping with a few projects that had already been underway when I arrived, Liana and I wrote a grant proposal together. The Peace Corps home office in Yerevan had sent out a call for proposals for the President's Emergency Plan for AIDS Relief, PEPFAR. The funds had been established by the US Government in 2003, and in 2009, funds were given to each Peace Corps office to disperse among volunteer projects.

I proposed to Liana that using these US funds earmarked for AIDS projects around the world, we should engage young people. We could choose two high school students from five of the twenty villages we worked in to make a team of ten youth educators. Those young people could hold peer workshops on AIDS in Armenia and how to protect yourself.

Liana was concerned about how we would choose just ten, and I offered that we could hold a writing contest and allow everyone in the office to vote. We could write the curriculum, hold leadership workshops, and train these young people on how to talk to their peers about AIDS.

To complete the application for funds, Liana and I typed out section after arduous section outlining the need for our project, the timeline, and who would work on the project.

We had to give intended outcomes and demonstrate community buy-in through surveys and quotes, which were gathered over a couple of weeks as I drove from village to village with Artavan, Petros, Vigen, Tirayr, and Melik. We outlined a budget, line by line. I gave Aram a list of items I thought we needed—pencils, notepads, empty paper charts, markers, Post-its, lunches for our meetings with team members we'd invite from the villages, gas to drive village to village. We wrote down as much minutia as we could think of, and Aram called and then visited shops throughout town to get handwritten or typed cost estimations to attach to the proposal.

I'd worked on these kinds of budgets already for other World Vision sponsored projects like the anti-human-trafficking project or the civic engagement project, but this was the first time the project had come from me.

In November, I sat down at my desk at World Vision and found an email from the Peace Corps assistant director. I read it, jumped out of my chair, and ran to Liana's office, knocking on the door frame but not waiting for her to invite me in. Afternoon light lit up her room through her window, and the sound of Yeraz typing made its way into the room through the open door.

I sat on the edge of one of the chairs opposite her desk, nearly shaking with excitement.

"We won."

Laina paused.

"We won!" I nearly shouted it.

"What?" she said.

"The PEPFAR funds. We won the PEPFAR funds."

"Really?" Her jaw dropped, realizing we'd just been awarded ten thousand dollars.

I didn't tell Liana that it felt like some kind of kismet, winning the grant. That here I was, a newly out gay man from Texas running an AIDS project in the oldest Christian country in the world with the largest Christian nonprofit in the world.

And I didn't tell her that at some point in the nights after I came out to my parents, but before I left, my mom had said, "What about AIDS? I'm scared for you. I lived through that time. You don't know how scary it was."

"Mom," I'd said, "being gay doesn't mean you get AIDS. Every kind of person in the world can get AIDS."

I knew enough to say that. And I knew about condoms, though I'd never had sex.

I would learn. I would teach myself. I would go to the Peace Corps library in Yerevan and find lessons and magazines and books left by previous volunteers who taught the subject somewhere before.

I would write a professional and youth-appropriate version of a curriculum outline about HIV and AIDS.

Someone in DC would know what we were doing and support it.

I made a mental note of these things. I was, in the cleanest and most simple way, proud of myself.

"I can't believe it," Liana said from behind her desk.

I grinned at her. "Neither can I."

13

"It will be great to see everyone," I told Zoe over the phone. "But really, what are the chances I'm getting laid at this thing?"

Zoe and I talked a couple of times a week, and our conversations were always relaxed now. She'd become the person I called when I needed advice, wanted to wax on about some angst, or simply wanted the feeling of proximity that a long chat can give.

On this night we were making plans for Peace Corps Armenia's annual All Volunteer Conference happening in a few days in Yerevan. All volunteers from every town and village, plus all Peace Corps staff would stay at a hotel for three nights. Google chats and Facebook chats between volunteers had been filled with chatter about it, the A-16s letting the A-17s know that the weekend would feel like one big party. One A-16 wrote, "Don't worry. You'll be hungover for every session."

I paced the tan tile of my cottage, hoping Zoe would be my wingwoman. "I don't care about the partying so much. I just... it feels like beyond time not to be a virgin, Z?"

"Well, you can only work with what you've got," Zoe said. "You're not into John?"

"John's not into me," I told her, thinking of Thanksgiving and my second trip to his apartment. That night's invitation to sleep in his bed went to Grace, leaving me on the living room couch.

Zoe asked about the other gay volunteers. "And not Kevin? Or Peter?"

"I don't think so."

"Then I think your v-card is staying intact, my man," Zoe said, a strain of annoyance in her voice. She could be annoyed, I told myself, but isn't the thing that really makes you gay the sex stuff? I felt that at any moment I could just jump on a man and ride him off into the sunset. But there was no man to jump on.

Still, I fantasized about a number of the handsome straight volunteers. I imagined sneaking into our conference hotel rooms on some break, the undressing, the falling into bed together.

In the years between puberty and Peace Corps, I presented as straight for so long that I let myself hope, just a little, that any of the straight guys in our volunteer group might be at least a little gay. I'd gone through life telling everyone I was straight, and I wasn't. So, couldn't there be some homosexual twinkle in one of these Peace Corps boys' eyes? I knew it wasn't likely, but I let my mind travel because I had no other place for it to go.

At the conference itself, the energy of volunteer togetherness melted all of us into a pot of relief mixed with joy mixed with a dash of sexual tension and another dash of that expat thing that happens when American expats converge in a foreign place. How do I describe that American expat feeling? There was joy in it after months of going through the Armenian streets alone, struggling to buy bread and milk (or, in my case, Coca-Cola and M&Ms). Practical things like going to the bank, grocery shopping or paying your bills could feel isolating. Making friends was even harder in a culture with expectations of relationships that took a lot of time to learn. Tuning in to cultural nuance took effort and brain power that was exciting but could leave you feeling tired and lonely some days.

We signed up for Peace Corps because we wanted the challenge, but the conference allowed us to let our hair down. Atheists could be atheists without having to defend it. No single person would be asked why they weren't married yet. And queer people could just exist without fear that some slip-up might force you out of the closet to your Armenian family, friends, or coworkers.

While I loved the ease we all felt with each other, what went on all around me made me jealous. As we mingled over coffee I noticed new relationships, volunteers who'd been placed close enough together to get to know each other, to start dating, to end up here sipping coffee and holding hands in the hallway outside conference rooms.

The sessions led by Peace Corps staff flew by. Vahagn, our extraordinarily handsome and beefy director of security, led a session on security protocols in case of a country-wide emergency. In another session, we all broke out into groups by sector—English teachers, community and business development volunteers, youth development volunteers—and brainstormed ways to collaborate and initiatives we might start in the next year, which we presented to the entire group.

On Saturday night, after more sessions and an all-volunteer dinner full of toasts over nonalcoholic beverages, volunteers rushed out into the city. Those of us in our twenties all the way up to those in their seventies went out for desserts or cocktails at cafés. We walked mostly, or shared cabs that drove under the yellow streetlights of Parpetsi or Tumanyan or Sayat Nova Avenues, breaking us up into smaller groups of friends, or wannabe friends or random groups left behind by those volunteers who had more closely bonded to each other.

Zoe and I and a few other volunteers let the still-bright evening sun fool us into sitting and then shivering at an outdoor café, chasing a round of shots with a plate of french fries. Then Zoe and I walked behind a group of volunteers across the street onto Northern Avenue, taking the stairs below ground to the dimly lit door of That Place, a lazily named bar opened, I'd heard, by a group of Armenian diasporans from California.

The thud of top forty American hits pulsed in my chest, and we could hardly hear each other talk. Zoe tried to ask me what I wanted to drink. I had to basically yell, "Vodka soda."

The air in That Place smelled aggressively straight, like Brut cologne and sweat and cigarette smoke because smoking was legal inside. When Timbaland, Nelly Furtado, and Justin Timberlake started singing "Give It to Me" over club speakers, I shuffled my feet onto the dance floor with the other volunteers, grinding our hips together, raising our hands into the air, and body rolling.

I danced smoothly enough that Danya, the sexiest girl in our group and the best dancer by far, rolled her way up to me, and our bodies pressed against each other's. Pride floated to the surface, washed over me like sun through a smoky haze. I could move. I could attract. I could play here in a world of sex and beats and bodies.

Zoe and I stayed long enough for that first drink and then a second. After a third vodka soda, Zoe and I quickly conferred on a plan to leave, eventually yell-whispering into the ears of other volunteers inviting them to walk to Cocoon with us.

When we climbed the stairs back to Northern Avenue, the cold November air wrapped around those of us who'd left and made our way through the dusk light. I'd thought through my drinking plans enough to know I wouldn't need a coat because, after four drinks, the cold couldn't bother me. I was anxious to be at Cocoon, to take my beating heart and pulsing-blood body onto that floor with men who might look at me, might see my body rolling and come up next to me and roll with it. I thought about the tall man in the black boots who'd played with my chest hair, and I walked to Cocoon like I was walking back to him.

Zoe lit a cigarette while we walked, and a few volunteers texted our plans to others and announced who was leaving where they were to come dance with us at the gay bar. The only married couple in our group, Nicole and Adam were there, the kind of couple you're jealous of because they are both gorgeous and found each other young.

Yerevan nightlife was unpredictable, I would learn. There were plenty of bars but not plenty of bar-goers. You could walk down the street, see a sign for a bar that seemed interesting, and go in to find the place empty. Even the most popular places on a Friday night might be empty because everyone in the city who went out were all connected in a web of social climbing. Friends would text friends where they were going.

I eventually preferred the strategy where you kept the right people together long enough that you'd have the numbers and the moxy to turn any place into a party. When this happened, when a group of us descended into an empty bar and turned up the hype meter to ten, it wouldn't matter where we were. We were going to have a good time. And inevitably, when passersby would poke their head in to see if anything interesting was going on, it would be because we would have already created an energy too enticing to leave.

So, that night, we created that energy at Cocoon.

Zoe and I, Nicole and Adam, Danya, Amanda, and so many more volunteers descended into Cocoon already inebriated and with our hype meters dialed way up. All the energy we felt getting all of us together at the conference, all the strength we felt in our numbers, all the freedom we felt to be ourselves among each other coalesced into a sudden frenzy of drink orders and dancing, all our faces smiling at each other while our bodies moved.

We ordered drinks to nurse while we danced. And when the bartender played "I Gotta Feeling" by Black Eyed Peas, we lost our minds. This song was all about having the best night, dancing with your friends, living a life full of joy without worry. And we shed all of whatever held us down. I started jumping at the bridge, the Black Eyed Peas yelling that tonight was the night, the bass pushing me into the air.

Zoe screamed up to me, cheering and laughing. Adam closed his eyes and wagged his hands out in front of him and his butt into the air behind him. Nicole put one hand on her heart and another hand toward the basement bar's ceiling like she was at a contemporary worship service, reaching up for something divine.

We felt joy in being away. Away from home. Away from culture. Away from whatever baggage we could leave behind. We were expats. No longer surrounded by the pressures of the US. Not fully aware or integrated into the pressures of being Armenian. And even on this night, our jobs and the pressure to make something out of ourselves as Peace Corps volunteers felt a million miles away. We were simply there together, having a great night.

Our party hype worked, and Cocoon became crowded with men and a few of their women friends. Zoe flirted all night with the bartender, who eventually encouraged a woman—who we all said was the most gorgeous hooker we'd ever seen—to climb onto the bar and basically do a pole dance with no pole while the bartender slowly cut the ribbons that held her corset on. We cheered when the last one was cut, and this beautiful woman slid her hips into the air, holding the open corset against her breasts before sliding down to the floor and into the bathroom, the applause of the room following her. She waved at us before she closed the door.

Borrowing her bravery, I tried to find eyes of handsome men to look into, spinning to the music, but found none. I wished for John, who'd gone to some other bar with other volunteers. I danced and swayed and felt incomplete, a gay man who'd never even kissed a man before. As I spun looking for men, the joy I'd felt in camaraderie and freedom with my fellow volunteers began to sour. I watched Adam and Nicole smiling and dancing together. I saw other volunteers kissing or dancing, their attention swallowed up by their new relationships. I watched Zoe at the bar with the bartender. And I found no male gaze to match my own. Loneliness crept in, like it did even on nights filled with joy like tonight.

I ordered more vodka sodas and then, as I began to lose my grip on decorum, rounds of shots for everyone. When some refused my gifts, I drank them myself. I was diving headfirst into this night so hard that I forgot nights ended at all.

I crossed over then. I'd known the extra shots were too much when I drank them. But I was drowning my loneliness and longing with liquor and joy, and eventually,

I was dancing so messily I felt I couldn't stop myself. Like I'd gone too far, knew it, but couldn't stop it now, the chemical reactions in my gut now simply following the laws of nature and clouding my mind until I fell to the floor and blacked out.

I came to consciousness outside and upstairs from Cocoon, leaning on the saloon doors of the western-themed bar next door. I had already vomited up most of the evidence I needed to remind myself that I'd drunk everyone, including myself, under the table. Most of the volunteers around me were in a drunken state many degrees less than me.

I couldn't find Zoe, could barely look for her as my eyes seemed to spin in many directions on their own. I was dizzy. I wanted to lie on the ground, but an A-16 I'd never said a word to, Michael, was standing next to me, holding me up. I looked through his long hair into his eyes while he rubbed my back, trying to say thank you without words. I thought the effort might make me vomit again, though. We would never speak again after this night, but I would think of him for years to come, his tall frame and square shoulders, cargo shorts, and forest green T-shirt, and his hand warming the skin of my back.

I blacked out again for a moment but found myself being pushed into a taxi, observing my body as if I was outside it, my limbs scrambling to get out of the door.

"Get in the car now," a volunteer nearly screamed at me, making me shudder in fear. I wanted out. I was certain I would barf in the taxi. Nearly a dozen volunteers were now standing around the car, trying to get me to get inside, and I was terrified.

A woman barely older than me with thick brown hair and freckles, Allison, was yelling from behind me.

"Get in the car now, Brent. Get in the fucking car," she said. "You are embarrassing all Americans."

I woke up in my hotel room, in bed with another volunteer, David.

"You had a tough night," he said to me, getting out of bed. He undressed to get into the shower. "So did I, honestly. We both slept through the first session already."

"I can't get up," I told him. "It hurts."

"Totally, man." From inside the bathroom, he said, "I get it."

I finally made it downstairs for the midmorning coffee break. I tried not to make eye contact, filling a white hotel coffee mug with coffee from a tall metal carafe. After a few more conference sessions and lunch, all of us would start finding marshutnis, the Armenian buses that would scatter us to our towns and villages.

"You told me to fuck off last night," Zoe told me, pouring herself a cup.

"No," I protested. "No, I couldn't have."

"Well, you did," she said with a grimace. "It wasn't pretty."

I put my head in my hands. "Zoe. Zoe, I'm so sorry."

I felt tears come to my eyes, my body unable to handle stress of nearly any kind, cramping and aching from the booze that seemed so deep in me it might never come out. I sipped from the mug, my free hand digging my fingernails into my palm.

"Oh, honey," she said. "I know." She looked at me and offered a smile. "We've all been there. You're still a baby in this world."

I smiled back. I walked to an empty seat and waited for Peace Corps staff to tell us what to do next.

14

On a Tuesday near Christmas time, Mom asked me to go into the office early to Skype. Without an explanation, I went in at 7 a.m. and opened the video call. There Mom and my sister Macey, twelve years old, stood by the Christmas tree, my mom's school laptop set up on a chair.

"We're decorating the tree with you," Macey said, pushing her glasses up on her nose.

"Oh." I let out a heart-pang moan. In the past few years, as our other sister and brother got married and had other traditions, I'd taken to making a big night of the two of us decorating the tree together. Our twelve-year age difference meant that I got to see the holiday through her child eyes, got to delight in the old ornaments and marvel at the lights when we crawled beneath the limbs to look up through them.

"She just looked so sad that you weren't here," my mom wrote me in an email the next day. She'd helped Macey lay out some of my favorites, and Macey asked me where I wanted to put them. Once the ornaments were up, Macey and Mom sang carols to me over Skype while I cried, missing them and missing home.

Over New Years, Zoe came to visit. She helped me wash Sanity, a heroic undertaking given Sanity's feral feline howling, and I bought us dinners of roasted chicken and lavash from the new grocery store called Yot Yot Yot on the main road.

I updated her on the AIDS project with youth educators. I told Zoe how proud I was of them, how quickly they stepped into leadership, how confident they seemed leading their peers in conversations about the kinds of activities that put you at risk of contracting HIV.

"They really only talk about drugs and 'bodily fluids.' Mostly blood. They don't really talk about sex."

"They have to talk about sex," Zoe said.

"I mean, I know," I said. "But maybe it's enough that they are talking about HIV at all?"

I felt like too much of an outsider to push the issue with my coworkers or teachers at schools who supervised the conversations.

Zoe and I made New Year's resolutions together and banged pots, standing on my snow-covered stoop at midnight.

This was our first time celebrating Nor Tari, the weeklong holiday at the beginning of the new year. We began with a visit to Naira and Vazgen's Nor Tari table before we visited coworkers' homes throughout town. We walked from house to house, sitting down to long tables set most often in living rooms each with food spread from end to end—dolmas, blinchik, baturma, kebab, lavash, fruit, and sweets. We drank toasts and coffee until we were miserably full.

A few hours after returning home, likely because of something we ate, both of us spent the rest of the first day of the year throwing up. We kept it up through the night. In the morning, Zoe, weak but determined, decided to brave the trip home.

I returned to my routine. I walked to work. I wrote project plans or newsletters or emails home. I walked home, sometimes stopping for coffee in Naira's kitchen or for nardi with Vazgen. Each night in my own kitchen I made one of three dishes—lavash burritos with homemade refried beans, lavash pizza rolls, or chocolate chip cookies. Some nights, I would just bake chocolate chip cookies and eat a dozen.

After one particularly cold day, I walked through icy wind and snow, opened my cottage door, and found Sanity eating another sponge. She was sitting on the corner of the counter on the kitchen wall, the sponge pulled from the sink and pinned under her feet like a trapped bird. Sanity ripped at the sponge fibers with her teeth.

Sanity wasn't hungry, I thought. She was mad.

"She's losing her mind," I told Zoe on the phone. She'd left New Years with her own share of pink claw marks on her hands.

Zoe and I had been talking a lot more since she left. I'd become anxious. The holiday season had left me wounded. I missed home deeply. Mom had sent photos from Halloween, Thanksgiving, and then Christmas. Everyone was together but me. I wanted to be there. I was afraid to be there.

And I wanted someone to know me. I'd fantasized about John. I'd danced at Cocoon and tried to find eyes to meet mine. I wanted to be known by someone. This me. This me that had come out and still wanted his dreams of learning by living abroad. But I was now someone, too, who had finally come to terms with a part of myself totally unexplored. What would it be like to love someone? To touch someone I wanted and to be touched by him?

"I just still feel like I'm on the outside," I told Zoe. "I feel like I'm on the outside in Armenia, and I'm never going to get in. I just don't have friends."

Zoe sighed. "I hear ya. I'm still not sure if the women I work with even like me. Your Armenian is better than mine. I just can't tell."

I felt for her. She had an Armenian tutor and had continued studying, but she wasn't able to follow along as closely as I could and didn't have a host family to practice with. She'd moved into an apartment by herself when the mandatory family stay had finished.

"But you have Chris," I said to her. I envied her American friends. "And Meghan and Patrick. And other people who live around you and come into town. You watch movies with people, for crying out loud."

"Yeah, three people," she said sarcastically.

I returned an emphatic, "Yeah, three people. Three friends. That's more than three times the friends I have. I have zero friends. I have no one to hang out with. I feel like no one knows me, and I really like the Armenian people I know, but I don't know how to get to know them. Back home, if I wanted to make a friend, I'd invite them to dinner or coffee or to go do something. Who would I ask? Where would I go?"

I slumped into my green chair. "Sometimes, I just don't want to try so hard."

Sanity scrambled across the tile floor after something only she could see.

Then I said something I'd already said before. But this time, when I said it, something shifted. "I think I might leave."

Zoe paused. "Okay. You're not serious, though."

"No." I stretched time, quiet moments that hung in the air. "I think." I paused again. There was a ledge I could step out onto. And I did. "I'm going to leave."

Zoe didn't say anything.

"I'm leaving."

~ ~ ~

The next morning, after a night of Sanity yowling outside my door, I called Liana and asked if she would meet me at the World Vision office.

"When?" she asked.

"This afternoon?"

I walked through the snow into town, thinking as I walked of the things I wanted. I wanted connections I couldn't name. I felt unmoored, and I wanted to be moored. I wanted to be understood by someone who wanted me after all that understanding. I wanted to be gay. And I wanted to live abroad and learn the kinds of truths you can only learn through finding common ground with people so different from you.

But I ached. I ached for some kind of gay life I thought I should have but didn't. I ached for a future I was scared of.

At the office, I found Liana working at her desk on her laptop. She looked up at me, her smile welcoming me into the room and her eyes watching for signs of impending news.

I sat down in a familiar black chair across from her desk and took a deep breath, my eyes drooping into sad resignation. "I've decided to leave Armenia."

"Vay, Brent jan," she said, her voice raised in surprise. "Really?"

"Yes, I think so." Tears flooded my eyes.

"Why?" she asked, sitting back in her chair and folding her arms

"I…" I struggled with the words. "I just don't think I'm doing very well here."

Liana waited, leaned further, and listened.

"I feel like I'm not doing enough. And I miss my family. I really miss them." I choked on these words, unsure of them, stumbling. "I worry about them, and I worry about being far away from them."

"Brent jan," Laina said. "I'm sad that you would want to go home." She put her hands on the desk, glanced out her window, and then looked back to me. "Do you need better projects? Do you want to do different work?"

"No. It's not that." Which was a muddy truth. I wondered if I could feel more connected to my work at World Vision. I couldn't say what was missing in my work, if anything at all. I wasn't proud of myself. I wanted to be.

"It's my family," I told her. "It's feeling so far from home. I feel overwhelmed by it." These words didn't feel whole. But how could I tell Liana about my family and my gayness and my loneliness and the need for friendship that somehow wasn't satisfied by anyone in this town? If I did, couldn't that break all of this anyway?

"I don't want you to leave," Liana said with an air of professionalism as if she were telling her employee to stay, which she was. "But I think you should do what is best for you. And if you think that is going home, I think you should do that. If you think it is staying here, I think you should do that. I think you have become a wonderful part of our office, and I believe you will be doing great projects with our team. You already are with the AIDS project."

I sniffled and used my bare hand to wipe my face, smearing tears instead of wiping them away.

"You are loved among our staff, Brent jan. If you do leave, you should know that we all really like you very much."

"Thank you," I said, looking up to her, her words a drink of water and the secrets I kept from her about being gay like vinegar. Her window was full of the grey sky, low clouds hanging lightly and cold. "That means a lot to me. Thank you for saying that."

"It's true, Brent jan. And we don't want you to leave if you don't mind me saying so."

"I don't," I told her. "But I think I have to."

We went on like this for a little while longer until we were laughing, and then I was crying again, saying what I knew would be a last normal goodbye.

"Tell them tomorrow, I think, Brent jan," Liana said. "You can leave, but you have to tell the rest of the team at our morning meeting. I think that's easiest. I think you should do that before you decide to tell Peace Corps."

"Okay, I will," I told her.

I walked out of her office, where, during our conversation, Artavan and Tirayr had met in the lobby, setting a computer on my desk to watch *Die Hard* dubbed over in Russian.

"Brent jan!" They both exclaimed, seeing me come out of Liana's office.

I smiled at them. "Barev dzez," I said.

"Barev, akhbers," Artavan returned, lifting a handful of sunflower seeds to his mouth.

"*Hello, my brother,*" Tirayr echoed. "*Sit down. Watch this movie with us!*"

God, I thought, *Die Hard? Right now? If you only knew I was about to upend my life again. Jesus. Die Hard? And sunflower seeds.*

"*No, thank you,*" I said and walked out into the cold.

In my cottage, I petted the cat, letting Sanity wrangle my hand, cutting just through the first layer of skin, no blood. I made pizza rolls. After dinner, I walked to Naira and Vazgen's house, thinking again that this would be the last evening coffee and then the last game of nardi before my life changed again.

In my cottage, I finally called my mom. I'd sent her an email telling her I was leaving the day before. I called to tell her I was still resolved.

"Oh, Brent," she said. Her voice was quiet and kind. "Oh, honey. I just want you to be happy. But if you come home, we'll be happy that you're here."

I cried into the phone. "I'll be a failure, Mom. Everyone will think I've failed."

Faces flashed in my thoughts, faces of family and college friends and church friends, of people who believed I could do this, people who would learn I was gay only after they'd learn I hadn't made it through Peace Corps. And Liana and the World Vision office full of people who'd asked me to come, to contribute.

"Have you made a pros and cons list?" Mom asked.

"Yeah, I have," I muttered, wiping my face. "Twice."

"Doesn't that give you some clarity?"

"It doesn't. I'm not trying to be difficult, but if I quit, I think I'll regret it. And if I don't quit, I think I'll be miserable. And I can't figure out which one to do."

"You have to do what's in your heart, Brent. That's all I can tell you. You have to do what's in your heart. Have you prayed?"

"No, Mom. You know I'm not really doing that."

"It might help."

"Well, maybe you can do that for me. Tell God I'm open and listening if he has anything to say." This came out with a twist of my voice that was meant to push her away.

"Well, you don't have to put it down."

"I'm not trying to. And I'm sorry I'm putting you through this."

"You're not putting me through anything," she persisted. "This is a big decision, and if you make it, just know that a lot of people at home love you and want you here. Nobody will think any differently of you if you decide to come home."

"Thanks, Mom."

"We actually went to lunch with the Blanks," Mom said. I hadn't thought of them since I arrived, that couple from church who always showed up when we needed them. My sister got married at the Blanks' house, and they showed up with a moving trailer when she got divorced. Mickey Blanks gave me my first job—organizing files at his law office—and my second—pulling mesquite brush on his property at the edge of town.

"They said they've be praying for you," Mom said, "and that you should definitely come home. We all miss you."

"Thank you, Mama." I paused, looking at my cottage, thinking suddenly about what I would take from Armenia and what I would leave behind.

When we hung up, I called Zoe and went through all of it again, all the reasons to leave, all the reasons to stay, mentioning more than I did to my mom.

"I am so worried that I won't find love, Zoe." I nearly whimpered the words.

"Me, too, buddy," she said. "We're in the post-Soviet closet, the closet inside a cement-block apartment with no windows. We're in deep."

I laughed. "I really feel fucked up about being out but then not really out and then feeling like I'm going to be alone forever."

"Well, you're not alone, B. You've got me."

I stopped for a second. "I know, Z. It's just, you know what I mean, I just feel like I don't know who I am. And I'm just like, what am I doing here?"

That night, I lay in bed awake, listening to Sanity howling outside my bedroom door. I fell asleep sometime when the moon had already moved well past my window.

In the morning, I made myself eggs and lavash and drank hot tea by the stove. It had been days since I'd changed the cat pan, and I was certain it was starting to smell bad, though because I lived near it continuously, I couldn't tell.

So, with the big leaving announcement on my mind, I put on my boots and coat, lifted the cat pan from under the table, and walked into the garden. I picked up a plank of wood a few inches wide and about a foot long from the shed next to my cottage. The weather had warmed enough that the top layer of snow melted and refroze, making a sheet of ice that crunched under each step.

I crouched on my knees and dug with my plank of wood, scraping first the layer of snow and then digging into the cold frozen mud. It didn't give at first, so I hit the ground harder, then harder, and finally with the full weight of me I raised the wood high into the air and banged it down until the dirt gave just a little, just enough to encourage me to keep at it. I raised the wooden plank high above my head, brought it down again, repeating this over and over, my breath getting faster, my lungs pushing with the rest of me, so I was heaving now, full body, at the earth, grunting.

I kept pounding the ground and started a final cry, warm tears rolling on my face into the snow. I cried, huffed at the cold air, and dug until there before me I'd made a hole big enough to bury my Sanity's shit.

I covered it with garden dirt and then snow and shifted my body to an untouched patch of white, to dig again the same way, chipping at the snow and then frozen dirt until I loosened enough dirt to fill the cat pan. In that hole in the ground, I placed my hand against the cold earth.

Armenia, I thought. *Armenia.*

I pulled my hand back and looked up past the leafless fruit trees and the yard covered in snow and my host family's cold clothes hanging on the clothesline, frozen and stiff. Then I looked to Naira and Vazgen's house where I saw a flash of Naira walking past a window and knew the kids were inside getting ready for school.

I'm not done, I thought.

I touched the dirt again.

I'm not done. I'm not done. I'm not done. I'm not done. The words rushed over me, and I felt them more than I thought them. I felt them in the cold air, filling my lungs, and the cold ice on my knees and the cold grit against my palm in the hole in the garden I'd dug.

As I picked up the pan of dirt and returned the plank of wood to Vazgen's shed, I thought of Tirayr and Artavan, that after all the talk of how lonely I felt, there they were on a Sunday afternoon inviting me to eat sunflower seeds and watch *Die Hard*. And Liana who'd said without hesitation how much she wanted me to stay. And the kids in my World Vision project. Then, Naira's coffees. The girls in the garden. And how Vazgen always said yes to this foreigner's plea to play nardi on his porch.

I pictured my hand on the dirt and thought, *What will I want to say that I did?*

In my cottage, I called my mom.

"I'm not leaving," I told her.

"Oh," she said, her voice tired like someone about to go to sleep. I wait for her to say more. "Okay," she continued. "Oh... I'm sad. Just promise not stay and be miserable. I know you wouldn't stay unless you thought it was the right thing to do. You're a good person, Brent."

"Thanks, Mom."

We both paused. The phone went silent. Then finally, "I've got to go to bed," she said.

"Okay," I said and hung up the phone.

On the walk on the icy road to work, the sun warmed my face and shone brightly on the snow.

15

On a Sunday morning in February, with snow on the ground and grey skies above, eight Armenian teenagers piled into a blue van, each with a small bag packed for a five-day trip. All of them dressed in contemporary Armenian style—black pants, slick hairstyles, sweaters with black and white stripes or accents. They were polished in a way I recognized—the cool preparation of confident teens who want to be seen.

I'd watched each of these kids grow like sunflowers toward the rays of their own promise. We'd started working with them for the HIV/AIDS project Liana and I had written together. In our first meeting together, they'd been timid, shoulders curled forward, reluctant to answer questions or share their perspectives. In the past few months, though, each of them had stood in front of peers in schools across northern Armenia and commanded each room's attention, teaching peers about a disease that so many of us human beings feared.

Liana and Artavan talked outside the van in Armenian that I didn't care to try and decipher. Surely, they talked plans, perhaps exchanged Armenian dram.

While I had already coordinated the locations for this trip to Southern Armenia, Artavan had managed logistics. He'd called the parents of each teenager to explain the trip and collect the permission slips, which Yeraz had translated. He'd explained to moms and dads that after teaching hundreds of their peers what they knew about HIV and AIDS, these teenagers were traveling to schools in the South to teach peers there. I'd set up classrooms near Zoe's town of Goris, and a town farther south, Kapan, where more Peace Corps volunteers had coordinated with classrooms to welcome these teens from the North.

I'd never been to Goris or Kapan and neither had any of these kids. We would travel the ten hours south to Goris in one day in this blue van that Artavan had reserved. He hadn't shared with me the details of the car hire. I found out that morning that the driver was Artavan's uncle.

The van had seat belts, which I'd insisted on multiple times to Artavan as he worked on transportation. It also had no windows. No windows in the back. No windows on the side. Only the windshield and windows by the driver and passenger. Small yellow lights on the ceiling illuminated the teenagers who smiled and talked in low voices, eager and excited for travel.

Artavan climbed in the passenger seat next to his uncle, his blue Rams Starter jacket rustling against the pleather. I climbed in the front of the rows of seats and sat in the middle for the best view out of the windshield. Liana had come to the office this Sunday simply to see us off and now walked to the open sliding door.

"*Are you all ready for this big journey?*" she asked them.

A chorus of "Ayo!" rang out of the van.

"*Did anyone bring food? Do you have something to eat on the road?*"

"*We'll stop, I'm sure,*" said one boy, Gregor, who seemed oldest with his deep voice and all-black style.

"Well, take these." And like the mother she was yet to be, Liana lifted up cellophane bags filled with packaged cookies, crackers, sunflower seeds, and bottled water, juice, and soda.

One of the girls, sitting closest to Liana, took the bags one at a time and passed them back, where they disappeared to the floor of the van.

I caught Liana's eyes. "Thank you," I said. "Thank you for supporting this project and for supporting me."

"You're welcome, Brent jan." She smiled at me and slid the van door closed.

The teenagers played a Russian card game called Durak, hollering at each other over their wins and losses while the three men in the front, including me, stared out the windshield hour after hour. We stopped in Aparan at the bakery, a place I stopped at on nearly every trip to Yerevan but which the teenagers had never visited. They were modest in choosing snacks, so I bought sweet bread and passed it out in the van.

By the time we were just a couple of hours outside of Goris, the teenagers had exhausted their interest in Durak and in talking, and the van grew quiet. I watched through the window as the road ahead curved into the mountains.

Snow fell lightly and had already fallen heavily at the topmost roads that snaked through mountain peaks. I'd been saving my iPod battery for the last few hours of the trip and pulled it out now. I turned on a new album, *Lungs* by Florence and the Machine. Florence Welsh belted her anxiety and transformed it into dance and some kind of levity that was powered by the heartbeat of drum. To the sound of that heartbeat, I thought about the hours I'd just spent driving through this snow-covered country.

Just weeks ago, I thought for sure I was leaving Armenia. And now, instead, I thought about how I'd been able to treat these kids to a trip they'd never imagined for themselves. I'd spent months working with them and then watching them grow in confidence, intellect, and joy. And in this moment, I realized I'd gotten into a van with twelve Armenians, none of whom spoke English or had traveled to the US. I'd not spoken a word of English on this trip. When I arrived in Armenia, a trip like this would have terrified me. Now, in this moment, I felt like this was where I belonged.

Zoe and I had already lamented the fact that she wouldn't be in Goris for my first trip South. She'd needed to go home to Maine. She offered that we could all stay in her apartment while she was gone. She left a key for us with Chris, another volunteer in Goris.

I felt the generosity of her offer to let a gaggle of teenagers descend into her home. And I felt a pang of wishing my American friend was there for me to hug and steal away for some fast-talking catch-up conversations while the teenagers did their teenage things.

After we settled, Artavan left me with the teenagers while he and his uncle went into town, coming back with pelmeni. I found a pot in Zoe's kitchen and boiled water, serving the pelmeni the way Arevik served it at her table—with sour cream and salt and pepper.

We ate together and then played Durak.

We slapped cards onto Zoe's dining table, and the kids leaned into the drama of winning and losing, whistling or shouting or throwing their hands into the air. I played into it, too, jumping up and throwing my hands on my face at my most dramatic losses.

At home, my family loved games. We played them every holiday, no matter if we celebrated with my mom's family or my dad's. I loved aunts and uncles and cousins and grandparents all leaning into the theatrics, dice bouncing on a wooden table, my grandfather shouting, "Hot dog!" after a great roll. As a tiny kid barely able to see over the table's edge, I loved the pats on the back when I won a game, the hands patting my hair, my mom rubbing my back while she watched her family admire her son.

I missed them, but now this feeling of missing didn't feel heavy. It felt like inspiration.

"*Do you all want to dance?*" I asked after another round of Durak finished.

The teenagers paused. Artavan threw up his hands. Jokingly but also with intent, he said, "*I'm going to get ready for bed.*"

"*I could teach you a dance from my home,*" I told the teenagers.

"*Yes, let's do it,*" one girl said. Then, she encouraged the others. "*Come on. Let's dance with him.*"

I stood up from the table. "*We need to move everything to the side of the room.*"

Very quickly, the teens pushed tables, chairs, and then the couch and lamp all against the wall, revealing the herringbone pattern of Zoe's dining and living room floor. The boards were grey with age, a few of them loose enough to roll out of place while we pushed furniture over them.

I'd brought my small set of speakers, so I plugged in my iPod. I spun my thumb on the circular pad until I found "Wide Open Spaces" by The Chicks.

I knew these Armenian teenagers wouldn't know how the song flicked a light on in my heart, a room as big as a Texas prairie full of memories of my family—road trips with all six of us to my grandparents' house, slipping The Chicks' first album into the CD player, the harmonies we all could sing thanks to years of growing up in our acapella-only church, the sound of my mother's alto and the way it felt to find the notes with her and blend our voices into a chorus that filled the car. How for years my mother distilled this feeling into memories she made with my littlest sister, the two of them singing on the way to and from the school where Mom taught, and Macey attended kindergarten and on and on.

"*Watch me.*" I looked at them and then turned around and started in on a grapevine to the right.

"*It's called,*" I said, and then in English, "line dancing."

"Line dancing," one of the girls repeated, her Armenian accent bouncing the words into the air.

I'd learned the Boot Scoot Boogie in elementary school in my small town in Texas, and the dance never left me. My feet shuffled across the floor in hiking boots, not cowboy boots, but I found my belt loops and hooked in my thumbs as I moved into the pattern, slapping my shoes at the end, and then swinging to do the whole sequence again looking a quarter turn in a new direction.

Gregor was the first to pick it up, stepping quickly in his pointy leather shoes that looked from the ankle down just like cowboy boots. He leaned when I leaned, and the seven others followed him. Soon, we were all boot-scooting in Zoe's Armenian apartment.

When most of them had mastered the dance, I asked them, "*Are you ready to dance to a faster song?*"

Many of them cheered. A couple decided to sit it out.

I went through The Chicks' songs I had on my iPod. The only fast song was "Sin Wagon."

I thought if these teenagers spoke fluent English, they might be offended by a song that connotes an old-timey vehicle moving down the road filled with transgressions. I assumed the idioms of the American West would be totally lost on them, the rolling in the hay, the mattress-dancing. And I wondered how they would feel about a woman singing flagrantly about her intention to build a life worth living, damn the damnation. But I knew the words. I loved them.

We danced until, on this freezing February night in the Caucasus mountains, we were sweating through our clothes.

When only Gregor was left standing, we all clapped for him as he took on the last few turns by himself.

"Any of you could dance in my town in Texas," I told them.

They eventually helped themselves to bed. I guzzled from a two-liter bottle of water and found my way onto a padded bench on Zoe's three-season porch just long enough for me to lie down on. I unrolled my cocoon-like sleeping bag, crawled inside and watched the stars through the wavy glass window until I fell asleep.

PART 2

16

I don't know if she wrote this before or after I came out, but when I opened a blank journal I brought with me, I found a note from my mother inside the cover.

Brent,

To tell you this family loves you would be an understatement! On these pages, you will write the story of your life away from us. How glorious the privilege to write!

Some pages will be happy, some sad, some questioning, some fearful, but all will be heartfelt and truthful. You are quite the man. And it's true this family loves you! May your pages be filled with good memories of your adventure.

I opened the journal over my lap in the green chair in my cottage after my afternoon coffee with Naira and Vazgen, and I filled the first pages with a memory only a few hours old. My coworkers had surprised me that spring afternoon with a birthday party in the break room, sparkler candles shooting little beams of light at their smiling faces. Liana gave a toast for me and then placed over my shoulders a necklace made of paper flowers. On each flower, my coworkers wrote kind words about me, showering me in encouragement and love.

I kept writing in my journal, following that happy memory with a painful one. On a warm day earlier in the week, as the snow melted, I decided to let my Sanity outside. She quickly disappeared.

Sanity had been named for what I needed but not for what she truly was. Her feral feline tendencies drove her to howl at night. She pounced on my head when I was cleaning and when I watched TV. I continued to find the occasional half-eaten sponge or kitchen towel.

I became certain my cat wasn't happy, and I couldn't blame her. I alternated between gratitude for my quickly heating tiny house and disdain for the walls that seemed closer every winter day. The pink walls grew mold that I treated regularly with bleach. I cracked the windows to let out moisture and turned up the heater to compensate for the escaping warmth.

When the weather warmed, I committed myself to letting Sanity outside. She certainly had the claws to protect herself, I thought. The lattice work pattern of scratches on my forearm was proof.

On the first afternoon, when the temperature rose above freezing, I opened the door, and Sanity walked quietly into the snow.

I did this every day, and she began to walk a bit further each time before coming in when I called to her. "Sanity," I'd say. Then I'd kiss at the air.

"The day had been so warm," I wrote in my new journal on the last day I saw her. I let Sanity out in the morning, and, with surprising confidence, she dashed away into the shed behind my cottage. When I came home from work, I kissed the air and called out, "Sanity! Sanity!" I waited for her grey tabby form to circle around out of the shed. Nothing. I called again. "Sanity! Sanity!"

Naira, shaking out a tablecloth over her porch railing, called to me. "Brent jan, *what are you doing?*"

"*Looking for Sanity,*" I said. "*Did you see her today?*"

Naira had not.

I took Sanity's tuna fish can full of dry cat food in my hand and walked out the heavy metal door through the heavy metal gate on the wall around the yard, starting my search on the wet dirt road. I shook the can with cat food, calling out, "Sanity! Sanity."

The food made a shka-shka-shka sound in between the calls of my cat's name. I walked around the block and past the cemetery next to Naira and Vazgen's house. I walked through parts of the neighborhood I'd never seen. Armenian neighbors I'd never met looked out of doors or windows as I yelled and shook the can.

I walked the neighborhood for hours shaking the can, and as dusk turned to night, I made a Hansel and Gretel style trail of cat food back to the cottage.

I did this for five days. Then finally, while Naira stood at the stove next to a boiling teapot, I told her and Vazgen that I felt pretty sure Sanity had gone back to the wild.

Naira put her hand on her hip. "*What a shame,*" she said.

Vazgen didn't say anything. I raised my eyebrows at him over the nardi board between us to see what he thought. He smiled a friendly smile and shrugged. "Ari," he said. "Khaghank." *Come, let's play.* And he rolled the dice.

~ ~ ~

After the success of our HIV/AIDS project, I suggested to Liana that I run a grant-writing workshop among the schools in all twenty villages.

"I love it," Liana told me. "But can we do more to get all the TDFs involved this time?" Artavan, the only transformational development coordinator who worked on the project, had been such a critical component to its success. He'd been the one to engage parents and schools in every village, making calls and explaining what we were trying to do in schools across the Marz. Liana hoped something similar would engage Petros, Melik, Vigen, and Tirayr.

I suggested a program where TDFs and I could teach grant writing and ideation workshops in each village. Students could write their small grant proposals, and ten of them would receive a thousand-dollar grant for a project in their village that we could execute over the summer. I also offered that I could move to their village for a week and be the students' own Peace Corps volunteer, mirroring the process Liana went through to make a position for me in Stepanavan. Liana approved, and I set out writing a project plan, budget, and curriculum that Yeraz translated.

"I mean, my job here is ultimately to make sure these kids feel like change is possible and that they can do it." I told this to Hayley, who I'd called after lunch just to catch up.

Hayley had been a fellow A-17 with me that first summer in Teghenik. Now, while Stepanavan was warming around me, her site of Sevan was still battling the winter wind that raced over Lake Sevan and crept through her apartment windows.

"But believe me," I told her, "I'm also really excited just to spend time in different villages. I'll get to live with different families, get to know them."

"I wish I could do something like that," Hayley mused. She was feeding two cats she'd adopted, Molly and Henry.

Hayley had spent a lot of time in her nonprofit writing grant proposals, all of which had been rejected.

"You'll get something," I told her. We'd talked before about how lucky I was to be in World Vision. There was no other Peace Corps assignment like it in the country. Every Peace Corps volunteer was either in a nonprofit, a village municipality, or a school. No other volunteer worked in a place that handed them money and asked them what they could do with it. Most other volunteers didn't even have radiator heat in their offices over winter.

"Molly, don't eat that," I heard Hayley command. Then to me, "It's starting to feel like I won't get anything."

"But look on the bright side," I offered. "Maybe we'll each be dating someone soon."

The two of us had already been chatting online about the new Peace Corps volunteers who were popping up on Facebook.

Before I even arrived in Armenia, Hayley had been the first Peace Corps volunteer I'd met. At the time, there was no official online place to connect with volunteers assigned to your country in your cohort. And these were the early days of social media. Facebook was only a few years old. Instagram was a sparkle in the internet's eye. TikTok was unimaginable.

As a millennial, I grew up on the Wild West of the internet, finding ways to navigate the unmapped possibilities for connection. So, at some point before leaving for Armenia, I searched Facebook for any posts or any content on "Peace Corps Armenia," and then "Peace Corps Armenia Summer 2009." In that way, I found myself in a Facebook group—Peace Corps Armenia A-17s—created by one of our cohort to connect with other people who had the same volunteer assignment. A for Armenia and 17 for the seventeenth Peace

Corps group to arrive in-country. When I joined, only five people were in the group, but Hayley was already active, commenting on the group's wall posts and sharing resources she found scouring the internet.

In that group I also met a number of internet-friendly A-16s who asked to join so they could share resources and advice after already living in Armenia for a year by the time we joined. "And to stalk us," I had told Hayley over Facebook chat.

"We should stalk the A-18s," I told Hayley now, a year after we'd arrived. "We need hotties to arrive, girl. We need them, like yesterday. We gotta find their group."

"Oh, I already did," she said. "I'll email you the link."

Unsurprisingly, someone had already made a group called "Peace Corps Armenia A-18s." The group was small. Just six people. "Okay," I told Hayley the next afternoon. "I don't see any of our group in here yet. Just people I don't recognize. We should ask to join, but don't tell any other A-17s. We don't want the whole group to pounce on them. Just us."

We giggled. We knew soon enough that every A-18 volunteer arriving would be going through the same things we were going through now—missing our culture, excited at the possibility of new connections. These would be people we might work with. We'd definitely party in the capital together. There might be new site mates in the group. There might be new best friends. There might be lovers.

"Oh, he's cute," Hayley said.

The afternoon light moved down the office walls while both of us opened up the profiles of A-18s who had no idea really what they were getting into.

"Which one?" I asked.

"The guy who started the group," she said. "Noah."

I navigated the group information to find the group owner. Noah Straid. "He is," I said, forcing calm into my voice.

I was being careful not to use "he" and "cute" in the same sentence. Yeraz hadn't left the office yet. Tirayr and Vigen were smoking on the stoop outside the front door, watching the sunlight dim on the town around them.

"Oh, he definitely is," I said, clicking into his profile picture. Dark hair. Face somewhere between square and round. Thin. Wide shoulders. A Green Lantern T-shirt. I clicked on his next profile picture. He was dressed as some kind of character I didn't recognize and wielded an over-large homemade cardboard sword. I wavered on my feelings about this and decided I would consider the childishness of it endearing rather than off-putting.

"Should I message him?" I asked Hayley.

Before she said yes, I'd already opened a chat window.

~ ~ ~

When we first started talking, Noah and I flirted like gentlemen from early America, as if we were in a parlor somewhere exchanging banter with our gloves in one hand and a drink in the other, which glowed from the light of a fire in the room.

When he missed a blog post I'd sent him, he wrote, "Please ignore the last message. My apologies for my momentary lapse of intelligence, though I shall not promise it to be my last."

And me in my first email to him after days of Facebook chat: "I can't really remember why you sent me your email, but alas, you did. You will be forced to continue this banter now for days to come."

In his reply to this, he reminded me that over chat he'd offer to bring me things. "I know you've been there a long time. There must be stuff that you need from home," which made my heart tingle. He told me to make him a Google doc, and he would bring me what I wanted.

My heart swelled. A man taking care of me. A man being serious about taking care of me. And in this version of the story, taking care of me meant I could ask for things. I salivated and wrote down a list. Hot bean dip and Fritos. Good maple syrup. The biggest bag of peanut butter cups he could find.

I wanted to ask for underwear. I rationalized this in my mind. The elastic of my current pairs had worn from a year of handwashing, and the styles here weren't the same as at home. Truthfully, I wanted to push our conversation there. I ultimately chickened out and asked for T-shirts in earth tones.

"A fine list," he wrote back. "There may be a few surprises in there, too."

Noah started waking up with me on his mind. In Armenia, I was nine hours ahead of him, and I got used to waiting for him to message me in the early afternoon. I'd refresh my browser window, and I'd see his email at the top of my inbox.

"Just woke up," he'd write. I'd imagine him rolling over in bed, his face lit by the light of his laptop screen as he typed a message to the first person he thought of in the morning.

He sent a link to an Owl City song on YouTube. The synth heavy, joyful, climbing bops of that band gave me a perception of Noah as a playful and perhaps painfully optimistic, boyish man. "Play this in your cottage," he wrote. "Dance all night."

I sent him back a video of Jane Lynch as Sue Sylvester in *Glee* singing "Vogue" by Madonna. And "Excuses" by The Morning Benders, which includes a lyric about licking the body of your lover.

From then on, every message included a link to a song or something else we loved. He sent me OK Go's Rube Goldberg machine video of "This Too Shall Pass," and I sent him, eventually, a video I'd made of me covering the Yeah Yeah Yeahs' "Turn Into" in an acapella four-part harmony.

"I miss singing with people," I told him. By then, we'd already talked about the Christians we grew up around—me in Texas, him in Alabama. I told him about my acapella-only hometown church in which I learned how to find the notes for every part, soprano, alto, tenor, and bass. I sang soprano as a toddler and landed in bass by college. "My mom sang alto," I told Noah. "That's still my favorite part to sing."

I started ending my emails with a list of questions like, "What does your time getting ready to leave look like? Crazy?"

"What are you most excited about coming to Armenia?

"What's it like to be gay and coming to Armenia?"

He did the same until our emails took an hour or more to write. I wanted to draw him out. I wanted to spin this time and stretch it like spun sugar I could feast on.

Days into these emails, he wrote, "I really have no intention of dating while in the service, though. To be blunt, I will probably come over and hang out with you and perhaps ask you out if you're much like you seem."

Noah shared this in between telling me that his favorite songs were all tied to his favorite memories and telling me he sticks his tongue out a lot in pictures because he sticks his tongue out a lot in general.

Noah wrote, "It tends to be my version of a friendly wave. I gauge whether people are going to be fun or not by their reaction to me. People who immediately stick their tongues out back at me? Those people are called potential friends."

No man in all my years of living had ever directed that kind of attention to me. Noah telling me he planned to ask me out in Armenia sent a shiver through me, like a never-used machine being plugged in for the first time.

Our email cadence picked up at an enormous rate. I would stay late at the office until 8 or 9 p.m. to write long emails back to him, answering every question and responding to every story. And Noah would do the same. He told me he would plan to go to India for Holi after I told him about celebrating Holi in Kolkata. He told me he'd bring me more books when I told him that I surrounded myself with books to feel at home. He sent me songs I'd never heard before. I told him about the people I loved that I worked with and the people who sketched me out like the security guard who came to sit at the office overnight, who, when finding me still at my desk, hovered around me until he finally decided to ask me if I had a girlfriend. Then he showed me a picture of a topless woman on his flip phone.

It was May. I told Noah, "It could be August before I actually meet you. You'll have training and then site placement. You're not technically allowed to leave the site for weeks, so you'll probably go to Yerevan for the first time in August."

"I try to go with the flow," he wrote back. "I tend to overcalculate, assume, make plots and plans, decipher logical termination points, etc. And that just wears me out and gets me nowhere."

"If I'd be able to convince you to listen," he wrote, "I'd send you a picture of me sticking my tongue out with the *Glee* version of 'True Colors' playing in the background. Because there isn't anything here that requires us to be serious. Or to worry. We're just two cool guys, talking (and not talking-talking) and just starting to be friends."

I thought about Noah constantly and wanted desperately to meet him as soon as I could. Then came an email from Garine, the same training manager who oversaw summer training when I lived in Teghenik. In her email, she included an application to help with preservice training for A-18s.

A week after sending in my application, Garine wrote back that I would be invited to join the welcome committee, greeting volunteers at the airport. I would be invited a month later to help teach a class on community engagement strategies.

This would be it. I'd see him when he got off the plane. Then, a month later, I'd figure out a way to sneak to his training village. I decided not to tell him and to surprise him instead.

Noah and I sailed through the next weeks writing and flirting and writing more. We Gchatted until we were both so burned out of Gchat and then emailed until we could hardly stand the distance. In the week leading up to Noah's flight to Armenia, his emails became shorter, sporadic, and sweetly scattered as he shared the frenzy of packing, the list of names of everyone who came to his going away dinner, and a long email about how gut-wrenching it was for him to leave his mom, knowing he wouldn't see her again for years.

On the day I knew he was flying out, I wrote one last email:

Hey, Noah, I just wanted to say that I have really, really loved all this, this emailing and gchatting and getting to know you. While these aren't my favorite media, I've never had so much time to get so excited to meet someone. I'm so glad you've been open to sharing with me about your life and who you are. You're about to get on a plane and turn a page, and I'm so glad you've allowed me to be a part of it.

I look forward to talking to you, online or otherwise, soon.

~ ~ ~

The flight full of A-18s arrived before sunrise, and Garine arranged for everyone on the welcome committee to meet at the Peace Corps office well before sunrise. I wasn't alone in my eagerness to meet newcomers. I saw Hayley's brunette ponytail wave behind her as she climbed onto the tour bus. Behind her other Peace Corps friends took the stairs up and found their seats.

I hadn't told anyone about Noah. I'd let the conversation drift off with Hayley. I certainly didn't tell Naira and Vazgen why I came home after dark from the office. And I kept myself from telling volunteers. I didn't want Noah to arrive with a shadow, the story of his arrival having something to do with me.

At the airport, we lined up under the dim, yellow overhead lights in the covered walkway that began at the parking lot and snaked up to a set of glass double doors.

One of the PCVs in the welcome group had made posterboard welcome signs that said things like, "Bari Galust!" and "Welcome, A-18s" in large, exuberant lettering. I didn't take one, committing instead to hollering and clapping when the arrivals finally made their way through the glass doors.

And soon, after about twenty minutes of standing in the yellow light, as the sun began to make its way through the grey clouds that obscured it, travelers that looked to us to be Americans began to emerge, and all of us started to yell.

We hollered and whooped and clapped as if this was a sporting event and our team was making its way onto the field. As we shouted and waved signs, we saw in their faces a tired but pleased look of recognition as they read the messages that welcomed them into the Peace Corps.

Hayley, standing next to me, recognized some of their faces from the stalking we'd done on Facebook.

"That's Matt," she whispered to me as a tall, thick, red-haired man in hiking boots walked at a surprising pace past us and toward the buses.

"Pat," Hayley said, as an older woman smiled brightly to those on her left and then her right with clear appreciation for our cohort's welcome.

And then Noah walked by so quickly I couldn't tell if he saw me at all. There he was, his dark spiky hair unkempt and greasy from nearly twenty hours of travel. His black polo loose and stretched from so much turning and trying to sleep on plane seats and airport concourse furniture. His khaki hiking pants still zipped at the knee where they could have been unzipped and made into shorts in the warm, humid summer air he was plunging through on his way to the van.

I hadn't told him I was coming. I'd wanted it to be a surprise. And it was such a well-kept secret that he didn't see me at all.

Garine kept the new A-18s on one bus and the welcome committee, including Hayley and me, on the other.

In our seats next to each other, Hayley turned to me.

"Well, they're here," she said. She pulled a granola bar out of her backpack and a bottle of water. She offered me half of her bar and added, "Our new best friends for a year." Though she'd been the one to point out Noah in the

Facebook group, she still didn't know I wanted more than just a new best friend.

We piled out of the tour bus at Zvartnots Cathedral, and the A-18s were already wandering blankly together up the ancient steps.

I was afraid to approach Noah, to let people in on the secret of our knowing each other. I saw the back of him but kept talking to Hayley and then to a new, young blonde woman whose name I immediately forgot as I saw Noah punch another guy in the shoulder. Both of them laughed, enjoying a friendship just days old, forged over the leap they both took into a new world. Two other guys were talking with them, and immediately I felt myself outside of them. Them—a group I was not part of. And in that group walked a man I was desperate to know, to look at. I'd fantasized about touching him, and now he walked and laughed ahead of me with a natural gait I could already tell I was wound too tightly to have.

Noah disappeared with those men behind the columns, and I hung back at the stairs. After the new volunteers wandered between the columns for a while, Garine called the group of nearly forty A-18s to the cathedral steps for a photo.

I watched from a distance, cheering with the welcome committee as the group formed. And in the back, Noah found a spot in the fourth row from the front next to the group of guys he'd walked into the ruins with.

And I thought, *Oh... oh no...*

And then Noah caught my eyes. Without too much exuberance, as if he knew I didn't want to give us away, he smiled at me. And he stuck out his tongue.

I forced myself to bury the fear that churned my stomach. I smiled back. No tongue.

I suddenly and desperately wanted him to stop looking at me, for no one in the group of sixty or so people to see that we knew each other, that we were connected.

Because, after all these months of writing to each other, spending hours pouring our hearts into silly flirting, deep sharing, and even a couple of relationship defining tête-à-têtes, after I'd told him I wanted to hold him after he'd called me a cocktease, after I told him I found myself falling for him over the internet, I was seeing him for the first time.

And suddenly, I was afraid I didn't actually want him at all.

17

"I think you're insane."

Zoe, on the other end of the phone, was still breathing heavily. When she'd answered my call, she was in her underwear moving furniture around her apartment, sweating and shoving.

"You've been talking about this for a year. You want to date. My god. You did the email thing. He's cute. Literally, what's not to love."

I was pacing, something I've always done on the phone. Had the floor been made of anything softer than its ceramic tile, I would surely have paced a rut into the ground like a wild animal in a cage.

"He just... I don't know... I didn't feel it. I wanted to run."

"Well, no shit," Zoe said. I heard her grunt accompanied by the scrape of furniture feet on that grey, hardwood floor. Another shove. "You've been running from this your whole life. You're good at running from it."

I laughed. "Fair enough."

I thought of our emails, Noah's and mine. He'd written: "Here's hoping I don't have something tragically wrong with me that you've yet to be able to notice." In another, he'd told me he loved cuddling and nature documentaries, and I'd subsequently told him I thought that a great first date would be watching *Planet Earth* together until we fell asleep. Then he followed by saying that whatever our first date was he wanted to be deliberate and even cautious because if things got physical too quickly, he was afraid he'd lose me. "Maybe it's just because I've been with the wrong people, but frankly, you're worth not risking it."

"I can't just sleep with him," I told Zoe. "He's been just… too sweet to me… these emails… it's too romantic. I am not sure what I want, but I don't want to be an asshole. I can't sleep with him if I think I might not even actually like him."

"And you thought this after seeing him once," Zoe countered. "After hours of international, sleepless travel. After he walked off a plane that he'd tried to sleep on, not even knowing you were going to be there, you saw him from far away and thought, 'No? This is not the guy for me?'"

"Oh god," I said. "That's not fair, I guess."

I could hear her exhale after another push against a sofa or a wardrobe. "Yeah, I don't think it's fair."

~ ~ ~

Before I left to teach my class to his new cohort of volunteers, I wrote to Noah, "Just so you know, I'm planning to pretend we don't know each other. I'm going to pretend that we talked a little online, but that's it. I don't want the rumor mill to chew us up."

The A-18 preservice training took place in the same town of Charentsavan, and my training village Teghenik was the site of a new set of the A-18s. But not Noah. In fact, another volunteer was placed with my Teghenik host family after I'd told Garine how incredible my summer was with Talin, Mikayel, Lala, Sona, and Hakob.

I traveled to Yerevan and got a ride to Charentsavan with the director of Peace Corps in a nice SUV with air conditioning that made the valley's summer heat feel distant instead of a single pane of glass away.

I taught the class to a group of strangers who smiled with me afterward and lazily asked questions that, after two weeks in-country, they'd already asked a million times. Things like, "Who provides the best internet?" Me— "Honestly, I wouldn't know. My NGO is one of the few placements that provides high-speed wi-fi, so I've never bought my own." Or "How do you get through winter?" Me— "Get into projects you love. Watch a lot of movies. I'd say get a pet, but that didn't work out well for me."

Afterward, I told the Peace Corps director I didn't need a ride back because I wanted to go visit my Teghenik host family. I walked alone on the streets of Charentsavan until I was able to find a taxi, which I asked to take me to that tiny village on the mountainside. I asked for the driver's number so I could call him when I was ready to leave Teghenik.

At the khanut, I saw Talin and Sona, who told me Hakob wasn't there. He had turned eighteen that spring and was completing required military service on the border of Armenia and Azerbaijan. The war over Nagorno-Karabakh had been won over a decade ago, but the border was hostile enough that Peace Corps banned volunteers from even visiting the region, which was just a day's drive away.

Sona looked at the ground while Talin told me this. Talin's eyes filled with tears as the words came out, and as soon as she finished saying it, she looked at my wet eyes, and she laughed, waving her hand as if she could bat away the fact of her son's absence.

"*Ice cream?*" she offered. The white, melting cream dripped onto our fingers and down to the khanut's white linoleum floor as the summer heat wandered in through the shop's open door and around the three of us sitting by the cash register.

I told them I couldn't stay long, that I had to get back to Yerevan. But the truth was, Noah had emailed me his new Armenian phone number, and I'd been texting him all day. I asked him to tell me the name of the village where he was placed and an easy-to-find place in the village I could tell a taxi driver to drop me at.

I called my driver, gave him the name of the village, and said, "*There's a school. Do you know it? I need to go to the school.*"

"T-shirt and blue jeans kind of guy..." Noah had written. And there, leaning on a pink-grey stone wall, Noah was looking at me now, his forest green T-shirt, his dark blue jeans with one foot cocked and pressed against the school wall like he just got out of detention and was waiting for a ride.

He didn't smile at me at first. *He's playing it cool*, I thought. *Or he's worried about the taxi driver seeing something in the way we greet each other.*

"Hi," I offered, my voice soft, a question implied in its vulnerability, like when a dog approaches with its ears back.

"Hi," he returned.

"Well," I pushed right into the awkwardness. "We did it. We broke all the rules. We're here."

I overlaughed, and he smiled. We did break all the rules, and suddenly a weight, like an accepting of something big into my hands, rolled over me. Peace Corps would not have approved this visit. Peace Corps approved every movement of a Peace Corps volunteer out of their work site, and they are incredibly protective of new arrivals. They wouldn't have liked me coming to see Noah. And while Peace Corps wouldn't have liked that for many program-related reasons, most of the world didn't want us to meet either. Two men who might actually like each other, two men who might want to kiss, to have sex. Not many people in the world would have wanted this.

But we wanted it. Noah and I wanted to see each other. Noah and I wanted to meet the other man behind the hours and hours of emails, the months of writing to each other the way a soldier from some very old war would write a lover they'd met just before shipping out. With longing. With hope.

Pretending in our emails that we were certain there was so much more below the letters on the screen, something stirring in our hearts.

The dusty road crunched beneath our feet, up a hill, into a shop.

"I'm getting snacks," Noah told me. "I told my host mom I was inviting a friend over to watch a movie. I need snacks. Do you want anything?"

Endeared to him by this gesture, I offered, "Sunflower seeds? And water."

He bought both for me, even though I knew he received so much less in an allowance than I did with my three-hundred-dollar-a-month stipend.

We walked into the kitchen of his host family's house, and I was grateful I didn't see a large family milling around. Only one older woman stood chopping a head of pale green cabbage in the kitchen. At the sound of the door opening, she looked up from the near-white strips, and after a second, she offered, "Barev, Noah jan!"

The sweetness in her voice, the belonging she offered him in her unambiguous cheer, touched me.

"Barav, Lilit!" Noah nearly shouted this back. Then he held up one of his bags, three tomatoes pushing against the translucent cellophane.

"Vay, Noah jan," Lilit said, her wrinkly hands letting go of both the cabbage and the long knife. She walked over to take the bag. I assumed by reading her demeanor that she hadn't expected these, as if perhaps there were a kind of gift from Noah to her.

"*They're pretty, Noah. Thank you,*" she said.

Noah looked at me to translate.

"She said that they're pretty," I told him. "And thank you."

Noah made a face of understanding and then said in Armenian. "*You're welcome.*"

Then he pointed to me and said, "*Friend.*"

"Ah," Lilit said. She wiped her hands on her apron and then took my hands in hers. "*Welcome,*" she said and then turned to Noah. "*Does he want to eat?*"

Noah made a friendly frown. In a thought as quick as lightning, I considered stepping in, talking easily with her, and answering that question for myself. And just as quickly I thought of her realizing I spoke Armenian well enough to talk with her, and I imagined she might ask me questions about who I was and where I lived. I didn't want any questions. The less I talked, the less opportunity there was to read something in my answers, to give myself away. I knew there was little chance she would see me as a gay man after a short conversation about whether or not I wanted a snack. But it was still nonzero. So, I stayed silent.

Lilit didn't even look at me. "Josh," she said, the Armenian word for meal, and mimed lifting food to her mouth and taking a bite.

"No, no, no," Noah said in English. *"Movie,"* he said in Armenian.

"Lav, lav," Lilit said and waved us upstairs.

Afternoon light found its way into Noah's room through a window that faced toward the valley. The sunlight was enough to see clearly the small room with cream-colored walls, the dark wood wardrobe that matched the bedframe for a long bed not quite wide enough to be considered an American twin. I sat down on it, stretched my arms back, and held them fully extended so I could lean back and look reclined, relaxed, which I wasn't at all.

"Well, you've been here two weeks, Noah," I said. "How has it been?"

Noah fumbled for a moment. I could tell he was unsure of whether to stand there by his closed bedroom door, take a seat at the desk, or sit down next to me.

"It's been good," he said.

"Do you like your group?"

"They're great, actually." Noah launched into describing them while he sat on the edge of the desk. Like his emails, he proved he loved people, sharing the names of A-18s and talking about their interests. He bragged that he'd become the dad of the group because he bought everyone ice cream after language class or provided beers when they hung out in the evenings. He knew their hometowns. He knew who'd already started dating.

"Started dating?" I asked as if this wasn't something that happened in our group. As if it wasn't, in fact, what we were trying to do now.

Eventually, he remembered he'd brought me something.

"I'll have to get you movies later. Amelia has my hard drive. But I did bring you the last two seasons of *Friends*

and the newest season of *Grey's Anatomy*. And I have this…"
He opened the wardrobe, lifting a few of his neatly folded
T-shirts to reveal a green shirt and another red one, both
from Target.

"Holy lord," I said. "New clothes."

I scanned the piles of neatly folded laundry on the shelves.
"All Calvins?"

Noah started, unsure, and then he smiled. He pulled
out a pair of Calvin Klein underwear. "I actually bought all
new underwear." He tried smiling slyly. "You never know
who you're going to meet. And it has to be Calvins. I have
to make sure there's plenty of room."

He smirked, and it took me so long to understand what he
meant that once I realized he was trying to tell me he had a
big dick, the moment had passed, and I was too embarrassed
to bring it back up.

I hadn't moved and my arms were starting to fall asleep.
But I didn't want to move. I was actually terrified. I had
never done this. Even with girls I'd dated, I'd never snuck
into their bedrooms. And in here, with Noah, I could sense
his maleness—the flat front of him, the square shoulders, the
unmade bed, the way he leaned back so that his hips were
pushing into the room without effort.

"Didn't you tell your host mom that we were watching a
movie? Maybe we actually should."

He laughed. "Maybe we should."

"I wouldn't want to lie, you know," I joked, and Noah
barely chuckled but turned to his desk and opened his
laptop. Without my asking, he opened *Blue Planet* and lay
down next to me.

I'm certain whales breached many different ocean
surfaces in the first minutes of our lying side by side on

his narrow bed, but I heard none of the splashes. I heard none of the narrator expounding upon the natural wonders of the sea.

Ignorant of the vastness of it all, my mind was so narrowly focused on that room in that house. I felt Noah next to me, my arm next to his arm, his hands folded on his stomach. My heart pounding against my rib cage as if that one muscle alone could propel me to turn and face him.

Noah wasn't moving, and my mind raced, scanning every part of my body to try and perceive the slightest touch. Months and months of emailing… two weeks of barely a message as he sought out a phone and eventually an internet connection. And now a physical connection made only where our bare elbows touched, my hand extended at my side, his still folded. Would he lean his foot over to graze mine? Would I feel a knee at my thigh?

He didn't move. I didn't move. As we lay there, I started to think of his host mom, tried to imagine a reason she might come upstairs and open the door without knocking to find us lying so close.

I chastised myself for not even asking how many other people were in his host family. In my mind, I made up a host brother who would walk in to see if Noah wanted to go drive around the villages and then cry out when he saw us. Maybe by then, we'd have hooked pinkies.

Nothing. Minutes and minutes went by. So many minutes that I started to feebly pay attention to the show. Whales. Then plankton. Then tuna. Then silky sharks. I hated every one of them. Could this man, this man who'd flirted with me for months online be so disinterested? Or worse, so emotionally terrified that he was paralyzed?

And then, quickly, I realized I'd also not moved. I imagined we were closing in on the end of an hour-long episode, and Noah's hands were still folded over his stomach.

I had to get back to Yerevan before dark, and I could tell by the way the color of his room changed that the sun was making its way toward the peaks of the mountains to the west. I'd come all this way, broken rules to be here. I was almost angry, angry that we could have been making out this whole time, but instead, he watched a sardine migration. I knew I wouldn't see him again until after his training was over in two months. I'd never kissed a man. In this room, on this day, in this moment, I wanted to be lighting fire to that part of my history.

As an albatross started building a nest on screen, I turned onto my side and looked squarely at the side of Noah's face. His eyes didn't move. His hands stayed folded.

I lifted my hand and glided a fingertip from the knuckle of his middle finger to the tip of his elbow. I traced my finger up his arm to his shoulder and then across his chest just below his clavicle. Then down his other arm and back up to his folded hands. He stayed still. I traced that course a few more times and then added a trip down his sternum, just past the bone to the surface of his soft belly, and then back up into the circle.

As a pod of orcas began pursuing a mother grey whale and her calf, I traced my finger to the side of his face and gently guided his chin until his head was turned completely to the left. His eyes were opened brightly all of a sudden, expectantly, almost demurely.

I leaned in to kiss him.

He kissed like a trout.

His lips were hard, the curve of his lips almost rigid. They opened and closed at a rhythm that seemed unchanged by any move I made.

His head was turned so completely that I imagined it might actually be impeding him, so I got up on one elbow to be above him. And then he kissed like a trout on its back.

I moved. I writhed. I'd been aroused and tried to excite him by rolling my body and pressing myself against his leg, though I was rapidly softening.

He didn't move. He didn't unfold his hands from his belly. His lips stayed hard and curved and moving with such a constant pace that I began to be able to plan my attempts at softening his lips, timing my tongue to slide over them and then back into my mouth before it got snapped.

I hadn't anticipated this, his lack of movement.

I stayed lifted until the orcas finally caught and ripped from the baby whale its lower jaw and its tongue. Something about the climactic music in the climactic scene of the episode cued a release of effort, and I settled myself with my head on his chest. I put my hand on his hands, and together we watched a final scene—hagfish slithering across the ocean floor to the carcass of another whale that attracted deep sea scavengers with a waft of decay. A year and a half later, the narrator said, nothing is there in that spot but the bones.

18

I dragged myself up five flights of stairs to a stranger's apartment in Yerevan. After three knocks, Zoe wrenched the red-painted steel door open and jumped through the threshold to wrap her arms around me.

"B!" she yelled, her voice echoing in the stairwell. "Tell me everything! Tell me what happened with Noah!"

I didn't say a word about Noah at first and instead let my jaw drop open at the apartment I found myself in. I'd just been in Noah's host family's modest village home outside Charentsavan. Now I stood inside the nicest apartment I'd ever been inside.

Zoe had asked a new friend, Phillip, if I could stay with her at his apartment. A free place to stay in Yerevan was gold to a Peace Corps volunteer. The hostel everyone stayed at was fifteen dollars a night, which is no small sum for people living on three hundred dollars a month. You could spend a tenth of your income on one weekend in Yerevan, just for a bunk in a room with twenty people.

Zoe had made friends with Phillip at Cocoon on a night I wasn't with them. She kept up with Phillip on Facebook and text and had already bragged to me about this wonderful man, the clean-water-centered nonprofit he ran, and his beautiful girlfriend. After hanging out a few times, Phillip offered to let Zoe stay at his apartment on the west side of the Cascade, where the sun crept through the windows of the guest room in the morning and tickled her toes.

"I feel bad," I told Zoe, following her over tiled floor, running my fingers over the stainless-steel range in the kitchen, and walking past a lounge with fur-covered chairs and mood lighting that accented a glass sculpture on the wall.

In the guest bedroom, while I dropped my backpack onto a fully extended sofa bed, I continued, "I just… I don't feel the feelings, I think."

Zoe listened but pointed to the door. "Outside?"

We walked to a tiny bistro set on the balcony overlooking the Cascade. Shouts of little children playing around the sculptures on the promenade rose in the summer air around us, followed by the murmuring of friends gathered at cafés below.

As the sun began to float toward the horizon behind us and the Cascade filled with golden light, I thought of the day passing. The day of my first gay kiss—a day I'd wanted to arrive so desperately for as long as I could fantasize—this day was ending.

"The kiss was… it wasn't good, Zoe." A cool breeze stirred in the shade of the building and made its way over us.

"Well, that's disappointing," she said.

"Yeah." I sipped a Schweppes Bitter Lemon, something I'd picked up at the shop downstairs. "I wanted it to be good. But Noah just lay there with his hands over his stomach, and eventually, when the kissing was bad and his hands didn't move I gave up."

"Geez, Brent. You gave up?"

"Yeah…" I flicked at the tab of my drink can. "It was bad enough that I wondered immediately whether I'm actually gay at all."

I looked up at her to find a shocked face, as if she didn't know what to say. I laughed. "Okay, but then I sorted that out. One kiss does not erase a lifetime of lust." I giggled but then continued soberly, "I'm not sure it's going anywhere with Noah."

"After all that?" Zoe asked, leaning back into her wire-framed chair. "After all the emails, the hours of typing, and the hours of talking to me about it, you're calling it quits with Noah."

"Maybe. I was really into the whole thing. The emails, the sweet talk, getting to know him. He's so reserved. He's been talking to me for months, and he just seemed like he didn't want to be kissing me."

I wasn't sure this was true. I couldn't tell. Was Noah terrible at kissing? Did he not know what to do with his hands? I didn't know what to do with my hands, but at least I tried. Maybe he was great at dating on the internet but terrible at dating in real life. I didn't want to have to try and figure it out. I was disappointed. I wanted something passionate. Something clandestine and exciting, full of serendipity and the passion of a man stirred by the same forces I could feel running through me.

"We're going out tonight, by the way," Zoe told me, looking out at the cafés below us.

"Seriously?" I threw back the last swig of Bitter Lemon, now warm, and looked down as a small girl ran, ice cream in hand to a tall man who lifted her up and then pointed to a statue of a rabbit on a bell. "I don't know," I told her. "I'm exhausted."

Zoe laughed, leaned back in her chair again and looked east. "Take a nap. I think you should meet Ana."

Ana. I'd been excited to meet Ana, who Zoe had been bringing up in conversation for months. Zoe met Ana first on another trip to Yerevan when Phillip invited Zoe to see Ana perform violin in Lover's Park. Phillip told Zoe, "She's one of us."

Zoe then waxed on about Ana's long dark hair, her scratchy voice, and the violinist's unexpected swagger, which sent Zoe into a swoon.

While I napped, Zoe made plans, and as soon as I woke up, she told me Ana would meet us at Lagonid, a Lebanese restaurant across town.

I could feel the power of Ana's charm as soon as I saw her outside the restaurant leaning against the wall, her arms crossed with one hand that gently waved when she saw us. In a world of Armenian women who wore black, beige, and white blouses that smoothed their bodies, Ana wore a baggy black T-shirt and circular sunglasses. In a country where most women stood in boots with heels that gave them inches and forced good posture, Ana leaned back in canvas high tops. She was not overeager to meet me, making her handshake feel like a kindness to me.

"Barev, Ana jan," I told her, still holding her hand in both of mine. "I'm so happy to meet you." And I was so happy, honored even, to meet this Armenian lesbian violinist in a country where homosexuality was treated as a mental illness you could be committed to an asylum for, a sin you could be killed for.

Ana smiled at my admiration of her, which was evident in my eager eyes. She said simply, "Barev Brent jan, how are you?" She was effortless.

However, I knew, having created my own facades of ease and comfort, that she'd had to run a never-ending gauntlet in Armenia, the threat of constant danger and insecurity around her always. I knew nothing about her life, but I knew it couldn't be easy to find a job or keep an apartment—both things you could be thrown out of because you looked like a lesbian, even if you said you weren't. All this I thought of in that instant, holding her hand. Where could she find love? Where could she be free?

Months after meeting her, I would ask her, "Where do you feel free?" And she would say, "Nowhere."

Ana and Zoe wrapped each other in a hug before Ana pulled back and gestured to someone behind her.

"Guys," Ana said, "please meet Vartan."

Vartan was silhouetted by the light of the setting sun that was trying to glide down behind city buildings. I couldn't quite make out his features at first, but his backlit shoulders made something wild rise in my chest and propelled me into a deep breath as if I could take him in through the air.

"Hello," he said simply and extended a hand with blunt fingernails and soft dark hair that grew from his wrist up over the top of his hand. Soft and still masculine. I took it in mine and held it. He stepped toward me, out of sunlight and into shadow, and I saw his face.

Kind, I thought. My age, I guessed, though perhaps a bit older. A bit taller than me, so that I felt just a hint of staring up at him. He had brown eyes as unassuming and vulnerable as birds alighting on a balcony railing. He looked directly at me without blinking, and I could tell immediately that he knew and I knew what we both were and wondered what we could be to each other.

Zoe said hello and then asked Ana, "How do you know each other?" Her voice pulled me back to earth like the tug of a string tied to a balloon.

"Vartan and I met at one of my shows," Ana said, her accent making her English bounce and turn in a way I instantly loved listening to. "He came to me and said hello, and I knew he would be a good person."

Vartan smiled, his tall frame bowing at the hips as if to say, "At your service."

Ana bowed back as if this was their own secret gesture, something they'd done since they were kids. Instead, they were two friends who had met making their way through the queer community in a place where it was so dangerous to be queer and shared a kind of camaraderie you make when the people of your youth are long gone—either because they abandoned you or because you ran.

The four of us walked together, down Northern Avenue in the fading light. Zoe and Ana paired off and walked ahead of Vartan and me.

He talked about his work in an IT center as well as his art. He painted, mostly portraits of people he remembered from his childhood in Tehran. He'd come to school in Yerevan, "to feel more free," he said. He told me his portraits were abstract, their faces irregular. I asked him what part of the face he liked to paint the most. He said he was fascinated by the mouth, all the things it does in a single day, and still, "It can be smiling at you."

We went from café to café to café, the summer night air warming us slowly until our bones were the same temperature as the air around us. We ordered sweet shots, beers, and then french fries. I told Ana and Vartan about my parents, their reaction to "my secret," a quickly made code to keep my homosexuality out of the ears of those around us. I told them about growing up in Texas, the fears and the freedoms. And they wanted to know about the cowboys.

"Yes, there are still cowboys," I said.

"Like, from the movies?" Ana asked, as if bewildered.

"Yes. The horses. The boots. The hats. It's all there."

We talked about Stepanavan, how peaceful it seemed compared to Yerevan, the fresh air, the green plants all around, the river that ran in the gorge to the east, the pathway down by the old fortress at Lori Berd where we could all carry a picnic, eat, drink, and then swim together in the hot spring.

"We will go. We must go," Ana said.

"Absolutely," Vartan said, smiling at me with his soft eyes.

We were all walking again, Zoe and Ana ahead of us leading us to another café. Vartan walked close to me, leaned in without touching me, and said, "You are so handsome. I want to get to know you."

Later, after I watched him pull Ana aside to walk around Swan Lake, he returned to me while I sipped on vodka soda and whispered in my ear, "Will you spend the night with me?"

Now, in this moment as I write, so many years later, I am surprised at myself. I am surprised that, after so many months spent dreaming of Noah, pouring myself into hours of email writing, sharing more sides of myself than I had with most people I'd known my whole life, that on the day I kissed Noah for the first time, I would also go spend the night with an Iranian-Armenian man named Vartan.

And I still wonder what power of the universe would deliver Noah and Vartan into my life on the same day, after an entire lifetime of dreaming of men, of beating myself up over my desire for men, after contemplating suicide and then instead deciding to build a life totally unknown to me… after deciding to leave the highway I was on for a tiny path barely visible on the edge of a forest… after all those years of being desperate to feel the sensual affection of a man, the universe would present two options on the same day. And I would have both.

At our last café, Ana offered that Vartan and I could stay the night at her apartment. While Ana and Vartan stepped into a twenty-four-seven supermarket to buy snacks, Zoe told me she was excited for me if I was excited. She hugged me, told me to be safe and have fun, and took a taxi to Phillip's apartment on the Cascade.

Ana, Vartan, and I took a taxi to Ana's apartment. While Ana told the driver what streets to turn on, I put my hand on the seat between Vartan and me. His hand followed, and in the smallest, most cautious movements we caressed each other's hands with our fingertips.

At nearly 2 a.m. in her apartment, while we all goofily made small talk, Ana moved about, flicking on lamps draped in wildly painted fabrics, setting out snacks on a coffee table also draped in a hand-painted cloth. The murals she'd painted on all her walls were illuminated by each lamp, and she left Vartan and me for a moment to dash upstairs, returning down the spiral staircase with sheets and pillows for a daybed in the corner of the living room.

Vartan took two bottles of water from the fridge for us and another beer. With the apartment appointed for us, Ana left abruptly for the staircase.

"I'll see you in the morning," she said.

To which I, with equal flourish, said, "Hajoghutyun yev shnorhakalutyun," which made both of them laugh.

Within moments of her leaving, Vartan lay on the bed and watched me walk over and lie down next to him. He put an arm around me and said again, "You are so handsome."

We were both lying on our side facing each other. I took one of his hands in mine, our fingers laced together and our palms touching. I looked into his brown eyes, his longish hair falling over them now in a boyish way that made him look shy.

I leaned into him. I kissed his neck. I kissed his cheek. I kissed his lips, which were still on first contact, as if he was hesitating, before he made small, and then larger glides of his lips against mine.

I kissed his neck again and then in Armenian said, *"I waited for this all night."*

We kissed for what felt like hours. We took off each other's shirts, our hands sliding over each other's bare shoulders, each other's chests, and bellies, and then along the waist of each other's jeans.

"Is it okay?" I asked, looking up at him as I began to kiss my way down his belly.

"Yes," he said.

The sun came up as Vartan came, and in the early morning light that crept in through the closed drapes of the apartment windows I searched the kitchen for napkins, finally finding some in a drawer with pens, scattered utensils, a wine opener, and a notepad. I took a crumpled handful of them and cleaned Vartan's belly.

I realized then, in that moment, how little Vartan had actually moved since getting into bed. In fact, he hadn't done more than to turn on his side and then onto his back again. Now, on his back, I lay next to him, my arm draped across his chest, while he pretended to sleep.

"Do you want to…" I whispered, "… you know…" And as he opened his eyes, I put his hand between my legs, inviting him to reciprocate.

He gently pulled his hand back to mine, squeezed it, and said nothing.

"That's okay," I said so quickly it surprised me. I knew I was disappointed, but I wanted to hide it.

Vartan began to fall asleep. I couldn't, my mind trying to make sense of the disappointment. Was it selfish that I wanted him to want my body as much as I wanted his? Like a door only half open, the evening felt so romantic. The night felt unfinished, not because I hadn't come but because when he finished, he'd simply gone to sleep.

I wouldn't ask him why. But I began to create a story on his behalf that he never actually told me. I imagined that it must have been hard in Tehran to be gay and that it was still difficult here now. That evening he'd told me many times how handsome I was, yet in the first hours of a new day, maybe he'd been afraid of having crossed a threshold for himself. That, in fact, hours after my first gay kiss with someone else, maybe I was actually his.

As hours went on, I imagined his coming to Yerevan, his finding a new home, his finding gay friends in a place still so unsafe for gay people, his fear of losing everything in this new life because of one night of letting down his guard for a handsome American. That he wasn't ready. That he needed time. That my own desires could wait.

I thought all of this as the sun rose, and we both pretended to sleep.

~ ~ ~

When Ana finally returned down the spiral staircase, she made both of us coffee and eggs.

We ate quietly.

When Ana went to the bathroom, I told Vartan, "I'd like to see you again."

"I would like that, too," he said. "Are you staying in Yerevan?"

"Yes," I decided instantly. It was Sunday. I should have been returning to Stepanavan that evening to work the next day. But it would be weeks before I returned to Yerevan again. "Do you want to hang out tonight?" I asked.

Immediately in my head ran visions of us together, repeating all of this, the cafés, the walking, the hearing over and over how handsome I was, the stealing of finger grazes in the backseat of a cab, and perhaps my own pleasure in a new night together.

Zoe had only arranged for her and me to stay at Phillip's on Saturday night, so I met Zoe at Phillip's apartment, packed my bags, and walked with her to Artbridge for brunch. We were both too hungover to speak much about the night. We each drank our second and third cups of coffee, ate eggs and french toast at Artbridge, and then called a cab for Zoe so she could make the six-hour ride home to Goris.

With my bag on my back, I went to the Peace Corps office to email Liana and let her know I wouldn't be in the office the next day and then to a café followed by another café followed by another café. At each of them I wrote in my journal, read my book, and waited until the afternoon, forcing myself to refrain from texting Vartan until 4 p.m., which I thought was a respectable time to reach out to a new lover without being too much in some way.

"Hi, Vartan!" I typed into my Nokia. "Want to meet for dinner? Do you like Indian food?"

When he didn't text back, I took myself alone to an Indian restaurant in a basement called Karma and ate a plate of samosas and mint sauce, realizing only after I'd ordered Chicken Tikka Masala that I had no cell service.

I ate and paid for my meal in ten minutes flat, went back to the surface of the earth, and waited for a text to come through, raising my phone in various directions as if trying to catch a firefly in a jar.

I texted Vartan again: "I'm headed to Calumet. Have a drink with me?"

Volunteers referred to Calumet as a "hippie bar" in a message to new volunteers on Facebook when they asked where people went out in the city. The bar had only recently opened, and I sat with my bag on a pouf next to a wall. I texted Vartan a few more times, drinking one single beer extremely slowly while finally beginning to let myself fear the prospect that not only was Vartan not going to text me back, but that I wouldn't be staying again at Ana's, having not asked for her number at all.

I left Calumet for the hostel where the front desk worker told me they were full. I walked back to Calumet, sat again on the pouf, and contemplated whether or not I could stay up all night walking the streets of Yerevan with my computer, a few sets of clothes, a couple of books, and groceries in a bag on my back. Tired from staying up with Vartan the entire night before, I set about trying to make friends in Calumet, gambling that some new stranger might let me stay with them.

A wave of desperation turned into luck when a group of European girls from a set a poufs next to me started to joke with me about the crazy things Americans do. "Yes," I told them. "We're obsessed with the Pledge of Allegiance. Everything goes quiet, and everybody puts their hands on their heart."

I eventually asked if there was any way I could stay with them. I inflated my story, told them my boyfriend and I were supposed to be spending the night together, but he dumped me. They told me they were staying with a group of Armenian friends they'd made in Dilijan and that they'd ask if I could stay at their apartment.

Perhaps to please these girls, two young Armenian men led all of us back to their top floor apartment, which they seemed to share with a number of other young people who, by the way they were dressed, all seemed likely to frequent the "hippie bar." One of the young men led me to an unfurnished attic room with slanted walls and old floorboards that bent when I walked on them. I barely was able to say, "Shnorhakalutyun," before he was gone back down the stairs.

I could have used the flashlight on my phone to read, but without an outlet to plug into, I didn't want to lose battery. I rolled my T-shirt into a pillow and lay alone in an attic in a building I couldn't place on a map.

I sent a final text to Vartan. "You could have told me simply that you didn't want to see me again."

In the morning, I scanned the floor with my cell phone flashlight to make sure I wouldn't leave anything behind and crept out of the apartment before anyone else woke up.

My taxi driver called and said he would be late to take me back to Stepanavan. Hours late. Which meant I'd miss another day of work.

I texted Zoe. "Vartan never texted. Never called. And my taxi won't show up until 2 p.m. And I need hangover food."

"Apsos, Brent jan," she wrote back. "Artbridge? Go eat your pain."

19

"I'm not sure I can make the trip, honey."

My mom said this to me on a phone call, me pacing cooly in my well-trod path around my cottage's tile floor. A summer breeze swept in gently from open windows, a soft aroma of cleaning liquid lifting from the freshly mopped floor, my laundry waving in the summer sun outside Naira and Vazgen's kitchen.

Though my dad and I rarely talked, Mom and I had been calling each other more. During the school year, she emailed updates a few times a week—a visit to her parents in Louisiana, Macey's band performance, Lisa's horse she was leasing on the ranch where she lived in a tiny little cottage like mine on the edge of our Texas hometown.

I missed them, especially in the summer days when I knew they were sitting out at night listening to crickets and talking about everything and nothing. I'd miss them and then shudder at the thought that if I was with them on their side yard, we'd be talking about my gayness, my choices, my future, and all the unknowns that scared each of us in different ways. It was better on this side of the world where the things that scared us could scatter like dust over all the land and water between us.

My mom had been talking since Christmas about actually visiting me in Armenia. She'd never been outside the US. She'd never flown across an ocean or gotten a visa or walked into a city where everyone spoke a language she'd never heard before. She didn't particularly want to, either. Except that I was here. And that was enough. In December, she started talking about coming up in the summer while she was on summer break from teaching fifth graders math and science.

When summer first arrived, she told me she'd come at the end of summer. And now the end of summer was a few weeks away, and she still hadn't bought a ticket.

"Okay, Mom." I sighed.

I imagined her agonizing over her decision not to come. The money would be a factor. The ticket prices were larger than most I'd ever bought over years of traveling, and no one else in my family, not grandmothers or cousins, ever traveled, so the price must have been a shock. The intimidation of making plans to fly to the other side of the world. The fear of going away from home alone. She hardly went out of our hometown without a friend, a child, or my dad.

And most of all, I worried that she didn't actually want to see me. Three nights before I came to Armenia, she looked me in the eyes and said, "If you choose this life, we will have to love you from afar."

And what did that mean? What life was I choosing? I couldn't have even told her then. Or now. I'd come out. And then I'd gone to a country that considered themselves the oldest Christian country in the world and been assigned to an office of the largest Christian nonprofit on the planet. I didn't bring this up on these calls with her. I assumed she might say something like, "That's probably God at work, honey." And perhaps she was right. What could I know about any god?

After attending church four or five days a week throughout high school and then studying ministry at the most revered Christian university in our Christian denomination, I came away feeling like all that studying and praying made God more opaque and unknowable than I'd felt before. I'd spent all those hours in prayer and Bible study and listened to preacher after preacher after preacher deliver sermon after sermon after sermon.

After all that, I had given up knowing who God was. In fact, I figured if God wanted me to know exactly who God was, if it was critical to my eternal life that I utter the correct answer to that one question, I'd done as much as I could. I supplicated with as much earnestness as a human being could muster. And if it was that critically important to know who God was, well, maybe God wouldn't have made it such a hard question for so many billions of people to answer.

So, I'd chosen to let go of knowing the right answer to that question. I suppose that was a choice, as my mother implied when she said, "If you choose this life." And then, since I wasn't going to choose Christianity, it didn't make sense to choose the common Christian belief that God doesn't want people to be gay. I'd stop praying my gay away. That was another choice.

But other than that, what else was I choosing?

I certainly wasn't choosing the way my heart beat around some men. My attraction to men was no more voluntary or optional than a compass needle pointing unerringly north.

So, no, she couldn't mean that. Maybe she didn't even know what she meant.

"You don't have to come, Mom," I told her.

She began to cry. "But I feel like I'm letting you down."

I paused. "Well," I said, "we don't get everything we want in life. But I have most of what I need, I think. I'm okay. You don't have to come."

~ ~ ~

Earlier that year, my summer project at World Vision had kicked off. During the last weeks of school, I spent my time meeting with students in villages all over the region. Each student had a vision for changes they wanted to make where they lived. They wanted gyms renovated, gardens planted, playgrounds constructed, and memorials built for the Armenian genocide.

I led classes on grant writing and project planning. I gathered the team at the World Vision office and asked them to judge the grant proposals students wrote. We picked five winners and gave them each a thousand dollars. They were asked to attend a series of project planning workshops with me over the course of a few summer weeks. And then, we made a schedule for me to go stay in each of their villages with a host, usually one of the students' families, where together we implemented their projects.

A year into my Peace Corps service, I was under no impression that I would make some kind of history-book-worthy change, that I would be some kind of Ghandi or Mother Teresa leader at the helm of a revolution that helped unseen people become seen. I had thankfully worked in enough cause-based organizations before Peace Corps to know people who would never make it into books, people who would be forgotten, though I could see their impact all around them. I knew I would live and leave Armenia without a great deal of fanfare from anyone who didn't know me personally.

But I hoped I would help a few people feel like they could be the heroes of their own lives. I hoped by spending time working with people to unlock their own vision, perhaps they would feel like they could change things around them, not just once, but hundreds or thousands of times by simply believing that some things around them could be better and they could use their power to help.

After teaching classes, talking about how change works in these specific, grant-bound ways, I spent week after week in a new home.

With these high school kids, I stood under a hot summer sun and dug post holes for a preschool playground. In another village, we dug rows in the dirt and dropped in seeds of chard, pumpkin, tomatoes, squash, and more. I watched them cup their palms to scoop dry dirt over the specks of life and then water them, hoping for a late summer harvest.

In Privolnoye, I met Seda, a woman only as tall as my shoulder with a shock of red hair and a round, expressive face that seemed always to either be smiling unbelievably widely or looking stern with concentration. At the World Vision office, Liana told me that Seda used to live in Yerevan, which seemed like another country when you compared it to the wealth, opportunities, and resources in Armenian villages. Seda left Yerevan, returning home to Privolnoye. Over the past decade, she'd built a youth center that was filled with kids nearly every day. She had no roadmap or money for any of it but was determined to find a way to grab any opportunity for the kids in her village. She had been one of them not too long ago.

She'd helped the kids from her youth center decide on a project, and together, they'd won money to build a memorial to the Armenian genocide. Privolnoye was the only ethnically Russian village I visited in Armenia. I never asked whether the village was as old as Armenia itself or whether the village rose up in this valley while the Soviet Union held all of present-day Armenia within its dominion.

We arrived for this trip with a khachkar, a stone cross not unlike those found throughout the Armenian landscape, some cement, others chiseled from stone. We stood up the khachkar in a small garden by the school where Seda had already led the students in landscaping, their flowers now watered and lifting colorful heads solemnly toward the new stone.

In the afternoon we put out chairs where eventually the people of this Russian village sat and watched as the children of the youth center honored lives lost in a tragedy I'd never heard of before moving to Armenia—a tragedy so many tried to forget or, worse, to erase.

But on this day, the youth center kids remembered. They read poetry, gave speeches, and danced, all in a dedication of this garden as a place to reflect on the genocide of Armenians in 1915. One small blonde girl twirled in a velvet dress, waving her hands above her head before finally walking over to me with a small yellow flower and holding it out to me by the stem.

When I wasn't working on projects in villages around Stepanavan or planning work at the World Vision office, I spent nearly all my time at home with Vazgen and Naira and their daughters, Nazeli and Ani. On weekends, while I cleaned my cottage and Naira cleaned her house, Vazgen was nearly always in the garden, planting vegetables or weeding, feeding the chickens or pulling cherries from the trees.

Outside my cottage door, the brambles bore raspberries, and I gathered them with Ani and Nazeli into a bowl, all of us splitting them apart with the tips of our fingers to look for caterpillars before we ate them. I loved settling into the warm summer afternoons, me reading in the orchard among the chickens, the sound of the girls running around the yard, giggling, and then bickering and then giggling again, and Naira hanging wash on the line. At some point, as the sun began to fall behind our neighbors' houses, I would walk across the yard to find Vazgen.

"Nardi khaghank?" *Should we play nardi?*

And then Vazgen usually saying, "Vay, Brent jan. *I still have a bit of work to do.*"

And then me, desperate for a little fun, calling back to him, "*So, after you're done with your work, then?*"

And his smile, "Lav, akhbers, *after the work.*"

And then shortly, he'd say, "Ari, akhbers. *Let's play.*" He'd open the golden board, the inlaid triangles catching the light in the lacquered wood. The black and cream-colored wooden draughts, both of us grabbing up our colors, me cream, him black. The pleasant smack of each draught as it found its place in typical backgammon formation, backgammon being our English word for nardi. And then, inevitably, Vazgen picked up the tiny ivory dice and handed one to me like an invitation.

We played nardi together outside on the skinny, west-facing porch all summer long, nearly every day. But the Saturday games were the best. Neither of us had work the next day. Neither of us had plans to go anywhere other than this porch.

Once we'd each rolled to see who would make the first moves, we traded the dice back and forth. I'd first learned nardi from a pair of Talin's nieces who lived next door to us in Teghenik in my first summer, both of them ruthless and more gorgeous than the world's second-most famous Armenian, Kim Kardashian. After that I'd been trained on the long, humble road of losses served up to me by Hovsep. And now, in my second summer, I won at least a third of the games Vazgen and I played. But I would have happily lost every time.

I'd never had such a friendship in my life—like an uncle or an older brother who expected nothing of me and who, it seemed to me, enjoyed this time as much as I did. A friend to simply sit on the porch and play a game with.

After nearly eight months of living in his garden, Vazgen became so comfortable that he would release small exclamatory shouts meant to give him luck, English phrases he'd learned from TV. He'd toss the dice with vigor at the board, punctuating the roll with phrases like, "Give me a dollar!" Or the more bizarre, "Toyota. Land Cruiser. Prado!" which he'd heard from a commercial. And then he would look at me, unsure if he'd actually said anything intelligible at all. I never confirmed or denied. I just laughed, smiled, and shook his hand at the end of every game.

Sometimes, on a weekend day, I'd make the whole family a batch of chocolate chip cookies, following a recipe some previous volunteer had entered in the well-loved Peace Corps cookbook. The book of recipes included contributions from nearly every one of the sixteen groups of volunteers who'd come before us and had an entire section on Armenian produce seasonality and substitutes for hard-to-get ingredients.

Naira loved the cookies even more than her daughters, sneaking another cookie from the plate for both of us after the girls had already had a couple and moved back outside to play.

When I made them at first, I didn't know the word for cookies in Armenian and told Naira so.

"*Tell me the English word,*" she said.

"Chocolate chip cookies," I said.

"Tokeens," she said.

"Cookies," I repeated.

"Lav, tokeens," she said again. "*Will you show me how to make* tokeens?" And I did, chopping up whole chocolate bars into shards and using the packet of powdered vanillin instead of a liquid vanilla extract.

From then on, I made them for every party, and every summer khorovats we ate with Naira's family, who lived in a village just outside of Stepanavan. Her mother, whom I called Tatik, wore her white hair short and donned a long jewel-toned dress and black sweater vest every time she came over. I called Naira's father Papik. His grey-brown mustache was so large and his smile so wide that I was immediately endeared to his strong and jolly presence at every visit.

And they did visit often. The first time, I was struck deeply by how confidently they embraced me, knew my name, wanted to know about my family. And eventually, during one of many summer khorovats dinners, they asked question after question about my family at home. I told them about my sister, twelve years younger, and how it was so good for me to spend time with Nazeli and Ani because I missed my own sister so much.

"*They love you like a brother,*" Papik told me, which stopped me so much in my tracks that I didn't know what to say next.

He asked about my parents, what they did for work, and I impressed myself with my ability to tell them in Armenian, "*My mother is a teacher. She teaches math and science to kids who are ten years old. And my father is a computer programmer at a factory that makes furniture for schools.*"

"*You must miss them,*" Papik said.

"*I do. I miss them every day. I think of them every day.*"

"*When will they come see you? They should come. We'll host them here at Naira's house. Does your father like to cook?*"

"*He does.*"

"*Then I will teach him to make* khorovats."

I imagined my father and Papik together, Papik's jolly demeanor as he held raw chunks of chicken in his hands and showed my father how to spear one after the other onto a skewer. I imagined he might give my dad the job of skewering lamb, the two of them sitting silently and proud together, making dinner without words.

I wanted them there, my parents. I wanted them to play nardi with Vazgen, drink coffee with Naira after work, make khorovats on the weekend with Tatik and Papik. I wanted them to play with Ani and Nazeli in the garden. I wanted them to pluck fruit from the trees outside my cottage door. I wanted them to see my cottage, the small, sweet, clean little cottage with pink walls, a warm gas stove, the bright blue tile of the bathroom. I wanted to show them how Naira taught me to hang my wash on the line in such a satisfying, controlled order, watching the sun do the work I'd only ever seen machines do before. I wanted them to walk in the afternoons with me, call out to Vazgen and Naira, and simply be with them, see what I saw in their faces that I couldn't hear in their words. That I belonged here. That I was fine. That I was better than fine. That I was happy. That I'd made a life I loved in a place I'd never heard of on a side of the world my parents had never considered stepping foot on. That here among the flowers of summer and the songs made of wind and giggles and Vazgen's rake in the garden, that I was okay. That after all this leaping out into the unknown, I'd landed somewhere soft, gentle, and warm.

And then, suddenly, an email.

"I've figured it out," my mom said. "I've figured out a way to come."

20

Zoe's sitemate from Goris, Chris, was in Yerevan, and she'd asked him to come with me.

"I'll totally come for moral support," Chris said. He rode in the taxi with me, both of us quiet.

At the arrivals door, Chris scooted closer to me as more people came to the gate, seeing the first of a new flight's passengers making their way into Armenia. We watched them push their luggage carts toward the plexiglass partition that separated those of us waiting from the people we waited for.

I tried to keep stiff arms around the flowers I brought my mother. I held them away from my chest and hoped they wouldn't be crushed. Feet shuffled. Necks stretched. Eyes widened. Small shouts of joy erupted from different cells in the crowd.

My heart pounded.

The last time my mom walked down a hallway with me she wouldn't touch me.

When I was a young boy in church, I only ever wanted to sit in her lap. During the sermon, I'd play with the necklace around her neck. A frosted glass oval was encircled with gold on a gold chain, a dove embossed on the glass. Above it, one star, a diamond. I would run my fingers over the shapes, over the diamond and swing the pendant back and forth on the chain. I'd hold the dove in my hands and lean into my mom, her arms wrapped around me. I'd snuggle with her until the Invitation Song at the end of the sermon when everyone stood while the occasional supplicant walked the long walk to the end of the aisle and asked to be baptized.

And now there. There she was. One roll-aboard suitcase. That's all.

She can't see me, I thought. *She can't see the flowers.*

I saw her smile, looking for faces in the crowd behind the plexiglass.

I jumped up in the air. I waved my hands. I lifted the flowers.

And then she saw me, and I saw her. And the emotion of the moment overcame us, the glint of the hallway lights bouncing off the tears coming down her cheeks.

"She's here, Chris!"

Chris and I ushered people aside so my mom could press through.

"Chris, would you take her bag?" I asked.

Then I hugged her. That's when I realized something had changed.

She'd lost weight, and it felt like part of her was missing. My arms stretched so much farther than I remembered.

"Mom," I asked, "Where'd you go?"

In the taxi, I couldn't let go of her hand. I kept looking at it. I didn't know I had this memory, the feeling of my mom's hand in mine.

I said to her over and over, "I can't believe you're here, Mom. I can't believe it."

"I'm here," she said triumphantly.

"But, like, right here. Right here in this taxi. Right here with me on the other side of the world."

"I am. And I am so tired."

I looked out to the city lights and wondered what she was thinking. "You know, I've never gotten to do this," I said. "No one from our family has ever come to visit me in one of the places I've lived outside of Texas. No one has ever come."

"I did," she said. "I made it."

Putting our stuff away at the hostel, she and I were both bewildered, her by fatigue and me by her presence in Armenia. Chris disappeared into the quickly darkening night to have dinner with friends, leaving my mom and me to our own plans.

"I can barely keep my eyes open, Brent."

"Oh, Mom, you have to. I swear if you can make it to 10 p.m. tonight without sleeping, you'll barely have jet lag. You might not get it at all. I never do."

She'd never crossed an international border. She'd never had a layover during a flight. She'd never stayed in a hostel. She'd never been in a place where most people don't speak English. She'd never seen me outside of the place she raised me.

After she showered, I walked her out into the Yerevan night, cool enough now for sweaters.

"I'll take you to all my favorite places when we come back to Yerevan," I said, "but I think tonight we'll stick close to the hostel." Up the street at the corner café, I dropped my backpack on a table to claim it and walked together with my mom to the ordering window. In Armenian, I ordered for her my favorite crepes—one with ham and cheese, one with Nutella, and two Jermuks, the local brand of sparkling water.

"You said all that in Armenian?" she asked me as we sat.

"Yeah," I said.

"Wow, Brent. Wow."

"Yeah, I speak Armenian, Mama. Can you believe it?"

"I can't. Brent, it's incredible. Seeing you here. Already, I'm amazed."

"And we've only walked half a block," I said.

She looked around. The café was just a small room in the corner of a large apartment building with one window on the wall outside to take orders. The tables and chairs with handwoven backs and seats were spread out on the corner sidewalk with room for pedestrians to walk by and around while people ate or drank coffee and beer. A few tall trees rose from the gap between sidewalk panels, and their branches barely waved in the faint summer wind.

My mom watched them wave and then looked at the small apartment balconies, some with laundry hanging over the handrails, some with small plants in big pots, some with lights coming through the windows out onto the street.

"Everything is so different," she said.

"Oh, it is, Mom," I said. "It's so different from home. But I love it. I've fallen in love with it."

We ate crepes with forks and knives, and like me, she delighted in the warm gooeyness of cheese and then Nutella, the chew of the crepe, the slide of chocolate over the tongue.

"I don't love the sparkling water," she said.

"I didn't either, but I try not to drink sugar all the time."

"Me, too. Oh my gosh, Brent. I barely eat any sugar anymore. Can you tell I've been working out?"

"Mom, really? You're small. You're minuscule. Seriously, it's insane. It's crazy."

"Really?" Her mouth twisted into a smile. Her head tilted in a question.

"I mean, come on," I said. "You know it's true."

"I know," she said, "but I look at me every day, so I don't notice the change every day. And you haven't seen me since before I started."

"Mom, it's incredible. I'm so, so happy for you. I feel like you're a real-life butterfly. You're emerging and flying around the world!"

"Ha! So true!" she said. "But I'm eating what I want over the next ten days. I'm trying it all."

"Good," I said. "Because there's all the Yerevan food. And I'd be very surprised if, at some point, you're not offered cake. And you kinda gotta eat it if it's offered to you."

"Why?"

"Because, Mom, people aren't rich. It takes money and time to make a cake for someone. It's rude if you don't eat it."

"Okay. Sure. Fine." She gathered her purse into her lap and leaned forward. I could tell she'd gotten a second wind. "So, what are we doing next?"

"Well, you gotta stay up until ten," I said. "It's nine. Let's walk to the Cascade."

I pointed at everything while we walked.

"That's the grocery store I come to a lot when I'm staying down here. Look at that billboard on the fence there. That's Kim Kardashian. She's Armenian. There are cafés covering so many city blocks in this part of town."

A kid in a plastic three-wheel bike darted in front of us by the Opera, lights flickering behind his trike seat.

"Why are these kids all out?"

"It's so hot during the day that families come out at night to get fresh air and let their kids play outside."

At the park by the Cascade, I pointed out the sculptures and more cafés.

At the bottom of the Cascade, she said, "Wow," again and then, "Yes," when I asked her if she'd be up for climbing some of the stairs.

I took her high enough to look out at the lights of the city. "Do you see them all, Mom?"

"What?"

"The lights."

"I see them. There are so many. It's beautiful. Just beautiful, Brent. Everywhere I look... it just blows me away. I can't believe you live here."

I took her hand. *She is here with me*, I thought. *Right here. In Yerevan.*

"All those lights are so many people's homes and businesses and places they love to be," I said. "Sometimes I just sit up here and look out at the lights and think about all the people living their own stories with their own families. Whole lives we'll never know about. And that's just here in Yerevan."

Mom moved slower going down, taking a step at a time. At the hostel, both of us brushed teeth and laid our heads down, falling asleep immediately, desperately exhausted.

In the morning, I bought us two cappuccinos at the bar at Artbridge, and took a seat at a table, ordering two plates of french toast. After we finished eating, I pulled her suitcase from under the table. "Do you mind if we walk to the Peace Corps office? It's a bit far, and we could take a taxi, but the city is so nice in the morning."

Cool air swept over us as we walked for blocks and blocks, light bouncing through the branches of boulevard trees. The wheels of Mom's suitcase clacked against the seams of the sidewalk, and we talked over the noise. I asked about Dad, about exercise. She told me that their exercise group meant the world to them.

"It's my new obsession, Brent. You know how I was obsessed with making jewelry for ages."

"How long do you think?" I asked

"Nearly a decade?" she said.

"That sounds right."

"Well," she went on, "I never even think about making jewelry anymore. I'm cooking all the time. Your dad and I are going to workouts at five a.m."

"Five a.m.?" I recoiled.

"Oh yeah. It's great. We get it done early and feel awesome all day."

We rounded the corner on Parpetstyan Street, where I caught sight of the Peace Corps and American flags waving over the security office. Our faces gleamed with perspiration. My T-shirt clung to my back between my skin and my hiking backpack.

"Mom, really, I don't think I remember you walking this far with me. Maybe ever."

"I know. I know. A new me."

In the Peace Corps office, I introduced her to Stepan, the program manager for my volunteer unit.

"He's one of the good ones," Stepan told my mom.

"Oh, I know," she said. "His father and I are so proud of him."

I beamed. I introduced her to Vahagn. I watched him cross his thick arms over his barrel chest while he listened to her talk about how long her flight was.

"We're just so proud of the work he's doing here. Everyone at home is," she said.

"We are, too," Vahagn replied.

I introduced her to the doctors and to the admin officer, all of whom told her that I was doing a great job.

"Gosh, they really like you," she said, walking across the back courtyard.

"Do you think?" I grinned like I couldn't tell, hoping she'd say it again.

"Air conditioning!" My mom laughed when we entered the Peace Corps office library, where she plopped down on the leather couch.

I laughed back. "Normally, people are in here. I'm kind of surprised no one is here. But I guess it's a Thursday. Most people are at their sites working."

She looked past me. "Is that the bathroom?"

"It is. Use the one on the left. The one on the right is much hotter for some reason, and the toilet doesn't always work."

"Oh, lord." She smiled and rolled her eyes.

Alone, I took to the bookshelves as usual. Someone spent time organizing the shelves into categories, but no one bothered with keeping them in any kind of Dewey decimal or alphabetical order. These books were sent to or brought by volunteers over the past twenty years. Pulp fiction and literary fiction and memoir. Mystery, nonfiction, and story collections. The collection changed as often as volunteers pulled books from the shelves to take to their sites and bring them back when they finished them or when their service ended.

I walked immediately to a shelf I knew, and the book I'd seen before was still there—*The Family Heart: A Memoir of When Our Son Came Out* by Robb Forman Dew. I'd imagined this moment since I saw the book on the shelf, though I never thought I'd be able to actually share it with my mom. I hadn't read it, but couldn't she use a memoir written by a mom who'd struggled when her son came out?

And this could be a way to broach the subject between us. I wasn't nearly as scared as I thought I would be. The airport pickup was barbless. The night and the morning were full of camaraderie and love as if I was still the boy coming home with a good grade on a paper, and she was still the perfect mom to celebrate it. We had missed each other, missed our friendship, missed the everydayness of being connected.

She'd changed. She was different. Lighter. Literally, yes, but figuratively. She was happy to see me.

I decided to break the ice.

When she walked out of the bathroom, I walked from behind the bookshelf. "We have some time," I said, "before the marshutni to Teghenik. Maybe twenty minutes before we need a taxi to the bus station. I always look at books. We can take any of them we want. They're free. Do you wanna look at books for a little while?"

"Oh, sure," she said. "I didn't actually bring one. I'd love something to read. I keep thinking of myself under the trees in the garden like you write in your emails."

"Totally," I said.

We walked silently among the books for a few minutes. I leaned books out, tilting them with one finger pressed at the top of their spines. I pretended to read the backs of a few, my ability to concentrate on the type leaving me.

I took a step to the side and pretended to discover *The Family Heart*. I pulled it from the shelf of tattered books and read the back as if I were reading it for the first time. I tried to hold myself there for the right amount of time, as if I hadn't considered some version of this moment, this confrontation, since saying goodbye in her dark bedroom the morning I left Texas.

"Oh," I pretended, turning to Mom. "Here's one you might like." And I handed it to her.

"Oh, thanks," she said, taking it. She read the title and took a deep breath. She looked up at me and handed it back.

"I don't want that," she said.

I took the book in my hands, looking at her. "Really?"

"No. I don't want it."

I leaned back toward the place where it came from, pretending to laugh the way I imagined, chortling, tucking it back into the hole in the shelf of books. "It was just a joke, Mom. I thought, you know, given the subject matter, you might find it helpful."

She paused. "I don't."

"You don't what? Find it helpful?"

"No. I don't find it helpful. And I don't appreciate it."

My heart churned.

"I thought you were over that." She crossed her arms.

"What do you mean?"

"I thought since you haven't talked about it with me since you left that you were over it."

"Over it? As in, it's not a thing anymore?"

"Yeah. Not a thing. Over it. Moved passed it. I didn't think we'd have to deal with it again. Or I was hoping."

I realized suddenly that there was no opening behind me to walk around. She was standing in the only way out, frowning with her arms crossed.

"Well, I'm not," I said. "I thought you were."

"Why would you think that?"

"I don't know. Because you didn't say anything about it either. Because you came here. Because we've been having such a good time."

She frowned more deeply. "I came here because my son needed me. But if you think I'm suddenly okay with what you told us before, I'm not."

"With me being gay? You're not okay with it."

"No."

I stopped moving. I thought about the day ahead of us.

"Mom, I'm having a great time. Can we put this away for now? This whole conversation."

She nodded. "I think that's a great idea."

"We should go. We should head to the bus station."

Mom turned, walking away from the bookshelves. "Is there a place to get water?"

"Here," I said. I lifted my bag from the couch and pulled out my Nalgene. "Here's mine."

~ ~ ~

Armenia gave my mom and me what it had already given me for over a year—a reason to ignore the past and the looming future and focus squarely on the present. Because out of the Peace Corps office, a hot sun heated us overhead, and the hot asphalt heated us underfoot on a busy street with Armenians driving quickly by the two of us and our luggage.

"Kilikia Avtokayan," I told a taxi driver, and he took us to the bus station with an afternoon bus to Charentsavan. We didn't speak on the bus while my mom stared out the window.

"Do you remember the first summer I was here?" I asked her as we pulled into Charentsavan. "This is it. This is the place."

"Whenever I emailed you, it was from an internet café in that town," I said in another taxi that took us from Charentsavan to Teghenik.

"Oh, wow, honey," she said softly.

She looked out the window at the golden grass and the tall cypress trees bustling in the wind.

"I had no idea where I was the first time I saw this place," I told her. "I couldn't have pointed it out on a map. I could barely get a sense of north, south, east, or west."

The church at the bottom of the hill came into view and grew as we got closer to Teghenik's main road.

"That's it, Mom," I said, gleefully pointing at the village on the mountain slope. "That's it. We're here. Remember all those calls. From this village. This is it!"

"Oh, Brent. It's just beautiful. Look at that church." She leaned into the middle of our shared backseat to look more clearly past the driver out the windshield.

"It's not that old," I told her, "but it's still beautiful."

Then, to the driver I asked in Armenian, "*Can we stop at the church? Just for a minute to say a prayer. Then you could take us up to the store?*"

In the church, my mom smelled the frankincense and walked slowly up to the icons with her hands folded in front of her and her elbows tucked closely to her body like a flightless small bird. I put a hundred-dram coin in a tin box and picked up two pencil-thin beeswax candles.

"Here, Mom. Come with me."

We walked together to the altar—a metal table with an inch-high rim filled with dark sand. A few candles stood burning, half the wax melted. My mom watched me, doing as I did.

"These are for your prayers," I whispered. "You say a prayer and light a candle."

I picked up a small box of matches from the corner of the altar table, struck one, and lit the wick. I leaned my candle to my mother's, and after I'd lit hers, she stood it next to mine.

Let her love me anyway, I prayed.

After prayers and candle lighting, my mom and I rode up the mountain until the taxi tires crunched on the dirt road in front of the store.

"Yntaniks!" I shouted. I rushed to Talin and wrapped her in a hug.

"*This is my mom*," I told Talin, gesturing to Mom, who was beaming on the road, bewildered, delighted, and overwhelmed and suddenly and immediately in love.

I introduced each of them, giving an extra firm hug to Hakob who, Talin had explained on the phone, was home on military leave. "Mom, this is Talin, Mikayel, Hakob, and Sona. *Where is Lala*?" I asked Talin in Armenian.

"*She's at the house*," Talin said.

My mom walked up to Mikayel and shook his hand. "Can you tell them thank you?" she said to me. Tears suddenly ran around her round cheeks and dripped from her chin as she looked into Mikayel's eyes, grabbed his hand again, and spoke to him. "Thank you for taking care of my son."

I translated. Mikayel looked bewildered. He nodded back to her, "Khndrem. Khndrem."

When Talin gave us both ice creams and invited us to sit inside, I pointed to the wooden stool next to the register and said to my mom, "Right here, Mom. Right here. I sat right here every day eating ice cream just like this, with my language books on my legs, reading and studying and practicing my Armenian with whoever came into the store."

My mom looked at me and then out to the hills, which she could see through the doorway. "Wow, Brent. Wow. That's just so special."

I turned to Talin, who sat behind the counter. She shifted her watchful eyes from me to my mother and then back to me again. Her smile was unbreakable, but her eyes searched for meaning in my gestures and the tone of my voice.

In Armenian, I said, *"I told my mother that I sat here last summer. With you and Hakob and Sona and Mikayel."* I caught each of their eyes as I said each of their names. *"I practiced Armenian. With people who came to the store. I learned fast."*

"Yes," Talin said. *"You did. And we laughed so much. Do you remember?"*

"Yes. I remember. Of course."

Talin looked to Hakob and Sona as if my saying so affirmed something.

I bit into the ice cream and said, *"You still have the birds."* And as we watched the budgies in their cage, a man walked in the khanut. The wrinkly sleeves of his windbreaker caught the wind from the electric fan by the door. His salt-and-pepper stubble matched the hair curling up under an old baseball cap.

"Akhbers!" Hakob said, taking the man's cellophane bag, which, though tied at the top, throbbed with moving crayfish alive and pressing against the plastic.

"Mom, crawdads," I said.

She smiled, both of us knowing that the other was thinking of crawdad hunting on the creek behind her grandmother's house in Louisiana.

After we finished our ice cream, Mikayel offered to take us in his car up the mountain.

"Can we walk?" my mom asked. So, we started up the mountain toward the house.

Hakob wrapped his arm around my shoulders, and our legs synced up, taking steps up the hill together. Sona took my mother's arm, and we all walked without talking, my mom and I quickly out of breath.

Lala rushed out of the kitchen when she heard me coming, wiping her hands on her apron before wrapping her arms around me. Flavored, savory air filled the house. Garlic. Oil. Fried rice, fried noodles, fried eggplant. We walked through the steam, and Sona directed my mom to my old room, the same wavy mirror and satin sheets welcoming her as they welcomed me.

At dinner, we sat at a table in the corner of the living room, a place I never ate a meal last summer. Over a white tablecloth lightly stained by decades of small mishaps, my mom tried every dish—the slimy, smoky eggplant, the pilaf, the roasted chicken.

"Brent…" Talin said, her voice lifting while she pointed to mashed potatoes.

"*My favorite!*" I exclaimed in Armenian. Talin leaned back laughing while I told my mom, "They know I love mashed potatoes. They made them for me."

"*And sour cream!*" Sona yelled, pointing to a bowl of sour cream between the potatoes, sliced tomatoes, and cheese.

Mikayel looked at me. "Brent jan," he said, pointing a finger at my mom. Then at the bottle of wine. Then at the bottle of vodka.

"Mom, would you like wine or vodka?" I asked.

She laughed and then said, "Oh, vodka."

I was struck by this. My parents raised me in a dry community. Drinking was against our religion. As a child, I'd seen her drink only once on vacation at a hotel pool and had a full existential crisis. After Mikayel's toast to family, Mom threw back the entire shot.

"You can sip, Mom," I said. "You don't have to do the whole thing."

She chuckled. "Yeah, right."

After the first shot, I asked for another toast. "Norits kenats," I said. Mikayel filled the glasses, and we lifted them into the air, looking into each other's eyes.

"Next week is my mom's birthday."

Talin tilted her head at me. *"Really?"*

"Yes. She came to Armenia to celebrate her birthday here."

"Apres! Apres Kim jan!" Talin cheered, and the table erupted.

"A toast," I continued in Armenian. *"Talin, Mikayel, Lala, Hakob, Sona… to you. I am so proud to bring my mother to meet you. You took very good care of me. You showed me how wonderful Armenia is. You make me feel that this is my home, too. And now my mom gets to have her birthday here. That makes me so happy. Very, very, very happy."*

"Vay, Brent jan!" Talin said, tears glistening.

"It's true. I am so very happy to know you and to introduce you to my mother. It is something I will remember all my life."

Mikayel now, his eyes glistening, said, *"A toast for your mother,"* boosting his glass another inch forward.

"Mayrikd," Hakob said.

"Mayrikd," Sona said.

Lala echoed, *"To your mother."*

The night continued with more eating, more drinking, and a cake with thin layers that Lala remembered me praising last summer.

"It's a cake for your mother's birthday," Lala said, which I knew she had just decided but said as if it was planned. I knew she'd made it for me.

"Should we dance?" Lala asked after we'd all eaten dessert. *"You liked dancing last summer."*

Hakob switched on a new stereo on the floor next to the TV. At first, it was Akon again, and over "Smack That," I said, "Hakob jan. *Not American music. Armenian music. My mom needs to learn Armenian dancing.*"

Duduks then sounded from the speakers, the soft reed buckling as the notes ran up and down. Drummers beat dhols, and I stood, taking again my mother's hand and pulling her to the center of the living room carpet. Hakob was there already, his long arms, elegant and strong, stretching out on either side of him, his hands pointing up, palms out, raising his knees in time with the dhol beats. He looked at me when I lifted my arms, and we danced together until he said, "Brent jan. Du hay es." Brent jan. *You are Armenian.*

Lala stood with Talin and Sona and the three of them beckoned my mother and then surrounded her, her feet a little clumsy from so many toasts. The women's arms undulated like blades of long grass in the wind. Talin watched my mother's feet.

Mom, like me, grew up in a Church of Christ church with standards I always said were, "like Baptist but conservative." No drinking. No musical instruments. No dancing. I found rhythm thanks to drumming in the school band. My mom did not drum.

I watched her with these Teghenik women. My mom. A woman who'd shed a quarter of herself since I'd last seen her. Maybe more. Her tennis shoes worn from workouts in the early Texas morning. Here now shuffling on the carpet, watching Talin's feet, trying to step in time, forgetting to move her arms, giggling, playing a bit of a fool for fun, for laughs.

"Ayo… ayo…" Talin encouraged her, stepping in time with my mom, both of them swinging their hands in the air. My mom watched Talin's feet to catch the rhythm.

Talin watched my mom's feet to help her find it. Every once in a while, they looked up at each other to see again that they were both still dancing together. And, suddenly, I realized that this was the first time I'd ever seen Talin dance.

21

In the morning, my mom passed on Lala's shiny scrambled eggs, and I showed her how to rip the lavash and use a piece to wrap tomato, cucumber, dill, and Lala's homemade cheese. Lala made the three of us coffee, and I warned Mom not to drink the dregs. Mikayel and Hakob had already left for the fields. Talin was already sitting at the khanut with the budgies. So, with no one else at home, Mom and I walked to the spot on the hill outside my window to look at the valley together.

I thought then of mornings growing up, my dad waking me and my brother in our shared room. Me wandering down the hallway and knocking on my parents' door. Mom welcoming me in, turning off her blow dryer, the air thick with hairspray. And me, climbing into her lap, sitting there, nearly falling back asleep in her arms.

I picked a purple and silver flower, handed it to her, and said, "It's been hard."

She took the flower, "It's been hard for us, too. But look what you've done, Brent. You're here. It's breathtaking." And we stared over the golden valley and watched a car drive slowly down the road from Charentsavan, passing the cypress trees.

Right before we gathered our things to leave, Mom and I walked with Sona in the cherry orchard and picked fruit from the tree. We ate until we were full of them, and I took a picture of Sona and Mom together. Sona wouldn't smile, so my mom tickled her ribs, sending Sona into peals of laughter.

Leaving Teghenik took taxis and marshutnis and then one long taxi ride in a five-seat sedan with three strangers. I sat in the middle in the back so my mom could look out the window on the four-hour drive to Stepanavan.

"Every time you tell us you're going to Yerevan," she said, squeezing my hand, eyes out to the mountains, "this is what you see."

I knew this road now the way I knew the roads of my childhood. Nondescript turns on roads no one in the car could even name. But the pull of gravity in the turn, the weight of my body against the seatbelt that held me until the car straightened out, those pulls and pushes, the forces of a journey made over and over again, known to me without names, just a feeling I could recall time after time.

I felt comforted by the field of cabbages, the field of sunflowers, the field of grass meant for hay-baling. Houses stood between fields, often just tin boxes with wooden windows left over from the poorest days anyone could remember. Then my favorite snaking path up to a crest and over it. Then rolling hills that seemed to go on forever. Green in the summer. Orange, red and yellow in the fall.

I wanted to talk to my mom about all these things, but I didn't because of the three others in the car. I wanted to reminisce about the roads to Lometa where my dad's parents lived or the road to Louisiana, where my mom's family had lived for generations.

"You don't feel your heart swell with anticipation until you cross that bridge over the Louisiana border," I wanted to say. "My heart starts to race when I can feel the bounce of the car going over the bridge panels."

I wanted to say to my mom, "Isn't it crazy that there are roads where we feel these things before we ever say them to each other?"

And then, "Isn't it crazy, Mom, that there are roads you know so well and others that I know so well—roads we know by the tug and pull of gravity, the turns, the rise and fall of the road—and we will never travel them together?"

As our taxi pulled up to the house in Stepanavan, Ani pulled back the living room curtain, pouring light from the living room into the night. Vazgen opened the door of the gate, already anticipating that we might need help with bags.

"Vazgen jan! Naira! Im mayriky yekel e!" I yelled, nearly jumping out of the car.

"Bari galust," Vazgen said, stretching out his hand to my mother while I paid the taxi.

He stood so much taller than my mom that she had to reach her hands up to him.

"He says, 'Welcome,'" I translated for her.

"Thank you," she replied.

We walked straight up to Naira's kitchen, where Naira had already prepared an assortment of desserts, knowing we'd arrive after dinner time. She offered coffee or tea, and my mom asked for peppermint. Naira set out cups, boiled water, and then filled each cup, moving a single tea bag from cup to cup to cup as she poured.

Alone in my cottage, I made my mom and me more tea, placing cups by each of the two green armchairs before lighting the vararan. I pointed it out to my mom and explained. "This is my heater. They say, 'vararan.' Most volunteers actually have to heat their homes with wood, but I've got gas. It totally freaks me out to light it. I'm always afraid I'm going to do it wrong and blow up in here."

I looked up at her to see that tears had welled in her eyes again. She sat crying, holding her tea with both hands, looking down as tears dropped from her cheeks.

"Oh, Mom. What is it? What happened?"

She kept her eyes down, taking in a deep breath that buckled with a voiceless sob.

"Mama?"

She pressed her thumb into the collar of her T-shirt, using it to wipe away tears. "It's just…" She looked at me. "They… your family. Naira, Vazgen, the girls… they just have so little… so little… not like we have. How can I go home? How can I go home, Brent?"

Her chest heaved. She choked down another sob.

"If I could, I would pick them up… if they wanted, you know… and just plant them in an apartment in our town in Texas. And put the girls through college."

She set the tea on the table and used both sleeves now to wipe her face.

"And if they didn't want that…" She heaved again. "I would hire the best architect in Armenia and build them a castle."

~ ~ ~

The next morning, my mother was reasonably adamant about bathing. She hadn't since we left Yerevan for Teghenik. "We can wait here until the water comes on, which doesn't happen until ten a.m.," I said. "Or you can take a bucket bath."

"Really?"

"Yes." I stood to pull water from one of the bathroom buckets, filling my pale green electric kettle. "It's actually very refreshing. It's not easy. But I can warm up a bucket of water real quick."

"Is that my only option?"

"No. We could wait until ten a.m. But then we wouldn't be able to go out into town until after you shower. I'm thinking lunchtime."

"Oh, heck no." She jumped up from her finished plate of eggs. "Show me how to do the bucket bath thing. I want to see as much of your life as I can."

I filled the electric kettle four times, boiling water each time to fill a bucket for my mom. The smell of hot plastic filled the cottage.

"Use this pot," I said, holding out the small saucepan with the long handle. "Just dip it in, lift it over your head, and let it pour."

"Won't the water splash everywhere?"

"Kind of. But there are no shower curtains here. That's what this squeegee is for," I said, pointing to the squeegee leaning up against the wall behind my washing machine.

When she was finished, she opened the door. She had dressed in jeans, a black long-sleeved shirt, and a draped grey sweater.

"Feel better?"

"Oh, yes. A thousand times better," she said. She moved to the bedroom and stood over the cot I'd slept on last night, which I borrowed from Naira and Vazgen. I folded up my sleeping bag and told my mom to use my cot for her suitcase while she got ready. She looked in my wardrobe mirror.

"My hair, Brent," she said. Her blonde hair hung in wet, temporary dreads, her eyes looking defeated. "What am I going to do with my hair?"

I'd been journaling while she bathed and put the book on the table. "I wonder if Naira has a hair dryer."

"Oh, that would be awesome," she said and left the mirror with a bloom of a smile, a rise in her cheeks, rosy below blue eyes.

I learned to understand my mother's smiles before I learned to read, to talk, or to walk even. I knew her smile with unchanging eyes—the stop-talking-about-that-please smile. I knew her smile with closed lips, her head leaning forward and to the side, wide eyes—the hopeful smile when she wanted to see you react to a gift or a surprise.

These sixteen months apart was the longest I'd ever gone without reading her smiles, and still, I knew them better than my native language. And this smile was my favorite—mouth wide, teeth gleaming, round cheeks rosy with a flush of happiness. Eyes open but soft. Happiness. A looking forward to things. And pleased. Known. Loved and loving in return.

"Brent jan?" Naira called, seeing me and my mother through the lace curtains after I knocked on the door. She stirred a porridge on the stove while Ani and Nazeli waited at the table.

"Bari luis, Naira jan," I said.

I'd never walked over to their house this early in the day. Hiding her body wrapped in a robe, Naira leaned her head out of the door.

"Naira jan, my mom's hair is wet. She wants it to dry. We have no machine."

"Ah…" She drew out that sound, which I recognized, one of her putting together my words like a puzzle to find a word I didn't know in Armenian. In this case, the word I didn't know was blow dryer. *"One minute, Brent jan. Wait there by the door."*

Down the porch steps at the door by the living room, Naira reappeared dressed, her curious girls trailing behind. The family shared one bedroom, which was actually a large hall between the kitchen and the living room with beds on both sides. Naira beckoned us in and pulled out a chair for my mother in front of a dark wood vanity at the end of the girls' twin bed. She unwrapped the cord from the blow dryer handle and plugged it into the wall.

"Ari. Nstir, Kim jan."

"Mom," I looked to my mother. "She's asking you to sit."

And Mom did, in the chair Naira had moved to the center of the bedroom. Naira reached over her, clicking on the dryer and raising my mom's blonde hair into the air with a round brush.

Mom mimed relief, telling me that she felt like she was at the salon.

I translated that for Naira, who said, *"Of course,"* and raised the next brush of hair with a flourish.

Seeing they were settled, I asked everyone if I could leave them and go bathe.

Immediately, my mom and Naira said in their own ways, "Yes, of course," raising their hands to me to wave me off, as if it were the obvious and natural course of things that the two women would be left together like this, Naira doing my mother's hair, their voices mingling like windchimes as they ushered me away.

In the bath, I ladled warm water from a bucket and let it pour over me. Cold September air had already moved into Stepanavan, and after I dressed, I journaled again by my gas heater.

When will we talk about it? I thought. I wanted to know what she thought now about my coming out. I'd come out over a year ago. And now I'd spent days with her, marveling at her taking in my life in Armenia and terrified at the same time of a conversation I knew was coming.

I found my mom at Naira's kitchen table with Nazeli and Ani on each side, the two women with coffee, the girls snacking on candy.

Wrapped up in my sweater and scarf with hair blown straight and with dark rimmed glasses on, she reminded me of her mother, Grammi, in a way that scared me. I could see her now, older than I remembered.

"Brent," she said to me as I sat across the table. "Look what she did to my hair." And, beaming, she let her hands fly around her hair as if she were modeling, sending the girls into chirps of laughter, hands to their tummies, giggling.

"Naira and I are like sisters now," Mom said. "What's the word for sister?"

"Kuyr," I said.

"Say it again?"

"Koo-eer."

She looked to Naira next to her, pointed to Naira's face and then her own and back again rapidly. "Koo-eer," she said.

Naira looked to me, and I translated, *"She says you're sisters now."*

"Ah! Yes, yes. Of course! Yes. We are sisters," Naira said. She lifted her arm and wrapped it around my mom's shoulder, pulling her in cheek to cheek. My mom closed her eyes as if savoring it.

At the World Vision office, my coworkers smiled and welcomed her. They bragged about our work together, which felt rooted in a desire to engender my mother's pride. At my desk, Yeraz told her she could also be Yeraz's *harevan*, her *neighbor* like me. Mom and I walked with Karine to our favorite takeaway window in town and brought pierogies back for lunch. In the afternoon, Ayda made us coffee and read my mother's grounds.

After work, I walked with my mom to my favorite spot in Stepanavan, the field at the foot of the mountains north of town.

Icy gusts of September wind whipped over us where we stood in the grass looking out over Stepanavan. I told my mom, "In June, this place is filled with millions of daisies."

She held my hand and said softly, "Brent, it's beautiful."

~ ~ ~

On the way home, Mom watched me while I checked in at my favorite vegetable stand, picking up tomatoes and cucumbers and dill.

We stopped at 777 bakery, where the women baking in the back greeted me by name when I opened the door. I felt honored that my mom could hear that sound, my name in the voices of people who cared that I arrived every day to say hello and buy bread. I wanted my mom to see that my life had become, in its way, more beautiful since I'd come out.

"*This is my mother*," I told the bakers, to which they all cooed or exclaimed praise to her for making such a trip, all while tossing lavash dough over their arms and stretching it before laying it out over a pillow, which they turned over and slammed onto the hot brick of the lavash oven.

"*I told my mom that I love to watch you work. It is so beautiful. Your work is beautiful*," I offered. This drew out laughter, and though no baker missed a beat, rolling dough, stretching it, slamming it, pulling it up from the brick to stack it and spray it with water to soften.

We talked with the women, me translating for my mom as she asked their names, if they've always lived in Stepanavan, if they have family here, if they like baking. One woman folded a freshly baked lavash and walked it to me. "Hats kerek," she said, inviting us to eat.

I held the lavash between my mother and me, and we pulled off pieces together, savoring the miracle of ingredients mixed with heat and time.

In the evening, after we'd played nardi in Naira and Vazgen's kitchen, and after Naira and Mom took pictures together posing as sisters, my mom and I made spaghetti in my cottage. After dishes were done with water from my bathroom buckets, my mom suggested we go to bed right away. When she climbed into my bed, I apologized again for the lumps of wool in the mattress. When I lay down on the cot, it shrieked, the canvas pulling hard against the wood frame. I zipped myself into my sleeping bag.

Now, I thought in the darkness.

"Mom," I said.

"Yes, honey?" With all the lights off and no light from the moon in my window, I could barely make out her shape across the tiny room.

"I'm scared."

A pause. "Scared?"

Another pause. "Yeah."

"Scared of what, honey?" I could feel the thud of her words, the way she laid them down with heaviness. She knew already what I wanted to say.

"Oh, being away from y'all," I said, avoiding a bit. "Of losing y'all."

"Brent," she said, "you can come home any time you want. You don't have to stay here if you're unhappy."

"I'm not unhappy here. It's lonely sometimes, but it's not that."

"Then what is it?"

"You know," I said.

Quiet filled the room, and I went on, "The gay thing."

The silence grew complete in the cottage. Though she was just a few feet away, I couldn't see her move. I couldn't see her face.

"We haven't been talking about it," I said.

"I know," she murmured.

"But I'm thinking about it. I miss you. It's so wonderful to have you here, and it reminds me how much I want to be home to see you and Dad and Macey and Lisa and Garrett. I don't want to lose you."

Another quiet. Then, I said, "When we were in the Peace Corps office, I saw that book, and I thought it would be a funny way to start the conversation. And maybe even give you a resource you could use."

"I don't want a resource," she said back, her voice short.

Lying on my back in the sleeping bag, I wrung my hands over my chest.

"I thought," she said, "that since you weren't talking about it in any of your emails that you were over it. That you dealt with it."

I wrung my hands. "It's not really something you deal with, Mom. It just is. I thought since you hadn't talked about it in any of your emails that you had come to terms with it. Maybe even changed what you think about it. Maybe you realized that God is okay with me being gay."

"Well, that's not what I believe."

I knew that saying my next question was like lighting a fuse. "What do you believe?"

The gap between her speaking and my speaking felt enormous.

"I believe in Jesus Christ," she said. "That he is the son of God and that he came to earth to die for our sins. I believe sin keeps us from God, and that when we have sin in our hearts, it will destroy our lives."

I replied, "Do you think it's destroying my life?"

We'd lay in the dark long enough now that I could barely make out the pink paint on the ceiling. My eyes didn't move from it as she spoke.

"It will," she said. "Maybe it is."

"Even," I asked, "with everything you've seen here?"

"I don't know, Brent. But I know this is not what God wants for you."

"Do you really think God doesn't want me to be gay?" I asked.

"Yes," she said.

And now a somehow harder question. "Do you think that if I come home, and I'm gay, do you think I'll lose you?"

With that question I brought to her the great chasm of loneliness, of all the years I knew I was gay and never told a soul, imagining this moment, this exact moment I ran from and then invited back when I was ready, when she might be ready, the one person in the world who made me feel the most loved, the most safe. I had imagined talking to her about this secret for decades. I imagined asking her if I'd lose her. I never imagined losing her.

"Yes," she said. "I do."

At that moment, something broke. *Do not wail,* I thought. *Do not wail.* I writhed into a fetal position and held myself. I dug my fingers into my ribs to keep myself from falling past the point of conversation.

The sleeping bag fabric became wet under my face. "I don't want to lose you," I said. "I don't want to lose you, Mama."

"I don't want to lose you either, son." There was no tremble in her voice.

"Mama," I cried. "Mama." Thoughts rushed out of my head then, my mind becoming unable to process. I had imagined this conversation my whole life. I had imagined the fork in the road, standing at it. And I had imagined no further. I was in someplace utterly unknown to me.

"Mama, oh, Mama." I dug my fingers into my sides, still holding on to myself. "This is so painful. This hurts." I turned onto my back, looked up at the ceiling, my eyes stinging with tears. "I'm so scared," I said.

And then, across the room, my mom said, "This is what happens when you let the devil into your life."

The silence fell then in a way that felt so final, like a sudden freezing of the ground that lasts for the rest of winter.

I didn't try to stop my tears then, not when they rolled down into my ears. Not when they piled up over my eyes to the point that they were completely covered, open, burning.

This could be it, I thought. *These could be the last days I spend with her.* I imagined now, my life anchorless without my mother.

"Mama, can I hug you?" I choked out.

"Yes, honey. Of course." Her voice so much softer than before.

I climbed out of my sleeping bag. The air had gone cold without the heater on. I lay down on the edge of the bed with my back to her, my head on the pillow, tears now pooling there.

She wrapped her arm around me, like every night of my childhood nightmares.

"It will be okay, Brent," she said. "It will be okay."

22

For the rest of my mother's time in Armenia, we didn't talk about my sexuality. On the day before her birthday, we explored the town, walking in every direction, tucking into shops, buying ice cream from a new cart in the park. I bought a paper cone full of roasted sunflower seeds, and we finished them before going back to the field again, where we sat in the sun.

We continued on, walking past the statue of Stepan and onto the bridge to look down at the river running through the ravine. I pointed out the old shell of an abandoned car. She pointed at a tree clinging to the cliffside.

We took a taxi to Lori Berd.

"This was an entire fortress," I told her. "Someone built it at the turn of the last millennium." We walked to the bathhouse, where I showed her the fragments of clay pipes in the wall.

In the church ruins I looked up through the perfectly circular skylight. The grass growing over the edge waved with the wind. Someone had left a pile of beeswax taper candles, and I picked up two, handing one to my mom.

With the simple intention of happiness, I lit mine, placing it in the altar box of sand to stand alone and burn. I walked out the door, leaving Mom in the ruin to pray and light her candle.

On the day she turned fifty, I sang her "Happy Birthday" when we were both still in bed. Naira had taken to blow drying her hair each morning, and on this morning, after she did my mom's hair, she presented my mom a gift, a silk scarf, before making coffee for us all.

My coworker, Hermine, had already been planning a birthday party for herself at the office and graciously folded my mom into the celebration. When Mom and I arrived on Saturday afternoon, desks had already been moved from offices into the foyer and set with tablecloths, lace doilies, and collections of bottled drinks.

Everyone wished my mother a happy birthday with at least one kiss on the cheek.

When Hermine arrived, her arms were full. She had dared to wear white pants while carrying a bag of drinks and a chocolate cake she'd baked and sliced into diamonds. And in another hand she carried a bag of candies meant as a magharich, a kind of gift you give others when you have something to celebrate.

My stomach turned. I did not prepare anything with my mom to bring to her birthday party. Guilt swam in my stomach. I should have told her about the magharich tradition.

Mom didn't notice my brief panic. She wore the nicest clothes she brought, including a black blouse that waved on her slight frame. She seemed buoyant, overtaken by the exchange of birthday wishes and general joyful energy.

When I walked her outside, she cringed at the skewers of meat Vigen and Tirayr grilled over hot coals on the ground.

"Mom, we haven't had khorovats yet. This is my favorite meal."

"Really?" she said, pausing with a pensive face.

"Mom, it's fine. This is how they cook it." Tirayr turned the skewers, grease dripping and sizzling.

When Vigen asked what kind of meat my mom liked, she said, "Chicken, but I'll like anything you make."

"Apres!" Vigen shouted after my translation, the two of them smiling at each other.

At dinner, Tirayr stood before the room full of coworkers and their families passing khorovats and dolma and a feast of food to each other. "Kenats!" he said. "*A toast!*"

"*To the beautiful women celebrating their birthday,*" he cheered. Yeraz whispered a translation into my mother's ear. Tirayr continued, "*To Hermine, our coworker who makes us so happy with her beauty, her kindness, and her great work. And who has thrown this beautiful party for all of us to enjoy and to celebrate.*"

Tirayr pivoted, pointing his shot glass toward my mother. "*And to Kim,*" he said, pronouncing her name "keem." "*To Kim, who came from far away to see us and celebrate this beautiful day with us. For being the mother of Brent, who has come to our office and made it more wonderful than it was before. Is she understanding me?*" He looked at Yeraz and then at me.

"Lav, Tirayr jan," Yeraz laughed. "*I am translating. You think I don't know Armenian?*"

The room exploded with laughter, except for my mom. I translated the joke poorly, and she simply smiled.

"Lav," Tirayr continued. "*To Kim, who brought our Brent into the world. You must be a good mother to make such a kind, wonderful man. We wish you a long life, a beautiful life, a life full of happiness and memories like this one. I hope you never forget this day and you never forget us.*"

Mom reached across the table and took my hand.

"Can I respond?" she asked me.

"Sure," I said, looking at Yeraz, who understood my silent request to translate for her.

"I just want to say thank you," Mom shared through her tears. She paused, knowing the translation rhythm now. Yeraz translated sentence by sentence.

"My son is very happy here. You make him happy. You take care of him when I can't. Your friendship brings him so much joy. And it is a great gift of my life that I get to experience that friendship with all of you. I miss Brent every day." She shuddered, exhaling. "But as a mom, I can feel so much better now knowing all of you. Seeing your faces. Watching my son talk to you like old friends.

"I will never forget any of you. I will always remember this day, your beautiful town, your beautiful faces, and the love you have wrapped around my son to carry him through his years in your home. Thank you." Her voice broke. She wiped tears from her cheeks, smearing them over her face with her palm. Yeraz delivered the translation, careful to mimic her tone.

When Yeraz finished, she turned to my crying mother, wrapped her arm around Mom's shoulder, and said, "Vay, Kim jan!" Yeraz laughed a comforting laugh, rubbing her hand fast over my mom's back, a gesture meant to reset her, to warm her, to lift her.

My mom smiled another smile I knew well, one that meant thank you and also that the mingling love and sadness cannot be so easily lifted.

Karine, sitting next to me, wiped her wet eyes with a napkin. I saw Hermine across the room doing the same. They didn't bring their children to the party. Both of their husbands worked in Russia. The quiet of the room reminded me that all of us know love and the distance of time and borders, and life that gives to us and takes from us.

After dinner, Hermine brought my mother a cake with the number fifty written in icing.

"You told them!" My mom laughed at me.

"Of course, I did! How many times does your mom turn fifty in Armenia?" I shouted, "Once!"

And my mom, more prepared than I had anticipated, brought out a bracelet she'd made at home, one she'd carried in case she needed to give a gift. She handed it in a silk bag to Hermine, who hugged her and clasped the rainbow of stones around her wrist.

Then, after all the toasts and the cake and the presents, we danced in the same foyer I'd sat and worked in for over a year. Ayda took my mom by the hand, my mom who grew up in a church where dancing wasn't allowed. And together they spun around the room to Armenian music my mom was only starting to love.

After a few songs, I sat back at the table and watched my mom dance with my Armenian friends. I wanted to feel the completeness of this moment, a dream I'd dreamed for so long. I had dreamed that I could find a way to be fully myself and to share that self with people I loved. And there they were, a room full of people I loved.

Yet, most of them didn't know, couldn't know, that I was still terrified that if they really knew me, I wouldn't be there with them dancing. I wouldn't be at this party. I had lived with this fear for so long that I could sit and watch and smile and feel happy as beneath that happiness, a sadness loomed while I clapped to music, while my mom turned under Ayda's outstretched arm.

~ ~ ~

We spent two days in Yerevan before my mother would be boarding a plane back to Paris, Dallas, and then home.

We rented a room in an older woman's tenth-story apartment. The woman had one hand and moved through her space in a wheelchair. Each morning she fed us toast and eggs talking in Armenian while we ate about her children and grandchildren spread throughout Eastern Europe.

Mom and I walked Yerevan again through perfect fall weather, the air crisp and brightly whipping down alleyways and over parks. We wandered between cafés, stopping at Swan Lake to people-watch, talking to each other about the people we saw—the couple sharing a bag of popcorn, the father chasing a child who ran frighteningly close to the water.

On the penultimate night of her trip, we walked to Karma for samosas and curry and to meet Zoe.

"You've got to meet her." I'd already told my mom so many times over so many months. "I wouldn't have survived here this long without her." I didn't tell my mom about Zoe's girlfriend, an A-18 named Arya. When I'd invited Zoe to dinner, she told me she'd bring Arya. I didn't want to object but worried about how my mom might react.

Down the stairs into the basement, a host escorted my mother and me past the bar and seated us in a back room. Red carpet purred when we pulled out our chairs, and Mom looked around at the walls draped with orange, reflective curtains.

Zoe arrived holding Arya's hand.

"Hi!" Zoe offered. She shuffled a few steps forward and leaned over the table to take my mother's hand. Arya put her hands in her grey hoodie pockets and waited quietly.

I jumped from my seat to hug Zoe, who then turned to my mom and said, "Can I hug you?"

My mom, anxious-eyed, said, "Of course." And Zoe wrapped her arms around my mother and squeezed.

"We already ordered samosas," I told them as they sat.

Arya was only the second black Peace Corps volunteer I'd met. Of everyone at the table, Arya was most visibly nervous, though she smiled and tucked her hands under her thighs.

"Brent has told me so much about you!" Zoe exclaimed, refusing to drop the energy she entered with, an energy she must have gathered on the walk here.

"He's told me so much about you, too," my mom replied.

When Zoe fed Arya a corner of samosa, locking eyes and tucking a corner of pastry over Arya's smiling lips, my mother looked away, turning her head so sharply it seemed to cut the air.

Zoe continued to ask questions, making jokes that I overlaughed at. Arya laughed, too, looking often at Zoe for comfort.

My mother spent a lot of the dinner looking at me or at the floor. She asked me about the food. She listened to Zoe tell stories about living on the West Coast of India but did not ask her any questions.

After we'd cleaned our plates and packed takeaway boxes, Arya tapped Zoe's leg and stared at her.

"We do have to go," Zoe said directly to me. "We're supposed to meet friends tonight."

"Well, thanks for coming to dinner," I said, our locked eyes, telling each other we'd talk about all of this soon. Zoe handed me dram notes to cover their side of the tab.

Mom and I walked in the darkness across the city, then to the singing fountains in Republic Square. Pushing through the crowd, we found a place to watch on the stairs, our arms linked watching water dance to "My Heart Will Go On."

Zoe would tell me later that she'd never been treated the way my mom treated her during that dinner at Karma. She told me how painful it was that my mom wouldn't hold her gaze, wouldn't keep eye contact while she spoke, wouldn't ask her questions about her life, wouldn't talk at all to Arya. She told me this and then said how sorry she felt for me that my mom would think of queer people that way, would think of me that way.

On our last morning, we ate again at Artbridge and then walked the Vernissage for hours looking at paintings, jewelry, and handcrafted souvenirs. I had thrilled at the thought of showing Mom what had become my favorite outdoor market in the world. But as she walked it, she asked every vendor the price of their goods and then, with me translating, told them all she was on a limited budget and needed to see the whole market before choosing something to buy.

For this, I yelled at her. Not for any of her reactions to my coming out. Not to her behavior at dinner with Arya and Zoe. Back at the apartment I yelled at her for wasting our last afternoon walking the Vernissage over and over, frustrating every vendor who she disappointed by showing interest in their wares only to leave them talking about her limited budget. I yelled at her for this, like a pressure cooker letting out steam.

Hurt, she began folding her things and packing her bag for her morning flight. I waited, fuming, not moving, until she walked to me and handed me a necklace—a small pendant with a tiny white flower she'd placed under resin before attaching it to a leather band.

"Will you give this to Zoe?" Mom asked. "Will you tell her I'm grateful you have a friend here who really cares for you. I know it must not have been easy for her to meet me."

I took the bag and said, "Yes, Mom. I will."

23

Zoe posed for a picture on Phillip's balcony over the Cascade, wearing my mom's necklace.

I thought about that photograph for years after taking it because Zoe looked so gorgeous in it. Her skin so perfect, her lips shining, her eyes closed but confidently pointed toward the sun, the cherished steps of the Armenian landmark behind her.

I thought how cruel it was of me to ask Zoe to take that picture the afternoon after my mom left. I would imagine Zoe never considered it cruel.

While my mom was trying to send a message of love through that necklace, perhaps trying to find common ground, it wasn't an apology. And that's what Zoe deserved.

Yet instead of asking my mom for that, I asked Zoe to pose with that beautiful but lacking trinket so that, instead of taking care of Zoe, I could try to tell my mom, "See. Gays are good. See."

Words that never should need to be said. Like saying, "See, Mom. Breath is good. Sunlight is good. Water is good."

I didn't take care of Zoe. I asked her to pose.

Afterward, I debriefed the entire trip with Zoe, walking through the streets of Yerevan to get ice cream at a café while I told her about the terrible night in my pink cottage, the charming dancing at my mom's fiftieth birthday party. Everything all the way up to the last night when we couldn't decide what to eat so we went to every restaurant I loved, ordering one small plate at each place and laughing at our cleverness.

"Mom said, 'We don't have to choose,'" I told Zoe. "We can have it all."

"I love that," Zoe said. "Restaurant hopping. We should do that more often. Why choose one place to eat?"

"We were out so late," I continued, pausing to lick chocolate sauce from my sundae off my spoon. "We were laughing and talking and just, like, enjoying the things we love about each other. But then, it's so hard because she said those things. About Satan and my life and how I could lose her if I keep being gay. It's a mind fuck."

"Yeah." Zoe wiped ice cream off her lip. "I don't know. I've never been treated that way. I don't know how you're going to keep it up. Why do you keep trying?"

A waiter took our empty sundae glasses, and I asked for the bill before going on. "I mean, most moms who believe being gay is some kind of sin don't travel around the world to be with their son. Mom came here," I continued. "Seeing her with my Armenian family, seeing them love each other. Seeing Naira blow dry my mom's hair every morning and walk arm in arm together. I love the way I got to see her with them.

"But then it's like all the wonderful things I love about her were here at the same time as the terrible things she said. Maybe it's an 'actions speak louder than words' thing. Like maybe she feels like she has to say these things, like she has to 'love me from afar.' But then she came here."

"Maybe." Zoe very gently changed the subject, and we spent the rest of the afternoon talking about Arya, who'd left that morning. They'd been fighting, she told me. She wasn't sure if they would stay together, but the sex was great.

"And there aren't a lot of options here for great gay sex." I laughed.

"Right?"

We went on, riding the night together from café to café. Earlier in the summer Cocoon had closed. Zoe had kept up with Siren, Cocoon's bartender, who told her a new owner bought the club and fired everyone. She said gays didn't go there anymore. I thought maybe the new owner hadn't known he was buying the only gay bar in the city. And now there were none.

Zoe and I passed by old Cocoon, stepping inside to see all the tables and chairs removed and mirrors installed on every wall. The place was empty, but for a new bartender neither of us recognized.

We both ordered shots, lingering to see if anyone would walk in. When no one did, I told Zoe, "Let's just go."

We walked across the city and then to Calumet, where people lingered outside the green door smoking cigarettes, which seemed silly to me because folks were inside smoking cigarettes, too. What did people love so much about this hippie bar to pack into it shoulder to shoulder? Zoe and I had to push our way through, both claustrophobic thanks to the crowded space and thudding music but also exhilarated by the connections this many liberal-minded people represented. While Zoe ordered drinks, I scanned the room, looking for cute guys or people we knew. It wasn't unusual to find other Peace Corps volunteers who you didn't know were also visiting Yerevan.

"There's Glenn," I told Zoe when she came back with drinks. "He's there in the booth."

We walked to Glenn, an A-18 with a large frame and loud voice, who gesticulated wildly, his hands high above the booth.

"Zoe! Brent!" He yelled our names loudly enough for a group on a set of poufs to turn their wide eyes toward us.

We pushed our way onto the booth seats, me next to two girls, one with a bandage across her face.

Imogen and Claire introduced themselves as Fulbright volunteers. While Claire kept running her hands through her thick dark hair, Imogen stayed still, leaning her face on her hand, trying, I could tell, to slyly cover most of her bandage. They'd arrived in the summer and had started teaching English at the American University in Yerevan. They lived together in an apartment at the north side of the city, Claire told me.

I looked to Imogen. "Can I ask what happened?"

Imogen lifted a hand to the corner of her bandage. "Car accident," she said overloudly. While the music made it hard to hear, it also meant that no one else could really hear the conversation if it wasn't directed at them. She told me of the visit she and Claire made to Glenn outside the city and how, on the way back, a truck had pushed their taxi off the road, making it roll three times.

"Holy fuck," I shouted.

"Yeah," she shouted back and then smirked. "I guess I'll have this badass scar from now on."

Glenn had been talking to Zoe about something I couldn't hear but interrupted us with a quote from *30 Rock*, which sent Claire and Imogen into a tabletop reenactment of an entire scene. They kept at it together, and I let my mind and then eyes wander around the room, passing the area full of people on poufs and then the bar where at the end, I saw him. Vartan.

With one arm around a woman I didn't know, he waved to another while he talked, his drink nearly sloshing out over them. The group around him listened to whatever he was saying as he told a story I couldn't hear.

I looked away. I hadn't heard from him. Not a word after that week in the summer when I'd kissed Noah and Vartan on the same day. Noah and I kept texting each other until eventually I felt like we didn't have anything left to say. And I ended it.

With Vartan, though, I kept searching for him in the city. I texted him every time I came in, hoping we'd meet up again as friends or lovers or anything. I was curious about him, even fantasized about him, but he hadn't so much as returned a text. After she talked with Ana, Zoe told me that Vartan wasn't out, that no one really knew about that part of him. But I hadn't wanted to out him. I'd just wanted to see him. To get to know him. To look at him in the eyes and smile.

And there he was. After all the unanswered calls and texts. *I won't*, I thought. *I won't talk to him. Not now.*

I didn't tell Zoe I'd seen him and forced my attention to the conversation at the table. They passed over usual expat topics like our favorite places in our towns and in Yerevan.

Glenn was waving his arms again, raving about his favorite shaurma place, when I felt a tap on my shoulder. I knew before I turned around who it was.

Zoe made wide eyes at me, but I waited to look back. I didn't want Vartan to catch anything in the way I responded to Zoe's look. I didn't want him to see the confusing mix of longing, hurt, and lust. I only wanted him to see the strength of my resolve, not to let him hurt me. I thought this was what I was supposed to do.

When I eventually turned to him, Zoe looked away, as if to give us privacy, the music so loud that even across the table she wouldn't be able to hear us.

"Hi," Vartan said and smiled softly.

"Hi," I returned.

Then he reached up and cupped the back of my neck, leaning up to my ear to say, "I miss you."

I thought, *You miss me?* And I would regret everything I did next. Not because of the magnitude of it but instead because of the simplicity of a decision I could have made to let go, to let myself stay curious and hopeful. It would have been easy.

Because then he said, "I'm sorry."

I knew the music was too loud for anyone to hear what we were saying, but I leaned to his ear and said, "Sorry for what?"

His hand stayed on the back of my neck. "For not texting. For not calling. I have so much in my mind. A lot is happening."

I wondered later if I would have been happier letting him let everything go. Sure, maybe he'd been a jerk. But he was also an Iranian-Armenian man straddling two countries where it was so dangerous to be queer. I learned later Vartan wasn't really out to anyone, that he was just now coming out to himself. In those months after I kissed him, after I touched him, maybe he'd retreated back, afraid of his family, afraid of this city.

No one had told me yet, not even Peace Corps, about the gay American who'd been stabbed to death in Yerevan six years earlier. I didn't know about the queer suicides and the murders and the attacks. A future queer-affiliated bar hadn't been fire-bombed yet. I know now that I was naive then. I only knew the teenage American version of this story. That Vartan had hurt me. That he hadn't texted me back. I didn't know anything about Vartan, really. And I knew nothing of what some queer people went through just to survive.

Vartan had been brave to walk up to me in a bar in Yerevan, his frame taller than mine and unmissable in a crowd. He'd walked right up to me, tapped me on the shoulder, placed a hand so gently on my neck and leaned in to tell me that he missed me.

I said back to him only, "I have a lot going on, too."

He leaned back and smiled at me, looking at my eyes for some sign that I might be happy that he was here now. I tried to look at him in a way that said I wasn't.

What principle drove me to that? To cling to an idea that he hurt me. I had no idea what was going on with him, really. But I was actually happy, honored, relieved that he was there now looking at me, his thick, dark eyebrows raised in hope, his thick lips in a smile, his olive skin a map I wanted to follow wherever it led. I could have at least let him take me out for a drink.

Then he leaned in again to my ear so close I could feel his dark stubble against my cheek. "Will you stay in Yerevan tomorrow? I want to take you to a restaurant. We can have dinner."

And all the hope and lust and curiosity and thrill retreated suddenly as if pulled by the snap of a rubber band. I had decided before he came over that he'd hurt me, and therefore, I was no longer interested. I had developed a principle: Don't let someone hurt me again.

"No," I said. "I don't think so."

And he scrambled, this time speaking loudly to my face. "No?" His smile dropped, but he maintained the composure I could sense was meant to keep from drawing attention. "I'm sorry. I need to try again. With you. I like you."

I became nervous, then, at the way he spoke to me so openly.

"No," I said again with a gentle but firm tone that he picked up as final.

He walked away without a word. I watched him move through the crowd, past his friends, who looked at me, puzzled. He smiled at them, patted one guy on the shoulder, and pointed toward the restroom, where he went behind the bar.

24

For the rest of the fall, I kept myself busy with projects at World Vision, engaging more community groups for small grants to improve more schools and kindergartens and community centers.

I spent a lot of time with Seda from Privolnoye, who had invited me once to her remote Russian village hours north of Stepanavan. She visited me at my desk in the World Vision office to talk about what we could do with her kids at the Privolnoye youth center.

Toward the end of October, the two of us decided that I could lead a workshop, a sort of ideation with the students at her youth center. I invited a new friend I'd made, a European volunteer service, or EVS, volunteer named Kristine from Latvia, who picked up Armenian so quickly that after a couple of months she seemed confident about teaching a leadership training to teenagers.

We arrived to a drizzle, the dirt streets of Privolnoye muddy and slick. A wet air clung to us all week and made me shiver so deeply I felt sure a winter snow would roll in any moment. We completed the week of training inside the youth center still wearing our coats and gloves, but the kids stayed so buoyant and unbothered by the chill that I became unbothered, too.

After the last night of training, Seda invited the kids, Kristine, and me to go for a mushroom hunt in the mountains.

In the back of the truck, the teens and I laughed as each pothole and bump sent us into the air, the five-gallon buckets meant for our mushrooms lifting and then clanging against the wooden truck bed.

When we arrived, the teenagers instinctively each grabbed a bucket and disappeared up the fog-covered foothills until only the sounds of their shouting to each other let us know they hadn't poofed into thin air. Kristine followed them, but Seda walked with me instead, showing me how to recognize mushrooms.

"*Look for a circle,*" she told me, moving her knife in the air to make the shape of a ring.

When she wandered into the fog, I kept walking alone, listening to children obscured by the mist laughing and then shouting Armenian equivalents of "Eureka" when they found a ring.

Within a few minutes, I found my own ring of mushrooms and slowly knelt into the wet grass to slice a few and drop them into the bucket. *This is the magic of this place*, I thought. Back home I would never have imagined myself hunting mushrooms in the woods, yet here I was with a kitchen knife and a bucket full.

In the mist we rode back to Seda's house, the flatbed truck making stops on muddy streets where each teen alighted and then sloshed home.

At Seda's house, we unloaded the buckets into the courtyard of the house, and when I asked to bathe, Seda told me to wait. I sat in the kitchen slicing mushrooms with Seda's parents while Seda fed a fire that heated a small sauna, leaving a bucket of hot water for me to bathe with. Clean and warm, I spent the rest of the afternoon with Seda, her father, and Kristine slicing mushrooms while Seda's mother cooked more mushroom dishes than I could count—mushroom filled blinchiks and dolmas, a mushroom soup, sautéed mushrooms with onions and a mushroom paste that I fell deeply in love with and consumed almost entirely on my own.

After dinner, with bellies full of fungus, I wandered out to the courtyard toward my guestroom when Seda interrupted my walking to ask if Kristine and I wanted to watch a movie.

"Of course," I said, leaning into the Armenian word with enthusiasm. I could think of nothing better after such a day.

In another spare room, I felt a wave of something like gratitude but also awe. As Seda set up a tiny computer on a side table, plugging in electricity and a set of tiny speakers, I marveled at the fact that I had arrived here. This day of teaching, of listening and encouraging kids to plan ideas for projects, of learning how to mushroom hunt and stuffing myself on gorgeous dish after gorgeous dish. The warm sauna that erased the chill of rain. The invitation to continue our time together into the night.

"I'll return quickly," Seda said, standing up from the tiny ten-inch computer screen. *"Popcorn!"*

We watched *Avatar*, a movie that had stirred such a global fervor that I'd already seen it in the news and all over my Facebook News Feed where friends raved about the film's special effects.

I imagined then, as we watched, my family sitting with 3D glasses in front of a movie screen where the characters and the alien animals and the floating flower petals all reached out to them, floated past their faces, their mouths open in awe.

No flowers floated out of the ten-inch screen, and still, I couldn't have been happier.

~ ~ ~

But then, the next day, Margaux called.

Margaux was an A-18 I'd seen dancing at That Place in Yerevan. I'd joined her and some of her fellow A-18s hopping from bar to bar. When all the bars closed at 2 a.m., we all stumbled to a twenty-four-hour shaurma place, and I told her in a clumsy, buzzed voice, "You should be my four a.m.?"

"Your what?" she said, her freckled cheeks half grinning.

"My four a.m. My friend who stays out with me until the wee morning hours." I snorted at my own silliness.

"Okay!" she had exclaimed back, but we didn't talk again until a month later, right after I'd returned from Privolnoye.

When my phone rang, I'd already spooned sauce onto lavash, covering it in shredded Lori cheese for pizza rolls. I tried to get the sauce off my fingers with a rag while Margaux told me, "My friend is coming to Armenia in December." I gave up and rubbed my hands on my pants.

"I want him to see the country north to south. And so, I was thinking…" She dragging out the word "thinking," pulling it like taffy, "that we could come to your house for a couple of nights."

"Oh, sure," I said, lifting my tray of pizza rolls into the oven.

"Okay, great," she said.

"I mean, it will be cold, probably snowy," I said.

"Well, it will be like that everywhere," she returned.

"I know," I said, "but my site tends to be one of the snowier ones. I mean it's fine, just not super dependable in terms of what you'll see around. But you can go over to the tenth-century fortress and go to the Stepan museum. And see me, of course."

"Well, duh." She laughed. "We're coming up there to see you."

"Obviously."

"But, seriously," Margaux said. "He's gay. So, you'll probably totally hit it off. That would be amazing. Right?"

"I mean… sure…" I said. *Hit it off?* The idea of me hitting it off with someone felt as likely as a lightning strike at this point in my service.

Later in November, she called again.

"I just want to make sure we can really come," Margaux said. "Because I promised him a booty call."

I guffawed. "Jesus, Margaux."

"Well, you'll sleep with anyone, though, right? We're slut positive."

I found myself remembering our night of dancing, the bravado I felt around her. And I'd been drunk enough not to totally remember what I'd said. Her joke made me quiver with fear and excitement. "No, Margaux." I put some laughter into my voice, but I called Zoe later.

"I don't want to sleep with just anyone," I told Zoe. "I haven't. I haven't slept with anyone in my whole life, so I'm not going to just sleep with someone she brings to my house. I'm not a booty call. Right?"

Zoe had been moving furniture again.

"God," Zoe said, huffing. She'd broken up with Arya shortly after my mom left Armenia. "I wish someone would bring a person to my house to have sex with. God. *God.* You've got a man falling out of the sky and into your house. Don't you want to just see what he's like at least?"

"Of course, I do. I actually already Facebook-stalked him."

"Really?"

"Yep. Margaux gave me his name. Chase Townsend. I looked him up. There he was."

"So, were there pictures?" Zoe still wasn't on Facebook five years after the platform first hit colleges.

"Yes, Zoe. There were pictures. He's cute. He's cute in most of them. There are these pictures from sideburn days, apparently. Not a great look. But he is actually really cute."

I thought of those pictures—Chase's dark hair cut short in a fade. His mustache. His sideburns in a school photo he posted when he got a new teacher ID. Chase in a white T-shirt, fishnets, pink American Apparel briefs and roller skates, his uniform for a roller derby match. His blue eyes blazed in every one of his photos. I clicked through them, back a couple of years and stopped on one of him sitting at the beach, his hands around his legs, his open-mouth smile with perfect teeth, those blue eyes staring through the camera to me.

"He smiles a lot in photos," I said to Zoe. "That's a good sign."

"Brent, go for it. Just see if there's a connection. If there is, just have sex with the man. For fuck's sake. Or don't. You'll know what to do."

25

When Margaux texted in the late afternoon, I left my desk at World Vision and started walking to where I'd said I'd meet Margaux and Chase at the feet of the statue of Stepan. I passed drifts of snow that covered the summer stalks of cosmos, my hands starting to shake with an energy I was afraid of. And there in the middle of the roundabout under tall Stepan, I caught the first glimpse of Chase, wrapped tightly in his grey hoodie to protect himself from the wind.

I tried to disguise my nerves with a boisterous, "Giiiiiiirl," shouting to Margaux over the cars that passed on the road between us and then running to her with a hug.

When we let go of each other, she turned to her guest and said, "So, this is Chase."

And he looked at me. Blue eyes. Blue like the deepest layers of a glacier. Blue under dark eyebrows that lifted and welcomed me to stare into his eyes, which I didn't. I couldn't. Because he would see that my breathing had tripled, breath I suddenly couldn't catch while looking at him. If I looked for too long into his blue eyes, he'd see the current behind me, and though he wouldn't know how long I'd traveled this current, he'd see me trying desperately to navigate it, like a boy on the Arctic Sea in a canoe.

"Nice to meet you," I said and shook his hand. Thick. Rough on the edges. Just enough to know he worked with them, not so rough he'd scratch the soft skin of my back.

"How was the ride?" I asked, mostly to Margaux but looking as much as I could handle at Chase. I put my hands in my pockets, slyly trying to raise my shoulders to make them broader, wondering if Chase liked broad shoulders.

"Fine, fine," Margaux said. "Right?"

"Yeah," Chase said. "It was great."

"You got to see a lot of Armenia that way," I said. "If you sat by a window."

"I did," he said. "Margaux made me."

"You might as well see the canyon now. We're right here," I said and led them for a short walk on the road that snaked north out of town. We stood over the canyon in the still cold, the grey sky low, the three of us staring over the bridge railing at the ground far below. I stayed away from the pair, fearing a lightning strike.

I stared at the shell of a car near the thin river below and braced myself against the railing of the bridge. I felt I might shake so hard with nerves I'd fall over, crash next to the car, become a ghost, and have nothing to haunt but this forgotten SUV.

As we walked toward my home, we talked about Chase's travel, Margaux's life in Kapan, other volunteers who'd quit or hooked up or done projects we admired. At the grocery store, Margaux walked straight to the counter.

"Pelmeni unek?" she asked the clerk.

And they did have pelmeni, which we bought frozen, along with sour cream and bread.

"He has to have this. Right?" Margaux asked me.

"Of course!" I said.

"It's full of cheese. It's a *duh*," she told Chase.

When we came up the street to my house, Ani, in pigtails, waved from the window, backlit by the living room lights. I watched her yell backward, point to us, and run from behind the curtains. Naira, Vazgen, and the girls rushed outside to greet us, wrapped in sweaters.

"*These are my friends*," I told my Armenian family, measuring my tone to sound as if I was so happy that my old friends had finally come to see me. "*This one is a volunteer in Kapan, and this one is a friend visiting from California*." I didn't mention I'd just met Chase.

"This is Vazgen, Naira. Their girls, Nazeli and Ani. Im yntaniky," I finished in Armenian. "My family."

Naira and Vazgen beamed at this. They welcomed my guests and then asked me if I had enough places to sleep in my cottage.

"*Don't worry*," I told them. "*We'll be fine*."

I spoke Armenian with more speed and ease than Margaux. Since Chase hadn't heard any American speak Armenian other than Margaux, I felt suddenly proud of my competency, walking with swagger over the rocks to the door of the cottage.

Inside, Margaux boiled the pelmeni. I opened the window above the stove to let the steam out, and the cool air steadied me, calming my nerves. The three of us finished the entire batch of pelmeni with ease and then dipped our bread in the mix of pasta water and sour cream.

After dinner, we talked about get-to-know-you things like Chase's students in Santa Barbara and his love for teaching math to middle schoolers. He recounted stories of the funny things they said to him, but I heard none of it. I

PART 2 · 297

simply watched his full lips move, his perfect teeth catching just a little of the overhead light.

"I'm in love," I said when he asked me if I had enjoyed the past year and a half in Armenia. "I love living here. I mean, I'll be glad to be home. And my dating life is nonexistent, but the place is beautiful. The work is good. And I am doing what I always dreamed I would do."

Which was almost true. I didn't include my dreams for love when I talked about the biggest dreams of my life. I never had. But I did dream of falling in love. I dreamed of romance. I dreamed of pressing my body against the body of a man I adored. I dreamed a lot of things, but I didn't say them.

We got ready for bed, brushing our teeth and taking turns in the bathroom. I laid out three of the seven mattresses on my bed, the best ones where the wool hadn't balled up, placing them on the floor in the living room.

"It's gonna get cold," I told them. "I'm too afraid to run the gas heater at night, and it's gonna be cold in here until we turn it back on in the morning."

"I'm not worried," Chase said, moving down to the floor. "I tend to be warm when I sleep."

"Okay," Margaux said, "but you'll probably want to sleep in long underwear."

"Probably not," Chase returned. "I really think I'll be fine."

Margaux and I rolled our eyes and kept our long underwear on.

Margaux lay down closest to the front door tucked inside her sleeping bag. I climbed inside mine, and Chase, in between us, pulled the duvets from my bed over his body, dressed in his boxer briefs, a T-shirt, and socks. They both rustled, changing positions a few times and then lay quietly.

My heart thudded in my ears. The thuds were so ferocious I could feel them change the pressure in my head. I became afraid Chase could hear the heartbeats.

As the night went on, I realized how easy Chase would be to fall for. His dark hair, his sloping jaw, his thick lips, and the eyes that had shattered my reservations.

But I had no moves. Not one. I had no practice. It would have been easier if I found him unattractive, if he'd been the kind of man I could ignore.

He's here, I thought. *Right now.* I spent the whole evening hoping something might happen. And now, as I listened to him shuffle in bed, turning in the mattress next to mine, I couldn't think of a thing to do.

In the morning, I thought, *they'll go. They'll go quickly.*

Zoe's words played in my head. "I wish someone would bring their friend to my house."

They'd leave in the morning, I thought, a panic starting to rise. The hottest man I'd ever been this close to. And the chance I had now would fly by like a cellophane bag in the wind, a regret.

The air turned quickly, and I became terribly, unexpectedly cold. More than usual. And I had to pee, which meant, I realized, I had a reason to disrupt the quiet. *Halle-fucking-lujah*, I thought.

I climbed out of my sleeping bag and opened the door to the bathroom, trying to lift it against its hinges so it would look like I was trying to stop it from squeaking on the floor. *In case they're watching*, I thought. My mixed-up mind wanted to wake Chase up but not have him know I wanted to wake him up, in case he didn't want to be woken up by me.

Watching steam rise from the toilet bowl in the bright light of the bathroom, I considered what to do next. I had to wake them. It had been a year and a half. I'd had a handful of chances to connect with men who might be interested in me and none of it worked out.

I didn't know how to connect with Chase. Could I hold his hand? Could we snuggle into each other? I didn't know what to do, but I felt like I had to do something. And while I had no idea what he thought of me, he was gorgeous. And here. In my cottage in Stepanavan.

When I opened the bathroom door, I let it screech against the tile. The sound, which I'd heard hundreds of times, did not fail me. It tore through the room, shattering any chance that Chase was still asleep.

I giggled because it worked, though I knew it sounded like I giggled because the sound was so absurd and disruptive.

"Sorry," I lied. Margaux and Chase laughed, too, at the awkwardness of waking them up because I had to pee.

The air had continued to chill, to freeze, the temperature dropping so rapidly that the cold stunned me, even in my own cottage. I climbed into my sleeping bag, which didn't seem to warm me enough. My toes were still icy, my arms tucked closely to my side trying to hold in warmth.

Chase did nothing. Said nothing. I said nothing. I stared at the ceiling. God. What next?

Then Margaux announced, "Well, now I have to pee." When she came out of the bathroom, the door shrieked absurdly again, and we all laughed. Chase hadn't moved, staying curled to his left side under my blankets.

And then came my last effort to keep this chance alive. As Margaux climbed into her sleeping bag, I spoke a convenient truth, "Are you guys cold? I mean, isn't it ridiculously cold?"

"I don't know," Margaux said softly. "I'm okay."

Lying on my back, looking at the ceiling, I said, "Seriously, though. Even in my own house, I just feel like this is really, really cold. I didn't think the temperature was supposed to drop that much today."

"I don't know," Margaux repeated.

"I just can't get warm," I said.

And then, like morning breaking over the horizon, Chase turned to me and said, "Come here."

I looked to him. He had turned onto his right side, facing me, and he'd lifted the duvet up as an invitation to lie under it next to him.

"Really?" I said.

"Really," he replied. "I sleep really hot. I've been told I'm like the sun."

I didn't believe him, but also I didn't care how warm he was.

"Okay," I said. I pulled myself from my sleeping bag, lifted my body along the floor to him, and slid under his arm which wrapped around me. With my back to his chest, little spoon, I relaxed into him.

The sun. He was the sun, a warmth all his own, which heated me through even though I could still see my breath in moonlight coming from the window. His warmth moved over me, across my back, from the tops of his thighs to the back of mine, from his arms around my sides and onto my chest.

I took a deep breath of the cold room air and tried to sigh it out slowly, attempting to slow my heartbeat. *He must feel this*, I thought, the pounding of it shaking my ribs, which he'd wrapped himself around.

Fear and lust began to swirl like divergent winds, and at once, I was trying to slow my heartbeat and aching for more of this acceleration.

And then, Chase's thumb moved, so slightly at first, I almost thought I was imagining it, and then wide enough to interpret circles, moving over the fabric of my shirt.

A rush of blood everywhere, as if after feeling the heat of him, my heart gathered that warmth and deployed it all at once.

Then, like a subtle crescendo, piano to mezzopiano, he moved the rest of his hand in the same circles, so gently that there was not even the sound of his hand brushing the fabric.

In a wave of thrill and relaxation, sudden heat and oxygen filled my belly, my legs, my arms, my face, my brain, my dick. On that river of blood, my consciousness left its seat in my head and traveled to every corner of me as if my mind dispersed to my edges. He was melting me. I wanted him to, and I wanted to feel every molecule of ice drip away.

He moved his hand silently to my waist and then pushed his hand inside my shirt, his fingers and palm over my belly and up to my chest. So slowly, so quietly exploring the right side of my chest, brushing his fingers over my nipple. Then the left. He lifted his hand away and then dove the tips of his fingers into my chest hair, following the line of my sternum until he could graze the base of my neck with the tip of his first finger.

His fingers moved to my belly, palming the soft skin in large circles as if to warm me, and then he moved his hand up in a diagonal, laying his arm over me. His hand tucked under my ribs so that with the full force of his arm he could hug me closer to him. He dipped his chin to the back of my neck, his stubble grazing the skin. He breathed in deeply, and I heard the rush of air, feeling it rush through my nape, tingling at the touch of his nose there.

I moved for the first time since he began caressing me, laying my arm over the one he had wrapped around me. I pulled his arm, hugging it and encouraging his grip. *Please*, I was trying to tell him, *please make this night a thousand nights at once.*

I pressed myself more deeply against him. With both our arms holding one tight embrace, I breathed as deeply as I could, filling my body with air so I expanded, pressed even more tightly against his chest, and then slowly exhaled, releasing, relaxing my body more deeply into his.

Then, like the earth turning, I rolled to face him.

And he was smiling. This smile showing me welcome, as if a long-extended invitation had just been accepted, as if he had been waiting for me, and I had finally arrived.

His eyes opened softly and asked a question I was unsure of, but I answered by bringing my face closer to his. Finding his lips with my lips, I pushed into a kiss that moved slowly, quietly while our arms found their place behind each other, holding on to something new we both understood could disappear like ice in the sun.

26

Margaux sat up, still inside her fully zipped sleeping bag, looking out from the hole that framed her face. The ends of her short, dark hair poked out the sides.

"Oh my god, yaaaay!" Margaux cheered over Chase and me, seeing for the first time that we were wrapped around each other, cuddled under blankets.

I shuffled to face Chase and saw Margaux on the other side, her eyebrows raised in a delighted question.

Chase opened sleepy eyes to me, and we kissed a small, deliberate, affirmative kiss. We stayed together under the blankets in no hurry to move. I let my mind travel down my body where it touched his—my hands on his back, his hand draped over my waist, my right leg tucked over his knees.

"Fuck, it's cold in here." Margaux climbed out of her sleeping bag and walked into the bathroom in her long underwear. She bent down to look at the gas heater. "How do you turn this thing on?"

With that, I broke the spell, moved from Chase, and felt so much colder immediately.

"Here," I said. I switched on the gas chamber on the wall, then the dial on the heater, which clicked wildly, harrumphing its way into a flame that burned behind glass, untouchable and blazing.

I turned to look out the window and saw my fortunate mistake.

"Damn," I said, "the window was open all night."

"For real?" Margaux asked.

Chase climbed out of the covers and stood in the middle of the room in his boxer briefs and T-shirt. A surge of pleasant, gentle desire ran through me.

"Yeah," I admitted, "we must have left it open when we made pelmeni last night."

"Pelmeni surprise!" Margaux said, drawing out the first-morning laugh from all of us.

Thank the lord good god hallelujah oh my god wow, I thought. The window was open. The window was open, and then the sun invited me in.

~ ~ ~

At the office, I couldn't concentrate on a thing, though there wasn't much to concentrate on. Armenian offices, shops, and families were already preparing to shut down for two weeks during Nor Tari. The office had started to slow with no new projects on the calendar. No big decisions to make before the new year. Some reports to write. And waiting for Nor Tari and then Armenian Christmas and then a long new year's winter into spring.

Margaux and Chase had taken a taxi to the old fortress of Lori Berd. The December sun shone bright and warm, and I imagined them walking through crisp air, dipping in and out of the Lori Berd ruins, imagining lives lived in another millennium.

I assumed they'd be talking about me. Margaux slept through our rustling under the covers. She didn't hear

Chase when he whispered to me, "I didn't know if you were even interested."

Margaux didn't hear me reply, "Yeah, I think I'm kinda like that sometimes."

He'd said back to me, "I couldn't read you at all."

"Read this then," I said and gave him another long kiss, my lips finding his again, my tongue slipping just barely into his mouth to the edge of his perfect teeth.

At my desk, I nearly prayed for the first time in a long time to any god who might keep Chase close to me a little bit longer. Margaux had asked only that I host them for a night in Stepanavan. I wanted another night. And maybe another. Maybe I could meet them in Yerevan when they returned from the south. Maybe he'd give me his number.

I knew their plan was to leave on the only marshutni to Yerevan this afternoon. Could Chase just leave like that? Last night had lit my cells up. And now I'd simply go back to my cottage alone?

While my mind was racing to find an option to stay connected to him, I spent a lot of energy trying to hide from my Armenian coworkers the fact that I might explode out of my office chair. I opened a blank email to no one, and I pretended to write. I barely looked up, and when Artavan walked in the front door and said, "Bari luis," I tried only to keep my face from flushing, to keep myself from giving away that my heart was beating for another man.

And then, a rush of panic swept in, a fear that my Armenian friends, my coworkers would be able to tell that this was, for me, a day unlike any other in my life. And then, at the same time, I longed to tell them everything, to jump up and down screaming with joy, fear, longing, and nervousness, a spark from Chase's touch lingering electric in my heart.

And then Margaux called on their way back from Lori Berd. "Would you want to come with us to Yerevan," she asked.

Stay calm, I said to myself. *Calm. Say nothing extraordinary.* It worked. No one in the office looked at me.

"Oh, that sounds wonderful," I said as if the thought of being with them again hadn't been on my mind every second since they left. "But I don't want to impose." I simultaneously praised and chided myself for giving them an out.

"No, honestly, please come," she said.

"Really?" I worried. "I mean, he's your friend, and he's come all this way to spend this time with you. Are you sure?"

"I'm sure. We would both love it. We'll laugh a lot, I know," she said. Then she whispered, "He wants you to come."

I died and then came back to life. Next to me, Yeraz simply answered emails, unaware.

I pretended to finish the email to no one and then walked to Liana's office, smoothing my sweater.

"Hi, Liana," I said. I wanted to holler. I wanted to shout to her that I met a gorgeous, sweet man. And he met me. And we spun around each other all night like we'd fallen into orbit.

She looked up from her laptop through her new haircut's triangle of curls. She folded her arms and sat back, looking at me warmly.

I mirrored her body language, crossing my arms as if I'd been thinking for a long time, weighing something very heavy. And it did feel heavy to me. It was the middle of the week, and I wouldn't be telling Peace Corps about the travel, a clear break from their monitoring rules.

"Inch ka, Brent jan," she said.

"So, you know my friend who's visiting from the States?" I lied, using the word "friend" so my upcoming request wouldn't feel too strange. A hiding trick. I hated to do it but was still too afraid of Liana knowing about me.

"Ayo," she replied.

"I'd like to go with them to Yerevan. There's not much going on here now, and I don't want to miss the chance to spend time with them."

Shrugging, she let out a soft, "Of course. How wonderful that they're here. Yerb kgas?" she asked.

"Now," I said. "I'd have to go now."

"Lav eli." She laughed, leaning back in her chair. "That's fast."

"I know. It's crazy. But I don't want to miss them." Which was true, but I hoped she read something untrue—that these were my old, dear friends from the States. Knowing she'd explain to everyone in the office where I'd gone, I hoped the story was a lie I didn't have to repeat. I was calculating, hedging, worrying still that my life in Armenia would crumble if my Armenian friends knew.

"Go," Liana said. "Have fun."

~ ~ ~

On the bus, Chase sat next to me. Our proximity attracted no questions from anyone packed tightly into the small marshutni seats. But when he snuck his pinky to hook into mine, I pulled my backpack from between my feet onto my lap to hide our hands. My ribs did their work, hiding my leaping heart.

When the marshutni stopped halfway in Aparan, I bought him sweet rolls at the roadside bakery. When we arrived at the bus station in Yerevan, I paid for the taxi to Phillip's, whom I'd texted on the ride for a place to stay.

In the evening, we eased into tipsiness, drinking cocktails with our samosas and curries at Karma. Then we downed sweet shots in a café by the Opera.

Margaux, Chase, and I laughed easily together at jokes that were made funnier by the delight we'd started to feel together—Margaux and I both outside administrative barriers of our Peace Corps assignments and Chase traveling, still on a great adventure.

At Republic Square, I leaned into Chase just slightly while we sat on the steps and watched the dancing fountains. We walked back the way we came, down an alley between two apartment buildings that lifted their tenants into the sky away from us.

Chase put his arm around my waist, which scared and thrilled me. He leaned into my ear to whisper, "I want to make out with you so hard right now."

"You guys need to make out," Margaux jeered from behind us.

"We desperately need to make out," I yelled back drunkenly overloud as we passed by a set of stairs that went down to a basement door with a padlock. "Down here."

Margaux responded with, "Go. Go. I'll stay up here and watch for people."

Chase grabbed me and turned me so hard I nearly stumbled before he drove his lips onto mine. I put my hands on his upper back and felt his back muscles flexing, moving as his hands found me, pushing over me until I fell against the concrete stairwell wall. Our lips moved over each other's, hungry, thirsty. His hands pressed me into the wall as he shoved them into my shirt, onto my chest, and then around to my back, pulling me to him. He reached down to my butt, held it in both hands, and then pulled my hips against his.

He pulled his lips away, stared at me, his skin shades of grey-blue in the moonlight, his blue eyes less potent. His face formed a question—How was that? How is this?

A joy, I thought. An invitation. A hope.

~ ~ ~

In the morning, as we drank coffee on Phillip's balcony over the Cascade, Margaux told me, "Chase is going to rent a car and drive from here to Kapan." Chase was showering, sending a soft sound of splashing down through the room and out the door while Phillip slept in his room upstairs. "That way we can stop where we want to stop," Margaux finished.

"Wow, that's perfect," I replied.

"You're coming with us. Right?" At this question, the air in my chest flash-heated. Chase and I had been in some kind of mating haze since our first kiss in my cottage two nights ago. But I hadn't asked to go with them south. Until now.

On top of that, I'd left Stepanavan without Peace Corps approval. And Peace Corps volunteers were not allowed to drive cars during service. Too much liability. But here was a loophole... Chase could.

"Oh my god, yes," I replied and then paused. "I mean, I feel like I'm really crashing your party."

Margaux sipped coffee, then said, "You're not crashing. He's happy. And honestly, Brent, we've never spent this much time together. I'm so glad he's here, but you two are hitting it off. It's been really nice..."

Lottery. I was winning some cosmic lottery.

Chase was staying until three days after Christmas. That meant we had nine more days together. I called Liana who heard me out, softly agreeing that things at the office were slow and there wouldn't be much to do until after the new year.

"You'll come back for our Nor Tari party, though?" Liana asked. "December twenty-ninth?"

"Of course," I said.

When I told Chase I'd be coming with them for the rest of the trip, he wrapped his feet around my feet under the table and said, "Good. At this point it'd be weird if you weren't with us."

We spent one more day in Yerevan. I tried to tell Chase about Cocoon, how it had been shut down, and how I still wanted to dance with him in the bar that had replaced it. When we arrived, we were the only ones in the black box that had once been full of dancing, exuberant queers.

"Vodka yev gasov jur," I ordered from the bartender. "Yerek hat." I passed the vodka sodas to Chase and Margaux.

"SexyBack" by Justin Timberlake played into the empty room, and without hesitating, we moved our bodies to the center of the room and danced like a crowd was on the dance floor. We wanted so much to make a night of it.

When the sound system started blasting Akon, I said, "Hold on a second," and walked to the bartender. "Lady Gaga unek?" I asked.

With a nod, he turned to a computer at the bar, scrolled on the track pad, and clicked.

Gaga's familiar call at the beginning of "Bad Romance" filled the empty black room, and I ran to Margaux and Chase. The light in his eyes flashed when he looked at me.

I stepped back to watch him. He ran his hands down his grey T-shirt, his American Apparel grey hoodie shaking from where he'd tied it over his hips.

I suppressed a tinge of disappointment as I watched him, unable to find the beat. I didn't know if he could tell how off the bass thuds he was. I could tell he loved it, giving himself to his movements, letting the music propel him. I went to him and tried to synchronize our bodies but couldn't. And I didn't force him. I closed my eyes, felt his hand travel up my back. He turned me around, pulled me with both hands against his body, tried to roll with me, awkwardly bumping into each other unintentionally.

When I turned around, he looked to the ground and then danced away on his own.

All the better, I thought. Better than too much gay in what felt like the tomb of a gay bar underground.

The next morning, in Chase's rented white sedan, we drove through the desert with the windows cracked, the sun bright enough to heat the car though the air was near freezing outside. We plugged Chase's iPod into the car stereo and played Beyoncé and La Roux while Mount Ararat towered over us from beyond Armenia's western border.

"That's where some Armenians believe Noah's boat landed after the flood," I told Chase, pointing to the mountain's peak.

"Huh," he muttered. "Noah wouldn't have even let us on that boat." We laughed, and I held down some inner voice, an old one from my youth that said to me, *He's right*.

We stopped for snacks at a roadside stand. We bought sharots, a treat made from meticulously strung walnuts dipped in grape molasses. We handed our dram to an older woman who asked us where we were from.

"*You speak Armenian?*" she asked us in her native language.

"*We do,*" I said, pointing between Margaux and me.

The woman raised her arms in delight and invited us to a stall behind her shop with a picnic table and a small coal heater, where she poured wine and fed us bread and fruit. A bright light of pride filled me then, proud to be able to connect with her, to ask her about her family, how long she'd had this roadside stand, her favorite treats to sell. At the last question, she brought out all of them—sunflower seeds, more sharots, halva, baklava. I translated all of this for Chase, proud also to show him what I loved about being here and finding camaraderie through a stranger's hospitality.

Back on the road, now on the way further south to Vayk, Margaux told us of a relationship she'd started with a volunteer who lived there, Adam, and we agreed to stop there for the night.

Adam greeted us at his house, his childlike, smooth face even more diminutive within his large house. Adam's house matched what I'd come to expect from volunteers who rented their own houses in Armenia. My tiny cottage was a complete anomaly. Some volunteers lived in a room in a host family's house, and most either rented an apartment or a house large enough for a family, available at an affordable rate because no families were around to rent them.

At dinner, Adam unscrewed a jar filled with a dry, crumbly cheese.

"My landlord dug this up from my yard today. He said he'd buried it ten years ago." Adam told us, pushing up his circular steel-framed glasses. "This is a ten-year-old cheese."

Sour, savory saltiness filled my mouth and nose. I will remember for years how it tasted and how it felt to savor another surprise from this country that felt familiar to me now and still delightfully unexpected.

"I wasn't expecting you guys," Adam said when we laid two flat, wool-filled mattresses on the wood-planked floor in his completely empty living room. "Could you use one of these as a blanket?" he continued and then left us, guiding Margaux by the hand to his bedroom.

Chase and I smiled at each other, and in the middle of all this empty space, he undressed me. Goosebumps raced across my skin as the cold air hit it. The golden red glow of the one space heater in the room tried at the impossible task of fighting off the freezing temperature.

We made love again without having sex, for the fourth night. Again, with passion, taking our time to discover each other. We tried and failed to keep the second flat mattress on top of us and braced our naked bodies against the winter air inside the room. When we finished, he looked up at me and melted me again with his smile.

We crawled under the top mattress, which fell over us stiffly, leaving gaps and exposing our bodies. Chase's warmth was enough to heat the space we held together, and I slept deeply as if, after just five days, our bodies were already home.

Late the next morning, Margaux and I sat in her sixth-story walk-up while Chase slept off the three-and-a-half-hour drive to Kapan. Margaux poured orange juice and vodka into pint-sized jars while I sat at her kitchen table looking out to the snow-capped mountains that walled the largest town in Southern Armenia.

"So, we're kind of having a Christmas predinner tomorrow night," Margaux said, taking a seat. "There's a hotel within walking distance. We ordered a huge meal, and everyone's meeting up there."

"Who's everyone?" I sipped half-reluctantly at my drink.

"Honestly, I'm not one hundred percent certain," Margaux said. "I kind of thought it would just be Kapan and maybe Sisian folks..."

I started making a mental list of the volunteers I knew who lived in the area. It was a long one.

"... and obviously Danya and Shereen because where are they going to go?" Danya lived four hours south from Kapan in Meghri, and Shereen, an A-18, had been placed an hour even farther south in a town on the Iranian border.

"But then, since I invited Danya, I invited Genya..." Margaux continued, referencing Danya's boyfriend, a Peace Corps volunteer who lived hours north by Lake Sevan.

"So, then you have to invite Lake Sevan people, and then I guess it kind of went from there because now Berd people are coming, which I didn't know until yesterday."

"Berd? Good grief," I said. "That's farther away than Stepanavan."

"I know."

A chill. "Who's coming from there?"

"I don't know everyone. But Landon asked to stay here. And Aaron. And Noah's coming."

My chill turned into a sting. "Margaux..." I held my breath.

"I know," she said. "But he's staying with Matt."

"Margaux..." I said again.

"I know. But I didn't even invite everyone. It's my party, and then Lizzie just started saying yes to everyone who wanted to come."

I knew Lizzie, Margaux's best friend in Kapan, was also close with Noah. "So, Noah's coming to the dinner tonight," I speculated.

"I mean, I think so."

"Fuck. Okay. And then he's coming to the Christmas party here. In your apartment."

"It'll be fine," Margaux said.

"Except I hooked up with Noah the last time I saw him." This was a secret I had only told Zoe. That a few weeks ago at my second All Volunteer Conference, after not really talking for months, I texted Noah. We flirted over text through every session. I'd followed him up to his room when everyone went out into the city. He'd had a cold and refused to kiss me, saying he didn't want to get me sick. We didn't go all the way, but our night together had ended with both of us sweaty, naked, and spent.

"I'm sure he's fine," Margaux said. And maybe she was right. That night in Yerevan he had, in fact, told me that what we were doing didn't need to mean anything.

Naked on the couch in his hotel room, Noah had said, "We just have needs. That's all this is."

I downed the dregs at the bottom of my mimosa and then rolled the bottom edge of the glass against Margaux's table in a circle.

"Should I tell Noah?" I asked.

"About Chase?" Margaux leaned back in her chair lifting the front legs from the floor. "I don't know. Do you think he still likes you?"

I told her I kind of thought he might. I didn't fully believe Noah in the hotel when he said hooking up didn't matter to him, though I wanted to believe it.

Margaux, Chase, and I spent the afternoon in town shopping a grocery list Margaux created for what had become a Christmas party for thirty people. Maybe more.

We split up, Margaux pointing us to where we could buy kilos and kilos of potatoes while she found a stand filled with bags of flours, picking up a cellophane full of cornmeal. At a vegetable stand a woman stuffed two cellophane bags so full of beets, onions, and cabbage I felt certain they would burst before we returned to the apartment.

Chase followed me closely most of this time, flirting as inconspicuously as he could manage. He slipped his finger into my front pocket while we were standing in line at a grocery store, tugging. While I tried to pretend this didn't thrill me, while I pushed down every longing I had to tackle him and touch his entire body with my mouth, Chase simply looked at me with a smile meant to remind me gently of the electric current that ran between us.

When we were nearly finished shopping, Margaux asked us to wait while she ran into one more shop for mushrooms. Chase and I sat on a green wooden bench, our feet encircled by the pile of bags. We left a full six inches of space between us, which felt forced and unnatural.

Speaking softly, I told him, "I'm having the best time with you."

He met my eyes and said, "I am, too."

Cars sped by us on the street. Pedestrians walked behind us.

"I didn't think this trip would be like this," Chase said, his voice still just barely loud enough for me to hear. "That I'd meet someone like you."

"Well," I joked, my voice low, too. "You did. And now there's an entire Christmas dinner right here in bags at our feet."

He leaned against the green wooden bars of the bench, falling a bit closer to me so he could whisper in my ear.

"I think we should have sex." He leaned close enough I could feel his breath on my ear. "I think we should have sex today."

Blood rushed instantly from my head to my lap.

"Today?" I said.

"Yeah," he said. "If you want."

My thoughts turned into a cyclone of joy and fear and what-ifs, but I kept at least part of my mind trained on the people walking around us, checking for any notes that anyone could perceive the truth of what was just now happening between us.

Simultaneous thoughts whirled through my mind. I was a virgin. I had no idea how to have sex. I wanted to so badly, but what if I hated it? Or what if he hated it? With me? And then the thought: *This is it. This beautiful man and me here. In a town in a country, I hadn't known existed until I'd been invited here by an institution that didn't know where I currently was.* This was it. A threshold I wanted to cross. And I wanted to cross it with him.

So softly, I returned, "I do want it. I do want to have sex with you, Chase."

He looked into my eyes, comforting me with a stare, eyelids down just enough to say, *I'll take care of you.*

"We don't have lube, though," I almost inaudibly whispered.

"Or condoms," he said.

"I have plenty of condoms," I said. I'd grabbed them at the Peace Corps office in Yerevan.

"Okay, but lube?" Chase said.

"There has to be some," I said. "Has to be. People are having sex in Kapan."

I scanned every storefront in view. The grocery stores, the stands, the khanuts.

"Look," I pointed. "That pharmacy. Should we go see if they have something?" Which really was meant as rhetorical. I would go because I spoke Armenian. But Chase stood up and crossed the street, walking right into the white building with the blue cross on the facade.

Margaux and Chase returned to the bench at the same time, her with mushrooms, him with a paper bag.

"Baby oil," he said.

Back at the apartment, without either of us saying anything to Margaux about our plans, she retired for a nap after we put the groceries away.

"Is that baby oil in your pocket, or are you just happy to see me?" I asked Chase after we were both in our room with the door locked. The afternoon light bathed us softly, coming in through lace curtains, turning the stripes of the yellow wallpaper orange.

I didn't know how to bring it up, so I said to him abruptly, "I've never done this before."

Chase smiled. "That's okay." He took my hand in his. With his other hand, he pulled the baby oil from his pocket and placed it on the second twin bed by our bags. Towering next to them, he lifted off his shirt without letting his eyes leave mine. He stared at me deeply, through years of me, and found the boy in me who wanted another boy. Then, the teenage part of me, standing there in front of him wanting to hold him.

I walked to him, closing the space between us, and held his hands, locking our fingers, raising them to kiss the backs of his knuckles. Then I kissed his lips, pulled his body to mine, ran my hands up his arms to his broad shoulders and down his back, across his olive skin to his backside, which I took in my hands and pulled so that his hips pressed into mine.

Our hairy chests together, I felt his heartbeat, and I breathed in a long, deep breath, lifting my hand to his cheek, his stubble prickling my palm, driving me again to stare into his blue eyes. I kissed him with the weight of years behind me, pushing against those soft lips that rose up to mine.

When we were both naked, wrapped up together on the twin bed, he whispered. "Merry Christmas, baby," which made both of us laugh.

"Merry Christmas, Chase," I said back.

Our bodies fell into a rhythm then. I'd heard my whole life that sex with a man would destroy me, bring destruction to my life, send me to a fire that would burn forever.

But when Chase and I finally connected completely, the rhythm felt like music, a song that felt new and so very old, like my cells carried a harmony to the melody of him.

And after the crescendo, I kissed him.

"Wow," I whispered, my hand sliding over the sweaty skin of his back. "I didn't know."

He kissed me again. I looked into his eyes and whispered again, astonished and in awe of the energy that ran through my body.

"I didn't know."

27

The next morning Chase and I showered in the clawfoot tub in Margaux's bathroom. Chase slid soap over my skin before rinsing away what felt like years and years and years.

With wet hair, I left him in the apartment and made my way down the stairs and outside, my pace quickening as I tried to find a place between all these apartment buildings where I felt no strangers could hear me.

"It happened," I told Zoe, holding my little Nokia up to my ear. I stepped between two windowless cars that seemed abandoned, shells with no parts. Clothes hanging from wires outside apartment windows flapped against the clear blue sky. Patches of snow hid in shadows trying not to evaporate, attempting to keep their particles from lifting, weightless, into space.

"Breeeeeeeeeeeeeeeeent!" Zoe shouted so loudly I lifted my phone from my ear. Zoe was already far north in Berd at another Christmas gathering with other volunteers.

"I know," I nearly screamed back. "Marking 'Lose my v-card' off my New Year's Resolutions, just in time!"

"Fuck, yeah!" she cheered. "I'm so fucking happy for you."

"I know." I felt I could jump onto the abandoned cars parked in the alley behind Margaux's building, bound from roof to roof like a man on the moon.

"Okay, so..." Zoe calmed and lowered her voice. "How was it?"

A rush of joy spread out through my arms and legs and back into my voice. "Magic," I said. "Total magic. I didn't know, Zoe. His body and my body and both of us together... I wasn't expecting it to feel that good."

"Awesome," she said, her tone reassuring.

Years of my childhood came to me in that moment, how often I heard that sex between two men was abhorrent, that it led to eternal fire, that God would never want that for anyone. I remembered people saying things like, "It's not natural," and, "You're not built that way."

"Girl," I said to Zoe, corporeal pleasure still sizzling like oil in a hot skillet. "I can tell you, my body was definitely made to do that. I mean, I've heard so often growing up that it wasn't natural. But my body was made for that."

Zoe laughed. "My god." she said. "Not everyone's first time is that good, you know?"

"Well, mine was." We both laughed.

"And how's Chase?" Zoe asked.

"He's good, Zoe." I held my breath and then went on. "He can be kind of intense. Like, while we were getting dressed yesterday, I mentioned that I wanted to trim my body hair. He replied so fast it caught me off guard.

"He was like, 'I don't do that. I won't do that. No one should have to change their body for someone else.'

"And I wasn't talking about him. I was talking about me. It was a little weird."

"Sure," Zoe said.

"But he... he looks at me, you know? Like, I'll look up from eating dinner or something, and he'll look up at me, as if he noticed me move in his periphery and wanted to catch my eyes. And he does. And I turn to mush because they're beautiful and he's staring at me like he wants me to know he's happy to see me. Margaux laughs at us, how much PDA there is. He's kind of all over me. Which I *love*."

I threw myself at that last part because I did. I loved that he was all over me. I loved that his hand traveled to mine as soon as we sat next to each other, that he wrapped his arm around my shoulders, that his hand rubbed my thigh when we sat together, that, in bed, his hands traveled the length of me under the moonlight coming in through the window.

"I wish it didn't feel kinda scary, though. Like, I keep worrying that someone is going to see us. An Armenian who hates gays or something. I don't know."

"Well, be careful," Zoe said. "But also, have fun, honey. Being gay can be really, really fun."

Later that afternoon, after our taxi swung a corner too fast, Margaux gathered herself next to me and said, "It's too many people."

"Zgush eli," I said to the driver. He laughed.

"It is a lot of people," I said to Margaux, trying to reassure her. "Where are they staying?"

"Most of them are staying at Lizzie or Matt's or Mark's. But they all couldn't stay there. Landon and David are the only ones coming to my place. And Adam. Who's been sick, apparently, since we left, so that will be fun."

"Oh, geez," I said.

"I just hope they actually all give me money tonight. I told everyone to chip in, and we spent so much yesterday I actually need them to pay me back."

Chase stared out the window, watching Kapan's lights pass by on the street. Snow fell softly through the streetlights, not sticking, and the wet sidewalks reflected shop lights still on. It was simply Monday for most Armenians, not the night before Christmas. My Armenian friends had told me that Santa Claus was called Zmer Papik and that he showed up each January 7, a week after New Year's Day. A few wreaths hung on light posts, and a few strings of lights twinkled over shop doorways. But there was no holiday frenzy except ours, the Americans, on our way to an American Christmas Eve feast at a hotel restaurant.

I told Chase about Noah before we left for dinner. "We had a thing," I told Chase. "It was short. Not much happened. But I do think he's kinda hung up about it."

"And you didn't tell him about me?" Chase asked, buttoning his shirt, looking up, his eyes wide in annoyed surprise.

"No," I said. "I mean, we don't talk now. Frankly, I'm kind of assuming the Peace Corps rumor mill has been tossing you and me around, and he'll have heard."

From the hotel lobby, a concierge led us down a nondescript hallway to a large room with pastel purple walls and long tables set for thirty. The hotel staff set the table in Armenian style—white table cloths, plates rimmed in gold, smaller plates with small coffee cups, a water glass and a shot glass and a juice glass for each person, soda and soda water and juice all room temperature in groups of three set every so often down the table runner next to unlit candles and bowls of candy.

When we entered the room, the volunteers already there screamed and ran to us for hugs. Then, as more people entered, we all kept screaming with delight to be seeing each other, to feel a particular but not complete kind of freedom among our cohort of expats. We all began feverishly updating each other, sharing everything from their road stories on the way to Kapan to how their work was going at site. Volunteers from every region of the country were descending on this hotel, and excited voices echoed.

I introduced Chase, grinning coyly. Some volunteers acknowledged him and moved on quickly. Some nudged me with good-for-you elbow bumps, and some even shouted with glee.

When I finally stood with Chase on the side of all the commotion, he reached to my hand, interlocking our fingers. A spark of pride ran through me. I had a hot date who claimed me in front of strangers by taking my hand. I squeezed and then let go for fear that the Armenian waitstaff might see.

Noah arrived in a group that received the same exuberant screams when they entered the room. I watched him, knowing Chase couldn't have picked him out yet, and anticipated when Noah would see us together. I let go of Chase's hand before Noah finally saw me and crossed the dining room to us.

Noah nearly knocked me back with an overeager hug, and when he said hello, I caught a whiff of alcohol on his breath.

"Hi, Noah," I said, stepping back. "Long trip?"

"Nine hours," he said. "But it's worth it. Who's this?"

I gestured beside me. "This is Chase. Margaux's friend from California."

"Chase!" Noah said taking Chase's outstretched hand and shaking it a bit too hard. "I heard you were visiting."

"I am," Chase replied. And both of us watched as Noah shrank a little, clumsily swinging into a different emotion.

"Welcome to Armenia," he said and then walked to a different huddle of volunteers, falling into a string of happy-to-see-you hugs.

At dinner we feasted on khorovats and salads and as much lavash and cheese and pickles as we could eat. The volume of our voices never decreased, and Chase wrapped his arm around mine as volunteer after volunteer stood in the Armenian tradition to say toast after toast. After plates were cleaned, someone plugged their iPod into the room stereo, and everyone left the table to dance.

I stayed at the table. When Chase wasn't watching me, I tried to watch Noah, looking for signs that I'd hurt him. I watched Noah stumble, saw him struggle to find a partner or a group to dance with, saw him dance alone with a beer in his hand, smiling and looking down at the floor, his feet completely missing the rhythm of the music.

I looked away. I found Chase's eyes, and I tried to forget about Noah or the rest of the party. I finally got up to dance, and I decided that for a moment, I would forget trying to hide Chase and me and our connection around Armenians. And I forgot, too, my family who, right then, were probably starting to gather at my parents' house for Christmas Eve. Games on the table. Cookie dough in the fridge to be rolled out and cut into shapes. Traditions kept for my thirteen-year-old sister still at home. I forgot that I missed them. I forgot that my mother said I might lose her.

I didn't think of any of it. I just looked into Chase's blue eyes and said, "Chase, do you want to head back to Margaux's?"

"Yes," he said, and we left, stepping out into the cold, wet air.

28

"I've got to be really quiet," I told my family through the Skype window on my laptop. My mom and dad, my two sisters, my brother, and his wife all sat around sheet pans of white sugar cookies, tubes of icing, and sprinkles.

I'd woken up at sunrise and snuck out of the room where Chase and I slept in a twin bed across from Landon. Margaux, Adam, and a couple of volunteers on floor mattresses were still asleep in Margaux's room, and I'd set my computer up on the coffee table in front of the living room couch. I lifted the computer and turned it to show my family a few people in sleeping bags along the outside edges of the apartment. I could hear my sister, Lisa, say, "Oh, wow," in my headphones.

"A lot of people are here," I whispered to them. "Everyone is still asleep."

With me on Skype, my parents, my sisters, my brother, and his wife all decorated cookies. In a square image rendered fuzzy by distance and technology, I watched them pipe icing and sprinkle sugar crystals on reindeer and stockings.

I'd carried my dice in my backpack throughout this entire trip for this moment. When my family was ready to move on to the next Christmas tradition, we played Pirate Dice, a game we'd seen in the second *Pirates of the Caribbean* movie.

I soundlessly let my dice fall to the couch cushions before letting out a barely audible whisper of "four sixes."

I stayed on Skype with them for an hour, telling them only that I was visiting Margaux for Christmas. I said nothing of Chase and tried to hide any sign of extra happiness that anyone could perceive. My mom could detect any lip quiver or elevated eyebrows and was unafraid to ask questions. I wanted no questions. I couldn't bear the idea that any judgment at all enter into this time with Chase. And my brother and two sisters still had no idea at all that I was gay.

I played games with them still, my lover asleep in the next room. When other volunteers in the apartment started stirring and climbing from their sleeping bags, I said goodbye and Merry Christmas and hung up the Skype call, putting away my computer along with the wish that I could tell them how happy I was with Chase.

Later in the kitchen, Chase and I poked at each other's bellies, tickling each other while we made coffee. We helped Margaux make breakfast burritos, which we set out buffet style for Margaux's guests while they talked and texted friends staying around Kapan.

Within the hour, everyone but Chase, Margaux, and I cleared out, leaving to go "see Kapan" or "meet up with people." Even Adam left, and Margaux started fuming.

"Thirty-three people are coming here for Christmas dinner tonight, and everyone just left. It's just the three of us here to cook everything."

I saw Chase grimace. "Are these people your friends?" He looked to Margaux, who furrowed her brow at him.

"Well, yeah," she said. "They're my friends. But like, they're just being jerks right now."

"I assumed they'd all be here, honestly," he said. "I mean, they're Peace Corps volunteers. I kind of assumed they'd volunteer to help with stuff."

"Not so," I said. "Peace Corps volunteers are opportunists." My tone lifted into a joke. I also felt miffed. "This group is looking at the opportunity of hanging out all day with friends, playing board games, drinking, having nothing to do…" I grinned. "But each other."

That got a laugh, and Chase looked up slyly to me from a pile of carrots he was setting up to dice.

For the next few hours, we made the best of it. Margaux turned on Christmas music. Together we mashed potatoes, reduced fat and spices into gravy and baked beets with goat cheese and dill. We roasted a turkey and sautéed brussels sprouts until the edges were crispy.

Margaux asked me to take on decorations while she and Chase made sugar cookies. We hadn't bought anything to decorate with. Margaux didn't even have a pair of regular scissors in the house. But she had a first aid kit. With a pair of bandage shears, I cut out paper snowflakes. From a Russian tabloid, I cut out the letters for "Merry Christmas, Bitches," which I hung with surgical tape over Margaux's built-in bookshelves.

Chase came up behind me, wrapped flour-covered hands around my belly and whispered into my ear, "It's a beautiful trashcraft, sweetheart." I jabbed him in the belly and then kissed his face.

Margaux, Chase, and I barely finished and changed clothes before the guests returned to Margaux's apartment, the three of us noting the few people who had bothered to bring dishes to contribute, including Lizzie, who handed Margaux a green bean casserole when she walked in.

As the party began, Chase went into service mode, making sure every dish had serving spoons and finding room among them for the few contributions from other volunteers. I didn't know how else to help, so I made myself a plate and found a place in the crowded apartment to sit on the arm of the couch, my heels lifted to elevate my knees so I could balance my plate on them to eat. I took a bite of Lizzie's casserole and looked up from my plate enough to see Noah walk past me, his eyes forward. He didn't even flinch when his leg bumped my plate. He didn't look down at all.

On the couch, Lizzie noticed me watching him and turned to me so quickly that her ponytail whipped the person next to her. "You really fucked him up, Brent," she said softly. "He's been at my apartment all day talking about it over and over. How you didn't say anything to him before he got here."

"Oh, no," I said. Was it really true that I'd hurt him? I'd thought I'd played by some kind of gay rules where no one was attached to anyone if they didn't want to be. That no relationship was serious enough to worry about hurting someone.

I looked up and saw Noah overdoing it while patting another volunteer on the back. He walked into the living room, looking for a place to sit. When I tried to smile at him, he pretended that he didn't see me.

Before we hooked up at the All Volunteer Conference, Noah assured me it didn't mean anything. And maybe it didn't. But maybe the months of online dating and my nearly immediate rejection did.

I felt like a child who'd broken something he didn't know could be broken. And then I realized that, of course it could be broken, a connection between us as precious and as fragile as glass.

The sound of everyone talking was so deafening, that I didn't notice at first when Margaux asked everyone to be quiet while she made a toast. No one stopped talking, so she tapped on her glass with a fork, which didn't work. I watched her face fall into disappointment.

Then Chase did something that caught me so off guard I almost choked. Perhaps from a sense of injustice, seeing not a soul listening to Margaux, the founder of the feast, and perhaps from his own sense of pride having helped cook it all, he filled up the space with his voice, yelling, "Everyone! Shut up!"

The room fell silent. Everyone looked at this visitor with sideways eyes and then exchanged smirks with each other.

Chase continued loudly, using a lot of air, "Margaux... has worked very hard to make this meal for you. Listen to her, for fuck's sake."

Margaux seemed embarrassed, fumbling through with a toast to friendship that landed awkwardly. The room raised glasses in halfhearted cheers.

I realized then that Chase wasn't getting a chance to see Peace Corps volunteers at their best—the volunteers who spoke clear Armenian after focused studying, the volunteers who showed up day after day trying to make something helpful happen out of a network of relatively few resources.

I wished Chase could meet volunteers that way, but he wasn't. He was meeting mildly or majorly drunk people who were clumsily excited to be together and didn't want any of that connection to end, though they knew it would when they all dispersed to their sites across Armenia.

Dinner flew by, people eating stuffing, roasted turkey, cranberry sauce, and roasted vegetables, with lavash in place of American dinner rolls. I sat alone on the arm of the couch, a plate on my knees, careful with my knife and fork. Chase sat across the room on the edge of a table, which surprised me. The chair next to me was open, and I felt a twinge of upset stomach because of the distance he chose to put between us.

After Chase took his plate to the kitchen, he returned to me and leaned down to whisper in my ear, "I want to leave."

"Me, too," I told him.

"I want to leave for the night," he said.

"Really?"

"Yes," he responded. "Is there a hotel here?"

"Yes, the one from last night," I said

"Do you think we could get a room?"

"I don't know. It is Christmas." But then I remembered today, December 25, wasn't Armenian Christmas. This was just a weeknight in December.

When I told Margaux, her face turned peeved. "You're leaving? For real?"

"Yeah, I mean, I want to go to bed," I lied. I actually just wanted out of this crowd, away from Noah, away from the Chase who had just yelled at everyone.

"Someone will probably need our bed," I told Margaux, making a drinking sign with my hand.

She rolled her eyes. "Someone's actually already in it."

"Who?"

"Paulie. He was drunk when he got here. Amanda said he barely ate dinner and just wandered into the room and fell asleep on your bed. I think Landon is in there, too."

Chase and I left with just my backpack, holding a few of our things inside. We drove in the rented sedan to the hotel. Looking out the window at moonlight on the wet streets, I broke the quiet and said, "I'm a little nervous."

"Nervous?" Chase asked.

"Yeah. You know. Two gay guys. A hotel in a small southern Armenian town. We're like, four hours from Iran."

"Iran? So?"

"Sorry. I don't know. I'm just nervous."

At the hotel, I tried to read every microexpression on the concierge's face when we checked in. I made a mental note of every person we saw. I wrestled with my imagination, which started to play scenarios out in my head, like the concierge asking us to leave. A guest seeing us, perceiving our gayness somehow, and insisting to the concierge we couldn't be here. Arguments ensuing. Violence.

In the room, with the door locked, I began to relax, though not completely. I whispered to Chase, "You make me so happy," while we lay together on one of the two twin beds in our room.

When we made love, the headboard knocked at the wall, and I couldn't stop fearing we were being monitored in some way by hotel staff. I asked Chase if we could change positions to stop the noise. It took me longer than usual to fall asleep in Chase's arms, fighting myself over the rationality of my fear that someone for some reason might walk in on the two of us naked and asleep in the same bed.

In the morning before we left, I ruffled the covers on the other bed that we hadn't slept in and then kept ruffling them until I was satisfied it looked like Chase and I hadn't slept together at all.

The day after Christmas, after everyone left Margaux's apartment, Chase drove Margaux, Lizzie, and me to the Armenian border with Iran to Agarak where Shereen lived. Curls of barbed wire traveled the length of the border fence.

Behind it, mountains taller than any I'd seen rose straight up into an intimidating wall.

We talked on the drive about the story we'd all recently read of American travelers currently being held in an Iranian prison for what was commonly perceived as an innocent hike over the border.

We stopped in Meghri on the way home at a restaurant that made a Peace Corps favorite, khachapuri. When I thought no Armenians were looking, I cut a piece of the Georgian cheese bread and fed Chase, lightly flicking his bottom lip with my finger.

It was our last night in Kapan. Tomorrow, we'd drive to Yerevan, and the next day we'd drive Chase to the airport for his flight home.

After days filled with so much activity, we decided to cuddle up together alone and watch *It's a Wonderful Life*, which he'd never seen. At the end of it, Chase cried quiet tears and squeezed me tightly when the whole town showed up to help the main character, George.

"I love that you love this movie," Chase said.

After the credits, we lay in the dark talking about friendship, about the people Chase loved back home in Santa Barbara, and how he missed them.

I talked about my family. I'd already told him about coming out, so I talked instead about the Christmas traditions I loved like decorating the Christmas tree or how all my siblings, even as recent as the Christmas before I left, fell asleep in the same room on Christmas Eve watching *The Nightmare Before Christmas*.

When fatigue crept in, I turned into the little spoon position and closed my eyes, focusing my mind on the rise and fall of his chest against my back.

When both of us were still, I thought about how he'd leave in two days. I replayed our trip in my mind. The drive through the valley to Iran, his hand on my thigh for hours, the sunlight on both of us as we rose with the road and fell with it into the valley. Decorating cookies, Chase putting icing on my finger then pressing my finger onto his tongue. His arm around me at Christmas Eve dinner at the hotel. The first night of feeling his warmth on my back in my cottage in Stepanavan.

Somewhere between waking and sleeping while falling into memories, I heard Chase speak. I felt the breath of his words warm against the back of my neck. In the quiet of the room, I pretended to be asleep. I pretended I didn't hear him whisper to me, "I love you."

29

After driving back to Yerevan from Kapan, and after putting Chase into a taxi to the airport, I sat in Phillip's apartment and found that Chase had left his grey American Apparel hoodie in my backpack with a note that said, "Wrap it around you. It will feel like I'm holding you."

I lifted it from the bag to my face. It smelled like him, and I called out to Margaux, who came in from the balcony over the Cascade.

"I feel sad," I told her, and she sat next to me on the bed and hugged me.

"It was just…" I trailed off. "It was just something I dreamed of happening when I decided to come out. Like… Margaux, what a crazy ten days."

"It really was," she said. "I mean, I thought you guys might hit it off, but you, like, really hit it off."

"Yeah," I said, wiping my face.

Now that Chase was on his way home, I'd be going back to Stepanavan in time for my last holiday party with my Armenian coworkers, who'd become my best Armenian friends. Liana had asked me to make sure I was back in time for it. She'd asked enough times that I felt touched it mattered to her that I was there. I felt grateful to be wanted, that she felt I belonged at this Nor Tari party.

Sitting on the bed, holding Chase's hoodie, I didn't want to tell Margaux that Chase told me he loved me.

I let Chase leave without telling him that I wasn't asleep when he said it. I let him leave without saying it back.

I wasn't sure if it felt too soon to hear him tell me he loved me. I wasn't even sure if I knew what it felt like to be in love. What did it mean if I said it back? And what did it mean that he told me when he thought I was asleep?

I missed Chase, thinking of this improbable connection that felt so precious and fragile. Who cared if it was too soon? I'd felt so good for so many days. I hadn't wanted to leave Chase's side once. And I wished he was here now.

And then my Nokia buzzed.

"They canceled my flight," Chase said through the phone. "I don't leave for two more days. Wanna go get Lebanese food?"

I paused, breathing in deeply while my jaw tightened. I felt pulled in two different directions.

Then, in that instant, I chose him over my Armenian friends, the ones I worked with, who'd welcomed me and made me part of their community. My last holiday party with them was tomorrow night. If I stayed with Chase for two more days, I would miss it. But wasn't that what you're supposed to do when you're in love? Chase had come in like a shooting star, one that still seemed to be shooting over a part of my heart that I'd hidden in the dark for so long. Wasn't his canceled flight a sign I should stay?

"So, you won't be here for the party, Brent jan?" Liana asked when I told her I wouldn't be home for two more days. I could hear the disappointment in the slight rise in her voice.

"No," I said.

"Apsos," she said. "Shaat apsos." *What a shame.*

"Please tell everyone I am going to miss them," I requested. "Tell them I'm sorry."

"I will," she said. "This is your last party with us. They are really going to miss you there, too."

My heart sank a bit, and that night as we walked through Yerevan's gift shops, Chase buying presents for his friends in Santa Barbara, I carried a sadness I couldn't quite name. I wished I didn't have to choose between being with Chase or showing up for my coworkers who had given me such a feeling of belonging with them. Walking from shop to shop I fantasized that I could just tell them about Chase, could bring him to Stepanavan for these extra nights so Artavan could teach him how to dance like an Armenian man, so that Tirayr could give a toast to our love, so Chase could meet them and see them the way I did, could understand why I felt honored to be loved by them.

Or could I have just been honest with Liana? Could I have come out to her? Could I have told her that I was gay and, for the first time, I was being swept up into a love I didn't understand, love like a wave and me, just learning to swim?

I could do none of those things. So, I stayed in Yerevan to hold on to Chase, making a memory with him instead of with my Armenian friends.

On New Year's Eve, Chase's last night in the city, the two of us and Margaux left the streets of Yerevan early, returning to Phillip's apartment to watch a movie and then go to bed. Margaux fell asleep on the couch, and Chase and I left to the bedroom and made love one last time.

When we'd settled down, lying against each other, our skin still moist with sweat, I told him.

I pulled his hand to my chest. "I heard you," I said quietly.

"You heard me?" His eyes scanned my face suddenly for clues.

"I heard you," I said. "The other night."

He didn't say anything. His eyes betrayed what was dawning on him.

"I was awake," I said.

Pleasant, hopeful surprise eased onto his face. "I wasn't sure. I thought maybe you were. But then you didn't say anything. You didn't move."

"I know."

He waited, watching me. In the dark, the streetlight coming in from the window panes lit him up in geometric shapes.

"I love you, too," I said.

He smiled, and I watched his tears reflecting the light.

"I love you," he said, tears starting to roll.

He pulled me against him. We kissed. When I pulled back, I told him, "I know it's a bit nuts. It's been less than two weeks."

"I know," he said, "but it's true. It just is. I love you."

Our eyes wouldn't leave each other as if we had nothing else in the world to look at.

"I haven't said a lot of things I feel," I told him. "For a lot of my life, I didn't say things I really wanted to say. And so, even though it's crazy, I just want to say it. I want to say what I feel. I love you. My whole body is filled up with thoughts of you. I feel consumed suddenly by you, by wanting you and wanting to be close to you."

Chase ran his fingers through my hair and over my cheek. "We can do this, you know," Chase said. "We can love each other. I'll call you. I can get on Skype. We can email every day."

A tear rolled then, falling sideways over the slopes of my face to the sheets. "I'm going to miss you. Like, a lot."

"I'll miss you, too."

"I'll miss holding you," I went on as if I couldn't stop, his hand stroking my cheek while I talked. "I'll miss reaching over to hold your hand in the car. I'll miss trying to steal away into alleys to make out. I'll miss holding you at night."

He kissed me again. "Maybe you could move to California when you come home."

"Maybe," I whispered.

Our voices went quiet then, kissing each other and then pulling back, looking at each other's bodies, running our fingertips over each other until we both went still and fell asleep.

PART 3

30

I left fresh prints in the untouched snow between Naira and Vazgen's front gate and the door to my cottage. I'd missed the first big snow of the new year. I'd missed it blanketing everything in Stepanavan, changing the height of buildings, the softness of cement sidewalks, the sureness of the ground, of the streets the cars now could slide on.

I'd missed, too, the holiday party with my coworkers they'd planned for Nor Tari. And on top of that, when I called Vazgen and Naira to tell them I was staying in Yerevan, without telling them about Chase, they told me that I missed their family's Nor Tari party that they'd hosted at their house. They thought I'd be home for it, but I wasn't. I heard "apsos," the Armenian way to say, "*What a shame*," so many times that it started to sting.

Naira, hearing me arrive from Yerevan and walk through the garden, called to me across the snow, "Brent jan, *you've come?*"

I turned to the sound of her voice. "*I'm here*," I said, my tone lifting at the sight of my friend. "*Can I come visit?*"

"Lav, Brent jan. Ari. Josh kutenk." *Come. Let's eat.*

I didn't even step inside my cottage but simply tossed my bags in the door and turned back to my footsteps, retracing them through the snow to the porch and then to the Naira and Vazgen's living room door.

"Dzun yekav," Ani called to me before running along the two long tables Naira and Vazgen had set up in the living room. It was now January 2, and from now until January 7, Naira and Vazgen would keep the tradition of having beautifully adorned tables spread with dishes and dishes of traditional Armenian holiday food.

"Hats ker, Brent jan," Naira ordered me, pushing a plate into my hand and pointing to the spread. I filled my plate with dolmas, blinchik, pickles, sour cream, lavash, and rice pilaf.

I sat at one of the long tables across from Naira while Vazgen made his way in from the kitchen with a loud, "Akhbers," that warmed my heart. "Bari galust Hayastan." *Welcome to Armenia.* A joke about my being gone for so long.

While I ate, I told them half of everything, drinking from a glass of Coca-Cola that Naira refilled each time I emptied it.

"In Tatev, they have a new machine," I said, struggling to find certain Armenian words. *"… big… how do I say it… for going from one mountain to the next over a big space…"*

Nazeli quietly sat in a chair next to her mom, already listening to my travel story, her six-year-old face barely rising high enough to see over the table. "Train?" Her English was new, and she rolled the R in "train."

"Train-i nman," I said. *"Like a train, but with one car on a rope.* Gondola?"

"Aaaaah," Naira and Nazeli said at once, recognizing a word I thought they wouldn't.

"It was mostly made of glass, and you could see in every way you looked…" I loved the way they looked at me, the way I felt like I could sit here and talk with them for hours, the way I felt honored by their curiosity over my trip and the smiles

they gave at the details I shared. And at the same time, I felt scared to let them know anything about Chase, the brightest part by far of my trip. I didn't tell them how, when I stood next to Chase in the gondola in Tatev, I hugged his arm, both because the height scared me and because I felt awe for the village on the cliff, its small buildings surrounded by dramatic crags like a city in the clouds. I didn't tell them how on one of those cliffsides, surrounded by mountains and clouds, Chase and I had clung to each other in a long kiss.

And I wanted to tell them. But I breezed through stories of Christmas, the foods we made and even the drive to the Armenia-Iran border. When I didn't mention my friends, Naira asked, *"The boy and the girl that were here, you went with them?"*

"They were there," I told her. *"We traveled together. The girl lives in Kapan. The boy went home."* And then, careful not to change my tone and to pause just the right amount of time, I changed the subject. *"I missed my family. I missed my family in America. And I missed you all, my family in Stepanavan."*

"Apres, Brent jan," Vazgen said, and then, *"A toast to our brother and his homecoming,"* and together we drank.

I struggled through the week to celebrate Nor Tari with my coworkers. I texted many of them to visit their houses but missed them as they left to visit other friends. I made it to Vigen's house and Artavan's, walking long walks in the snow to arrive at their homes for their versions of holiday favorites like dolma and baklava.

The days became lonely. I walked to the empty World Vision office to read emails and scan the new Facebook feature, the News Feed, which was filled with updates from my friends in the US. And I lived for Chase's emails. He sent the first as soon as he was back at his home in Santa Barbara.

"I find myself sitting here," he wrote, "still so surprised that I'm here with love in my heart for a man who makes me laugh, who makes me light up. I keep looking at pictures from my camera. And there he is, the handsome man I fell in love with, wishing for the day I get to hold him again."

Chase and I wrote sweet things to each other every day. But as full of love as I felt, I had an ache, a disconnection with Stepanavan, as if the combination of being gone from this town for so long and hiding my new love had changed something. Or perhaps just brought it to the surface. I would leave the World Vision office, walk by all the businesses closed for the holiday, and make pizza rolls before sitting down to watch season after season of *Friends*.

On the last day of the Nor Tari week, I called Karine, my coworker who'd become my friend, to see if I could visit her home. She worked at World Vision translating the letters Armenian children wrote to their sponsors in England. Over the last year, she was the only person in the office I ate lunch with nearly every day.

She wasn't home, she told me. But when she found out I had no plans for Christmas Eve, which for Armenia lands on January 6, she invited me to come stay with her family.

"Really?" I said.

"Yes," Karine replied. She told me that her husband, Hovannes was back from Russia and her parents were coming, too. "You will not be alone on Christmas," she said.

On January 6, I packed a small bag with overnight things and set out on the icy sidewalks to make my way across town to Hovannes and Karine's house. My bootlaces came loose, and I stopped in front of the closed vegetable stand, removing my gloves to bend down and tie my shoes.

As I stood, my knee hurt with a pain so bright I cried out before thinking, my yelp echoing in the quiet, empty streets. As I tried to stretch out my leg, it seemed to pop, and suddenly, the pain disappeared almost completely. This had happened a couple of times when I'd taken up running in Stepanavan. The second time it happened, the pain lingered long enough into the afternoon that I simply stopped running at all.

Worried it would happen again, I walked softly and deliberately on the ice, making the long walk across town much longer.

When I arrived, sweat lingered under my coat and sweaters, which I peeled off before greeting my friends and presenting two chocolate Kinder Eggs filled with small toys for each of Karine's boys. Clattering dishes in the kitchen signaled the dinner preparations as Karine's mother worked on a Christmas Eve meal. Karine's father and Hovannes sat in the living room, watching the boys eat chocolate shells.

Snow fell after the sun went down, and white flakes sparkled in the porch lights while I helped Karine and her mother make cookies in the shape of moons.

At dinner, Hovannes made a toast to our health in the new year. I followed up with another toast for friendship.

In bed in their oldest son's room, I heard the family shuffling up and down the hall, getting ready for bed with the two boys while whispering to them of Zmer Papik and his impending arrival with gifts.

In the morning, I heard the kids rush by the door to my room and rose from the bed quietly to join them in their living room where the boys opened Christmas gifts. Afterward, I made them pancakes, showing Karine's mother my measurements for flour, milk, and butter. Just after I served them, it started to snow again. After we ate, we all put on our winter clothes and followed the kids outside to make snowmen before devolving into a snowball fight.

When Karine had taken too many hits, she stopped to catch her breath under a shelter of thick, winter-barren grapevine. I joined her, thanking her for welcoming me for Christmas. "I'm glad you're here, Brent jan," Karine said.

"Me, too," I said, healing a bit from a Nor Tari full of missed connections with my Armenian friends. And then I added, "Thank you for making sure I wasn't alone."

~ ~ ~

My routine finally resumed when offices and business reopened for their first work week of the year. I went back to meeting with Liana and TDFs about projects that could happen in villages in the region. And every morning, I walked in to find emails from Chase. In one, he explained why he didn't text me back much.

On Gchat he said, "Text messages cost me seventy-five cents to send and twenty cents to read yours, but I'm trying to figure out if I can get Gchat to go to my phone... without actually telling people I'm online because I don't want everyone I know to be able to text me at school."

I imagined that he must have a smartphone. Even though I'd only ever seen one, apparently they'd become a big deal at home. I tried to imagine an iPod that was also a phone and Chase trying to figure out how to get Gchat to work on it.

I messaged him back. "So, when could I get online with you and just talk and talk without worrying so much about the time difference. I mean, I could talk to you every day." I typed out these words, still always watching closely to see if anyone might walk behind me, might read my words to this new love across the planet.

"I think about you all day," he said. "I'm not sure when the best time to talk would be. I'm not sure I could do every day. And nights are hard because I'm usually eating dinner with friends."

I wanted any time with him and as much of it as I could get. "Totally," I typed. "I could do early mornings. Or I could stay late at the office." I immediately regretted the offer, knowing the latter meant I'd miss my after-work coffee and nardi with Naira and Vazgen.

"I don't think so," Chase replied. "I need my mornings alone."

I counted time zones backward in my head and then offered, "What about when you get home from work? I could come into the office early."

"That could work."

Then, no words. I waited, watching the white space on Gchat and my own cursor blinking at me like a question. Then he replied, "It would have to be kind of early for you, I think. I get home at 4:30 and eat dinner by 6:30, and I'd like to have some space in there to decompress from my day."

Something about that stung. I'd move anything to talk to him. Decompress with me or something, I wanted to say. Just give me a time.

We settled on talking every other day at 4:30 a.m. Armenia time. I would have said every day, but I wasn't sure how I could explain a sudden daily Skype call that early to my coworkers. I thought every other day was somehow more explainable. I could tell anyone who asked that I just really missed my family. I'd been away from them for so long.

And so, on Monday, Wednesday, and Friday, I woke at 4 a.m. in the dark cold of my house. I wouldn't turn on the heater and got dressed in the freezing air. I put Yaktrax on my hiking boots and walked the icy roads and sidewalks, the scraping of my shoes the only sound in town, bouncing in the night between closed shops and unlit houses, my body moving in and out of the light of streetlamps.

Chase filled my mind on these walks. I thought of him bicycling home from his job teaching middle school, past a beach I'd never seen to an apartment where he'd sign on and wait for my name to appear with a green dot next to it. My heart would leap, and I breathed deeply the winter air, this romance like a feast I'd waited my whole life to eat.

In the office, I'd walk past the security guard, who at first needed me to explain why I was there, to which I said I was calling my family. I'd make my way upstairs to an empty office where I thought the security guard couldn't hear me and talk to Chase for an hour or so about anything at all. He'd stay on, sometimes cooking dinner with me on video, introducing me to his roommate or to friends he'd invited over.

Chase never stayed on past 6:30 a.m., so I'd linger upstairs in the dark office writing on my blog or web surfing until the sun rose and the rest of my coworkers arrived.

My work days started to feel scattered to me. I became tired, asking Ayda for extra coffees. Weeks went by like this with very early mornings followed by days of meandering work with no projects really getting off the ground.

I started to get antsy. Without active projects, I wasn't going out with Vigen or Artavan or the other TDFs to work in the villages. I felt listless like I was losing touch with my Armenian friends at the office. I started to feel shame about being so unfocused at work, my energy and enthusiasm anchored in my calls to Chase in the dark early morning.

I wanted to talk to Liana about it. I wanted to tell her why I felt disconnected. I even wanted to apologize for what I felt was wasted time during all these weeks that went by without a significant project to work on.

I wanted to tell her that I was gay and that I'd fallen in love, that I was distracted by it, swept up in it. And perhaps I wanted relief. I wanted to tell someone in Stepanavan what was happening. I wanted a friend who would understand, who I could talk to about how much I felt like I had to hide from my coworkers. I wanted to tell her what it was like to hide my computer screen from Yeraz in case she could read my messages to Chase and find out the truth about me. I wanted to talk about life in Stepanavan in the closet with someone who knew both me and this town.

I played out scenarios over a few days, running them in my head. I thought about coming out to Liana. I knew the worst scenario would be that she hated my being gay, that this fact alone would upend her opinion of me.

And then, I rationalized my worst-case scenario. If things got too hard because I came out, I felt close enough to the end of my service that maybe I could get through the hurt of having to leave.

After lunch on a sunny day, I asked Liana for time to talk. I sat in the same black chair across from her desk where I'd sat to hatch project ideas with her, where we'd laughed together about our family stories, where we'd become friends. And this time in the chair, I started talking to her right away, beginning with an apology for my work being scattered and my mind being elsewhere.

I rattled on, Liana listening and gently rolling a pen between her fingers while I talked. "I've had a lot going on," I finished, and then so quickly that I couldn't back out, I said, "I'm gay."

The expression on her face didn't change, but I caught an involuntary widening of her eyes. Before she could respond, I went on, "I fell in love over Christmas. That's where I was. I was falling in love with someone while I was gone. That's who I talk to in the mornings. My family is not supportive, and I think about them all the time. So, I'm really nervous about going home."

Liana's eyes barely moved. She seemed to be studying my face while considering the tone of the room so carefully. She changed almost nothing about the way she sat, the way she looked at me, the volume or pitch of her voice.

"Okay," And then she changed her voice just enough to let me know I was safe. As imperceptible of a moment as the first peek of the sun at sunrise. She breathed in deeply but not out of rhythm. Her shoulders relaxed. She smiled but only just slightly. Her eyes warmed. She held the room there and then said, "I knew something was going on when you missed Nor Tari."

My breath left my body, and as it did, I uttered, "Yeah."

"I actually thought," Liana said, "maybe he's fallen in love. Love makes you crazy. You forget everything in your life but the person you love, and you can't think."

"Oh my god," I said. "Yes. Like everything else just falls out of your head."

Liana giggled, just barely. She shifted in her chair. "You know, I think maybe I'm falling in love, too."

"Oh my god, really?" And then, with the relief that comes with shared vulnerability, I felt like I could lean in, which I did, like girlfriends talking about boyfriends.

"He's someone I didn't know I would feel this way about," she said. "And he says he wants to marry me."

"Do you want to marry him?"

"I think so." She paused. "But you know, I don't know love well. Love has not come easy to me."

"Are you kidding?" And I relished this, a chance to praise her, powered by gratitude and admiration for my friend who'd invited me to this life in Armenia. "Liana. You're beautiful. You're successful. You're fun to be around. Where's the line? There must be a line of men."

She smiled and rolled her eyes. "There isn't. But this one. He makes me feel different. Maybe I'm falling in love like you."

I burst into a laugh. "Lian jan. I highly recommend love, but maybe don't fall in love with someone on the other side of the planet like I did."

She joined my laughter. "Maybe you're right."

We broke eye contact, and I began to stand up. But then she said, "You know, I thought you were going to tell me this on the night of the khash."

I met her eyes, mine surprised, maybe a little delighted. "Really?"

"Yes."

"I was actually going to tell you, but I was scared."

"I thought you would. I wondered why you came to talk to me on that night, but I thought, 'Okay. Well, whatever it is, maybe he'll tell me another time.'"

"I was very drunk that night, Liana," I said. "That was a great night, though. I love being part of this team." I thought about it for a moment. "I wished I could just come out to everyone. But I couldn't do it."

Liana's smile turned then, a sad look coming over her face. "I don't think you could have, Brent jan."

"You don't?" I said. I felt my heart deflate a little.

"No, you couldn't have. You shouldn't," she said. "It would be too hard for people to accept at our office. And in Stepanavan, really. I don't think you would have been able to do any work here."

"Okay. Yeah." And I found myself then in a swirling current, the one that brought Liana and me together, and the one that kept me and everyone else I'd come to love in Stepanavan apart.

31

The end of January brought on the real beginning of me considering the end of my Peace Corps service, and the changes around me started sooner than I expected.

Not long after I came out to her, Liana announced she'd been promoted to a new position in the World Vision office in Yerevan. She also announced her engagement to Yaren, a man I remembered visiting Stepanavan, who had greeted me and everyone else with kind handshakes and warm smiles.

Karine, I was told both by Liana, would be my new counterpart.

I'd barely adjusted to this news when Yeraz told me she'd be leaving for Russia. Her husband, who'd not been able to find work for over a year, finally did what so many Armenians do without a job; he answered an invitation to work in Russia.

At her going away party, through tears, I told Yeraz, "I would not have made it this far without you. You never made me feel embarrassed about any question I ever had to ask. Anytime I needed to know a word, you never made me feel like I was bothering you when I asked for a translation. And every project I've thought about doing, if you weren't helping me, I felt like you were cheering me on."

"Oh, harevans," she said. *My neighbor.* And I was touched to see tears in her eyes. Her desk stayed empty for the rest of my time in Armenia.

Not long after that, Kristine, my European volunteer service friend, invited me to a party at her apartment in Vanadzor. Shortly after I arrived, I crouched down to change the music playing on her computer, and when I tried to stand again, I couldn't. I screamed in pain, and Kristine and a host of other European service volunteers rushed to me, carrying me to the couch, my knee unable to straighten. Kristine ran downstairs while I called Dr. Torosyan, the Peace Corps doctor. Kristine returned holding a cellophane bag filled with snow that she packed around my leg.

"Brent jan, you are saying you just stood up and it hurt?" Dr. Torosyan asked through the phone. It was Saturday night, and though her voice was professional, I could hear an incredulous tone in the way she spoke. She'd always been sharp. She dressed sharply. Her jet-black hair fell in a perfect bob, slicing the air in front of her eyes. She was kind, but she suffered no fools. And she'd seen Peace Corps volunteers behave badly, calling her in various broken and drunken states.

"Yes," I told her. "I can't bend it now."

"You need to take ibuprofen, Brent jan," she said.

Pain rang up my leg to my brain. "I can't stand. I can't walk. This is not something for ibuprofen."

"Are you in a safe place?" Dr. Torosyan asked.

"Yes," I said. I looked at Kristine who sat next to me, waiting to hear what the doctor said and how she might help execute the doctor's instructions for care.

"Take ibuprofen now. I will send a Peace Corps vehicle for you tomorrow."

The next morning, in the back of the Peace Corps Lada, I rode with my foot propped up on my hiking backpack and a fresh cellophane bag of snow pressed and packed around my knee. By the time I saw Dr. Torosyan, I felt almost disappointed that the pain had almost completely subsided. There had been no popping or clicking like before, but I could bend it again, even walk with caution.

I stayed for two days in a closet-sized room in the Peace Corps medical office in Yerevan. During the first, Dr. Torosyan tapped her fingers against her desk and asked me how much I'd had to drink at the party. I told her the truth, that I hadn't drunk anything though I'd planned to. She circled back to the question again later, certain I'd hurt myself while drunk.

When the MRI report came back showing no injury, the Peace Corps doctor sent in a male doctor to counsel me. Certain I was faking this injury to go home, Dr. Torosyan thought I might be more comfortable confessing the truth to a man.

He closed the door behind him when he entered my tiny room. The fluorescent light bounced off his bald head. "You can quit if you want to," he told me. "You don't have to make up an injury. It's okay to go home if you need to."

I fought back fumes. This stranger didn't know me. He didn't know that I'd come to love living in Armenia.

For so long, I dreamed of the feeling I had now in Armenia, this belonging I started to find in this place I didn't know existed only two years ago. I loved my friends at World Vision, though now two of my closest friends were leaving. I savored my walk home, the welcoming shouts of "akhbers" when I arrived at the vegetable stand, the warm lavash always handed to me when I stopped at the bakery to talk to bakers as they tossed sheets of lavash dough, stretching it over their arms. I adored Naira and Vazgen. I cherished nardi games and coffee in their kitchen that marked the end of each day. I loved hearing the giggles of Ani and Nazeli, who played in the garden outside my window. I loved my work. I loved that I could speak Armenian now, that I could travel and talk to strangers. I could teach in Armenian, lead community meetings. I could tell people I loved them in Armenian, that I was grateful for them and the way they'd given me a sense that I was meant to be here in some way.

And furthermore, I'd fallen in love with Chase. Keeping that secret from Naira and Vazgen and from my friends at World Vision hurt me. It made me feel a distance from them I longed to cross, to be fully myself with them.

I wasn't lying about the pain I felt in my knee. And I wanted the *opposite* of going home. I longed to fully belong in Armenia. I wished more than anything in those days that I could simply come out, live as myself, love who I loved, and enjoy this new country that had, in a way, come to feel like home.

At the end of two days in the Peace Corps office, I Skyped with Chase and filled him in on the days and my confusion about what happened to my knee.

"I really couldn't stand up," I told him.

He smiled softly through the screen. "I believe you, Brent."

We caught up on his roller derby team, the new relationship between his roommate Rafael and their mutual friend Sophie, and his plans for his spring break in March.

"I wish I hadn't promised my friend I'd spend spring break with her. If I didn't have plans already, I'd just come back to Armenia."

I felt a twist, a bit of hope. I'd only taken one weeklong vacation since I'd been here. I had saved up thirty-five days of time off and had no plans to use them. "Well," I said. "If you feel like you can afford a plane ticket, I've got a ton of time off. What if I came to Santa Barbara?"

The next morning, Chase sent a flight on Aeroflot to my email inbox, leaving in March.

Zoe cheered for me over the phone when I told her.

"My god," she said. "Brent, I'm starting to get jealous. This is a serious love affair."

Margaux told me she was jealous, too, but only because she felt like she could use a vacation.

And after worrying over it for a while, I told my mom. I felt like if I was going to be back in the US, she should know. This meant telling her about Chase. Telling her that I'd fallen in love over Christmas. And that I would fly to him.

I waited until I was back in Stepanavan and then waited a whole extra day to build up the courage.

My pulse raced while the phone rang. And after I told her everything, she went silent. I paced over the tile in my pink cottage, the windows dark with night.

"Why would you do that?" she said.

"What?" I replied. "Visit Chase? I love him, Mom."

"I don't believe it," she said.

"What do you mean you don't believe it?" I asked.

And she dug her feet into the ground. She told me that men don't fall in love with other men. She said that I probably thought I was in love, but God doesn't let that happen.

We kept on for a while. I could feel my temperature rise and my tone get tense. I didn't want this. I was in love. This was a shadow, this worry about my parents, their judgment, the fear about where I would land after Peace Corps.

I didn't know if my parents would want me in their home, knowing how much they didn't want me to be who I was. And now this disdain for someone I'd just learned to love.

"And honestly, if you have time to take off from Peace Corps, why wouldn't you come here?" Mom asked.

The conversation grew wider with me telling her that at some point she might actually meet a man I'm in love with.

"I won't be able to sit in a room with you and any person like that who you're dating," she told me.

"Mom. Mom!" I nearly screamed. "It doesn't hurt. Anyone. Not anyone."

She went quiet. "You keep saying this doesn't hurt anyone. But it's hurting me."

The next day, the Peace Corps doctor called me.

I took the call and walked outside the World Vision office where, under a bright, clear sky, the white snow sparkled in piles covering up park benches and flowerbeds.

"Brent jan," Dr. Torosyan said. "I have news." While she talked, I looked toward the statue of Stepan, where snow covered his shoulders while he looked past the canyon into an infinite distance.

"It is Peace Corps policy to send all medical test records to Washington," she said. "They have another doctor examine them. I'm sorry to tell you this, Brent jan, but they have found that you have a torn meniscus."

She paused, and in the pause, it felt like a wind left my chest.

"Okay," I said. "What is a meniscus?"

"It's a piece of cartilage in the knee. Yours is torn. And they have said that you need to return to the US as soon as possible to have surgery."

The bottom dropped out of my stomach.

"Surgery?"

"Yes," she said.

"And I have to leave soon?"

"The day after tomorrow. Tonight, you should pack. The office here will buy the ticket and send it to you. Tomorrow you come to the Peace Corps office in Yerevan. Then the day after tomorrow, you fly to DC."

"Sorry," I said. "This is coming on very fast. I have a torn meniscus in my knee?"

"Yes."

"And I need to have surgery to fix it?"

"Yes."

I considered whether I should ask if she believed me now and why they couldn't have diagnosed it in Yerevan. I quickly decided that would be fruitless. I was being medically evacuated. "Medevacked" we called it in our Peace Corps circles. It had happened to one other volunteer I knew of who'd had to go to Thailand for gallbladder surgery.

"And I need to fly home the day after tomorrow," I repeated.

"Yes," she said, "and, Brent jan, in this situation, it is important for you to know that they may decide to terminate your service early depending on the results of the surgery and the necessary recovery time. If your healing time is longer than forty-five days, you will not return to Armenia."

"Wait," and I felt tears suddenly come into my eyes. "Like, not return here. To Stepanavan."

"It is possible, Brent jan." She kept saying my name in a way meant to soothe me.

I thought of my body. Of going unconscious and the slicing of it during surgery. I thought of this town, the place I stood right now, and that tomorrow I might have to leave it and not return. I thought of Chase and the ticket in my name indicating a flight I should be taking in just a few weeks from Yerevan to Los Angeles, where this beautiful man who told me every day that he loved me would be sweeping me off my feet at the airport and driving me home to his bed and his California town and his life.

"Sorry," I said. I knew she could hear me choking back tears. "It's just a lot."

"I know, Brent jan." She sighed. "This is life."

32

I had to take two flights on the way to the US. The first, from Yerevan to Paris. The second from Paris to Washington, DC. From Yerevan to Paris, I listened to the voices of Armenians around me, sometimes catching their words, often simply comforted by the sound of the consonants we don't use in American English—the vibrating air on the back of the throat, the scraping r-like sound made by pushing air over the arch of your tongue and the edge of your hard palate. Hearing those sounds on the plane, I could instantly feel myself moving farther away from my life in Armenia and simultaneously nowhere near the life I left in the US.

I wrote in my journal, "Americans are so loud." I couldn't understand the difference in sheer volume I heard on this daytime flight from Paris to DC.

The man sitting next to me asked me what I was doing in Paris. I told him I was simply on a layover on my way to DC for medical leave from Peace Corps.

"My sister was in the Peace Corps," he said. "She spoke the language perfectly, and she got to know the locals."

Like a frisbee from nowhere, a woman across the aisle interjected, "And it didn't matter. Did it?" she snarled.

"It absolutely mattered," my seat neighbor clapped back.

She returned, "They see an American, and they just see walking money."

What a colossal asshole, I thought.

I was, however, happy to sit in a soft seat. I was happy to be served a hot meal, happy to peel back the food tray's aluminum, watch the condensation roll from it onto steamed vegetables, couscous, and chicken. Someone had added grill marks on the chicken breast for style, I assumed, and I was grateful for the touch. I was grateful for seemingly endless water and movies just released in American theaters served to me on the seatback's tiny screen.

"This sucks," Chase said.

I thought of those words, how they had comforted me like we were on the same team. Then, the comfort I felt flipped over when he followed with, "That ticket was expensive. Almost a thousand dollars, Brent. Can you get it refunded? I don't want to be out that money."

"Okay," I'd said. I'd wanted comfort for this journey I was taking alone, but it was replaced with guilt that swarmed me as I thought about his teacher's salary in Santa Barbara, one of the most expensive places to live in America.

"That was too selfish of me," he emailed me later. He followed in another email, "I'm going to spend the next week thinking about how to make your time in SB amazing." He sent me a photo of a handwritten list he was making of things he wanted to do with me in California, his hand over a section titled, "Sexy Stuff."

While the plane descended into Washington Dulles, I thought of two things.

First, I thought that being medevacked wasn't how I thought I'd return to the US. I felt broken and out of place, like I should be in Armenia or Santa Barbara or Texas, even. Not DC.

And I thought about the emails I'd written home to tell my family about my surgery. I told them I didn't know the details. A torn meniscus can sometimes heal itself, the internet told me. And often, it's just a bit of cartilage hanging off that can easily be trimmed. This made me think of eating the khash and chewing tiny bits of cow cartilage that hung from the ankle in my bowl.

My oldest sister, Lisa, immediately told me she didn't have PTO to use to come see me in DC. She said she was thrilled I'd be only an hour's time difference away. She promised to call, and said, "I am secretly hoping your healing time will take longer than forty-five days so you will come home early! But I know you'd be sad not to finish your time in Armenia."

My brother and parents both wanted every detail necessary to try and plan their own trips to DC. My dad told me this in an email asking what my hotel address would be because there were four possible airports to fly into, and he wanted to plan his route from the airport to the hotel. I didn't even know they were considering coming and was so caught off guard I wrote back in all caps, "YOU'RE SERIOUSLY CONSIDERING COMING?" which is the email equivalent of a spit take.

I wasn't sure I wanted them to come. I was afraid of surgery, afraid of pain, and afraid of negotiating our relationship with only one good leg.

And as for my brother, I hadn't come out to him at all. We'd emailed during the past year, but the thought of him physically in front of me in a hotel room scared me. I considered keeping my gayness a secret even though now I felt willing to tell strangers.

When I landed, a taxi took me straight to a high-rise larger than any building I'd seen in nearly two years. Inside the Peace Corps headquarters office, a woman named Janet with silver-rimmed aviator glasses and spiky blonde hair told me I'd be staying at a hotel in Georgetown, that I'd get thirty dollars a day in per diem, and not to ask any of the other Peace Corps volunteers at the hotel what they were here for.

"If they tell you, it's fine," she told me over her desk, "but some people are here for very sensitive things. So, please don't ask."

For the next forty-eight hours, I settled into a room with two queen beds and central heating, which I turned up to fight the wet cold outside.

I left the hotel to find takeout and met a few Peace Corps volunteers who were also coming and going. I kept Janet's rule and didn't ask anyone about their injuries. Some were obvious because they came with crutches or a wheelchair. A surprising number of women walked around without any injury I could see. One woman who'd come from Botswana invited me to her room. She brought out a yellow jerrycan, offering me a glass of banana liquor. She held out the drink to me, and her arms and face were covered with red boils.

The day before the surgery, I met my surgeon in a brownstone building. I felt lost in his office and sank into the leather chair. I looked up at a screen where he pointed at images from my knee.

"See this," the surgeon said. "Your meniscus is torn down the center. It's the best kind of tear to have because we don't have to trim anything off. But the recovery is a lot longer."

In my hotel room, I stared out the window and watched people walk up and down the street while I called Chase.

"The surgeon said the recovery could take more than forty-five days," I told him. "And if I don't heal in forty-five days, I can't go back to Armenia."

"What?" he said.

"I know," I tried to reassure him.

"Oh my god," he said. "I'm sorry. I'm just really, really annoyed."

Annoyed? I thought. *I'm about to go under and be sliced open and then heal for a month and a half. Maybe more. And he's annoyed.*

"I'll figure it out," I told him. "I'll go after my surgery. I could change it. If I can make it back to Armenia, I could just come later." This felt like a stretch even to me. After forty-five days it would be the beginning of April. I was supposed to finish my service in Armenia in July.

"Yeah, okay," Chase said. "I hope your surgery goes well. I love you."

I ended the night with phone calls home. I felt like I had some kind of calling campaign to do before going to the hospital in the morning. I was so tired my nerves stayed at a simmer.

I started with my parents. Dad wished me luck. He told me he loved me and that he wanted me to call after surgery.

Mom cried into the phone.

"We just can't come, honey," she said. "It's just too expensive." I could hear her voice trembling, like she was torn between what she wanted to say and what she actually said. "But we love you so much. You'll be all right. We know you will."

I felt like I needed to come out to my brother and oldest sister before surgery. *In case I die*, I thought.

Lisa made it so easy it was almost anticlimactic. She'd had a hard time through high school and only a couple of years earlier had gone through a divorce. "I don't feel like such a black sheep anymore." She laughed.

I couldn't tell my youngest sister. Macey was thirteen. I wanted to protect her from having to take a stand, something I knew she'd feel pressured to do because we were so similar. I knew what it was like to grow up in our small Texas town. She'd think there were sides to take, and she'd feel like she'd have to tell me what side she was on. I didn't want her to say something she couldn't take back.

So, I ended the night of phone calls with my brother. He, too, said flights were just too expensive for him to come.

"There's something else," I said to him over the phone. "It feels weird to talk about. But I'm about to go under, you know. So, I'm just going to tell you. I'm gay."

And then silence. I watched strangers walk silently down the sidewalk outside, a cold drizzle starting to collect on their coats.

"Okay," he finally said. "I'll always love you. But I think I'll need some time, you know."

And I thought, *Time. I could use some time.* Though, in that moment, I wasn't sure what I would have done with it.

33

I woke up in a stupor, pain soaring through me with meds that held that pain at a distance, like the sensation you get when you're under an umbrella in a rainstorm. I couldn't see my leg under the sheets. With one hand, I searched for it and found straps and metal bars. I called a nurse, and when she came, I asked her how to pee. She handed me a plastic jar with a curved neck. She showed me how to use it and held it while I rolled over on my side and peed into it. I heard her empty it into the bathroom's toilet. She told me to press my call button when I needed to fill it again.

The drugs were powerful. I had no sense of time. I fell asleep and woke up in what felt like short increments of both. Flashes of longing would peek through my haze of drugs. A wish for my mother to stand over me to rub my hair. A fantasy where I heard Chase ask for a chair to sleep in so he could be near me. At one point, I woke almost fully, felt the fantasies evaporate into the reality of my empty, dark room, and wept quietly. I longed for the nurse visits, so grateful for a human to visit me in the dark. Tears pooled in my ears because I was too afraid to turn on my side alone.

In the morning, when a grey light from the overcast sky outside made its way into the room, Janet from Peace Corps Washington DC headquarters came by to check on me.

"You're looking good," she said, her bracelets jangling when she reached up to pat my healthy leg. She asked if I wanted to stay in the hospital overnight or go back to the hotel. She said the cost was irrelevant, that insurance covered either option. I opted to stay another night, afraid that this pain and dysphoria would be tripled if I was alone in the hotel in Georgetown, not even a nurse to bring me food or empty my pee jug.

The next morning, I felt more coherent. They'd backed off the drugs. I slept more between waking up in pain.

And then, John appeared in the doorway. John with his burly hands. He'd shaved off his chin strap. I missed it instantly.

After he'd left Armenia with the rest of the A-16s, John moved to DC. I'd emailed him about my surgery. Seeing him in the doorway, I cried again. "Thank you," I told him. "Really. I needed someone." He spent an hour with me before he got up to return to work.

"When you can walk, I'll show you around DC," he said.

When Janet returned, she asked the nurse if I could leave and told her that she'd drive me to the hotel to recuperate. The nurse told me then that I couldn't take the brace off. Not even to put on pants.

"It says 'under no circumstances' in the discharge notes," she said.

My straight-leg jeans weren't going over the brace. Pantsless, I waited for Janet while she searched for over an hour looking in the hotel gift shops and asking staff until finally she found a pair of extra-large scrub pants from a different hospital in the lost and found.

When she returned, I pulled on the green T-shirt Noah had given me and covered it with Chase's grey hoodie. Janet then pushed me out of the hospital in a wheelchair, my drugs and my crutches in my lap.

At the hotel, Janet rolled me to my room and helped me get to the couch. She left and then returned with groceries—frozen burritos, sandwich bread and meat, Honey Nut Cheerios and milk. She brought my computer to the coffee table in front of the couch and plugged it into the wall. She asked me if I needed anything else. When I said no, she returned a motherly smile.

"I've asked some of the other volunteers who've been in the hotel to check up on you over the next few days. So, you'll probably hear a knock at the door."

The next few days blurred by.

Most days, I called Mom, who asked for all the details: the hotel room, my phone number, even Janet's phone number. "In case of an emergency," she told me.

Wasn't this an emergency? I thought.

Like I'd done in Armenia, I tried to catch Chase on Skype in the couple of hours he was open to talking between when he got home from teaching and when he started dinner. But unlike our conversations while I was in Stepanavan, Chase would hardly stay on the call longer than thirty minutes, and sometimes not at all, excusing himself for roller derby practice or to meet a friend for happy hour or to clean the kitchen before one of his friends arrived for a visit.

He still said he loved me, but this felt different. In the days right after he left Armenia, he'd thrown his emotions toward me with such power I could feel his love completely on the other side of the planet. Now, just a continent away, that love came mixed with other feelings, ones I couldn't name that felt spikey and new.

After a couple of days, I finally tried showering. I'd been instructed not to take my leg brace off, even to bathe, so I stood in the shower on one leg like a cast member from Cirque du Soleil, balancing and twisting my head and then body with my left leg always extended out of the tub, the shower curtain draped across my upper thigh, constantly adjusting the curtain with my hand as I twisted and turned. I was terrified and kept fending off my own flights of imagination, brief visions of myself falling, hitting my head, and lying unconscious in the water, Janet finally discovering my lifeless body when I didn't come for my per diem.

When I felt strong enough, I went to Trader Joe's on my own, where I felt my first thrill in days by sitting in one of the motorized scooters, gently gliding down aisles of groceries I'd only fantasized about for the last two years. All the various types of juice. The potato chips. The twelve kinds of sliced bread. Bagels. Cream cheese.

Other volunteers did eventually visit my hotel room, prompted by Janet, who knew I was alone. A woman who'd left her service in Guatemala. Another from Belize. One from Peru. They'd all been here a while. They brought me coffees from the Starbucks next door and cupcakes from a shop down the street that had its own show on TLC. Sometimes they sat with me in my room, bringing me food from the kitchen. They demonstrated such kind patience playing spades with me while the Percocet sent my thoughts in loops and slow waves.

When I finally felt I had enough strength, I called Aeroflot to reschedule my flight to Santa Barbara. I was dismayed to find that I could not reschedule over the phone, and I could not process my request over the internet.

"The only way to change your flight is to go into an office and meet with an agent," I was told, speaking into the phone, anxiously fiddling with the curled cord in my fingers.

"Where are your offices?" I asked.

"There's one in Chicago. One in New York. And one in DC."

"You only have three?" I asked. I was surprised. "What if I'm not in one of those cities? Or what if I can't make it to an office because, I don't know, I had surgery on my leg or something."

Without missing a beat, she said, "We recommend that you select a personal agent who can go into one of our offices on your behalf."

I had no such agent. I waited two more days. Five days after surgery, I searched the internet for bus routes and wrote down the three buses I would need to take to get to the Aeroflot office. Then, a bit stronger and high on Percocet, I took those three buses to parts of the city I'd never heard of until I got to a skyscraper that held the office. Sweating at the reception desk, I asked for options. I chose a new flight, one that, if I stayed in DC the full forty-five days to heal, would leave a week after I returned to Armenia. If I returned.

After I got back to the hotel room, I called Chase. He didn't express any gratitude at all, but instead, simply a sense that I had done what was required of me, what I should have done given the circumstances.

"Great," he said, though he still sounded upset. And then soon after, "When will you know whether or not you're actually going back to Armenia?"

I winced, having to tell him something that, at this point, I knew he didn't want to hear. "I won't know," I said. "The surgeon said it will probably be right up to day forty-five before he makes a decision."

My days started to even out for me as I became stronger and had a very, very small routine. Once a week, I crutched onto the bus, riding to the Peace Corps office to check in with Janet and receive my per diem. Three times a week, I crutched onto a different bus to a physical therapy office where I practiced lifting my brace-straightened leg into the air in different directions with a very nice Pakistani physical therapist who ended each session by sticking the ends of her E-Stim machine to my leg and shocking my muscles with even bursts of electricity.

"I think Washington, DC, is really a walking city," I told Chase over the phone from my spot on my hotel living room couch. In my fingers, I twirled the cord on the hotel phone. From the way his short one-word responses sounded, I could tell he had me on speakerphone. He asked about my plans for the day. He expressed a playful jealousy when I told him about my routine.

"Honestly, I'm not sure I can think of a better way to recover," I said. "My only responsibility in life right now is to take care of my body and go to physical therapy three hours a week. Otherwise, I don't have to do anything I don't want to."

This was my line I told everyone. None of my family had come to DC for the surgery, and none of them planned to come now while I waited to recover, hoping I would be healed enough to return to Armenia.

I kept my tone cheerful with my family and with Chase, perhaps as a way to leave the door open for them to show up. Even if they didn't plan to, who would want to visit me, limping and weepy and stuck in a beige hotel room.

But I did weep alone sometimes, mostly watching a show I'd heard about on a podcast—*RuPaul's Drag Race*—which aired on a tiny business-card-sized window at the LogoTV.com website.

"I'm just so grateful for these drag queens," I wrote in my journal in a Percocet haze. "They're brave. They are who they want to be without apology. I want to be brave." I cried when they lip-synced for their life. I cried when they talked to each other about the families that rejected them, redoing their eyeliner after wiping away tears. I cried when, from the side of the stage, these men in dresses cheered for each other, snapping their fingers in the air, their eyes and smiles wide and glittering.

On one of my weekly per diem trips to the office, Janet pulled her lunch out of a canvas Peace Corps bag.

"Are there more of those somewhere?" I asked, somehow emboldened by my physical situation to ask if I could have one.

"Oh, we don't actually make these," Janet said, explaining that in the next high-rise over I could find the National Peace Corps Association office, a nonprofit that lobbies for Peace Corps because, as a government agency, Peace Corps can't lobby for itself. I actually knew the National Peace Corps Association. I'd followed them on Twitter throughout my service and joined many of their live-tweet sessions where their communications director, Erica Burman, invited currently serving and returned volunteers to talk with each other about a new subject each week. I had no idea I'd already been so close to their HQ.

I rode the elevator down many floors to the street, crossed it, and rode another elevator high up to a small, much more unassuming office, where I asked a receptionist on his way out if Erica was still here.

"It's you!" I said to her. I'd never seen her before, didn't know she wore wire-rimmed glasses or nearly red lipstick. When I told her who I was and what handle I used on Twitter, she recognized me and invited me to sit for a few minutes. I told her about being medevacked and my wait to see if I would be able to go back to Armenia.

"Take a bag for sure," Erica said, tucking her long grey hair behind her ears before leaning forward over her desk to hand me one.

A week later, Erica invited me to cohost a live-tweet with her at her office. I over-enthusiastically accepted the invite. I'd participated in them for over a year, and I knew how to get into the conversation, tag people into a thread and draw people into sharing their perspectives, which were always fascinating because they came from different parts of the world.

With the help of my physical therapist, I'd started walking without crutches, though I was careful not to overdo it, looking up bus routes on my computer and writing them down before leaving the hotel and planning places and times I could sit midroute to prop my leg up and take a break.

In Erica's office, I sat next to her on a blue couch as she took a selfie of us, and tweeted out, "Look who's here! @heybrentlove who's temporarily with us from his service in Armenia!"

Erica centered the conversation during the live-tweet on languages. Volunteers around the world shared their favorite words.

"Mercel," I tweeted. "I love it because it means to be cold but also to be sick with a cold. Armenians take winter health very seriously!"

I recognized another volunteer from past live-tweets. Erikson had served in Kenya and was present as much as I was for nearly every live-tweet. He always shared generously and encouraged other PCVs and RPCVs in the chat. I remembered he worked at the Smithsonian because he'd shared that he was on a break during many of these events. And he'd shared he was gay during a different live-tweet. What I hadn't known until this conversation on language was that he was deaf. Those of us participating in the live-tweet got into a conversation, asking Erikson a lot of questions about learning Kenyan Sign Language when he arrived and what it was like to try and teach and build relationships at the school he worked at for deaf students.

Erikson's tweets filled the feed, and I felt a pull to him. I started to feel a glow of admiration. The bravery to be gay, to move to Kenya, and teach in a language unknown to so many people. I wanted to meet him. And I hadn't ever made an out, gay friend in the US.

I'd had a deaf friend growing up, a boy I looked forward to hanging out with at summer camp every year. During camp, I'd picked up enough sign language to feel confident saying hello and carrying on a conversation. It hadn't occurred to me at all that there must be so many different sign languages in the world.

I wanted to meet Erikson. I private-messaged him. He told me he could take a late lunch.

On the bus to the Smithsonian Museum of Natural History, I tried to warm up my rusty fingers. I spelled my name a few times. I tried to remember the signs for "know" and "sign language." I tried to think through possible conversations I might have with Erikson. I knew he didn't have a lot of time. But I wanted to let him know how cool I thought he was, how much I was grateful to have met him over these live-tweets, and how much I admired his service in Kenya. "K-E-N-Y-A," I spelled with my fingers.

I didn't have a cell phone or mobile internet, so I simply arrived on time and hoped he would, too. I had no idea what he looked like. In our private message, I told him I was tall and blond and wore a leg brace over my blue jeans. I figured he couldn't miss the leg brace, and he didn't.

While museum-goers wove their way past both of us, Erikson smiled at me, his charming dimples giving away a kindness and a gentle welcome.

"Thank you for meeting me," I said with nervous, jumpy hands.

His eyes widened. "You know sign language?" he signed.

I nodded.

"I didn't know," he said.

"I learned when I was…" And I didn't know the sign for "small" so spelled it with my hand. "I had a friend who was deaf."

I didn't tell Erikson how much that friend had meant to me. I didn't know how to sign that well, but I had been fascinated by the way my friend's hands had moved. I couldn't tell Erikson that as a child, I found sign language a far easier way to say words like "beautiful," to imbue more meaning into your words by the speed of your fingers, the earnestness of your eyes, the gentleness of your smile, all that personal meaning entering into the word as you signed it to a friend.

And I couldn't tell Erikson about the boy at camp, how something in me recognized something in him, a way he looked at everyone else with a whole world of thought he couldn't tell anyone.

Standing in the lobby with Erikson we talked about the countries where we served in Peace Corps. I asked him what it was like now to be home after a few years. He told me he loved his job and his bike ride to work. He was proud to be part of the Smithsonian, grateful to continue a career of service after two years in Kenya that had meant so much to him. He asked me why I loved Armenia, and I told him that most of all I felt loved by the Armenians I lived with and worked with, and I felt like maybe I was helping build... and I finger-spelled "imagination for what's possible" ... for the kids I worked with.

Erikson was kind enough to watch my stuttery hands and my slow fingers. He looked at me so warmly while I signed, the gentle connection between us warming up in the sun that came in through the lobby windows. I tried not to notice my own imagination flashing with the thought of me running my fingers through his thick, dark hair.

I could feel us slowing down, running out of things to say to each other. I began calculating the signs I needed to say goodbye when, unexpectedly, Erikson extended an invitation.

"Would you like to see the museum?" he asked.

A brightness flushed over me. A connection, a first real connection to a new gay friend in the US. A friend. This was something a friend would do, I thought and then quickly buried the idea that maybe he was interested in me, though a tour of the Smithsonian was pretty romantic, after all.

I signed a very enthusiastic, "Yes!"

I expected then to be walked to some of the highlights of the Natural History Museum to see Erikson's favorite displays.

But as tourists went through the main thresholds, Erikson turned to a nondescript door on the side of the lobby. He scanned his badge and waved me through.

Surprised and then wide-eyed, I stepped with him into the staff hallways of the Smithsonian.

Erikson stopped first by a canoe on display outside a room filled with artifacts labeled "The Americas." "This is very old," he signed.

I didn't know how to ask about what I was seeing, but I knew this was not a hallway any tourist would walk down.

Down another hallway and through a white door, Erikson waved his hand toward cases and cases of insects behind glass. He pulled open a drawer, inside of which were dozens of stick bugs of different sizes, organized by length and color, pinned to beige paperboard with tiny labels next to each one.

"Who comes here?" I asked. "Why is this here and not out in the…" and, not knowing the sign, I resorted to finger-spelling, "M-U-S-E-U-M."

Erikson signed something I couldn't understand, and I shook my head.

He finger-spelled, "R-E-S-E-A-R-C-H."

After the canoe and the stick bugs, Erikson continued on. He showed me room after room of specimens. I didn't touch a thing, afraid mostly that if I moved wrong and broke some dried-out crustacean from Antarctica that Erikson might be reprimanded. But he seemed unafraid. He pulled out a drawer in a room full of dead birds. In the drawer three dead green macaws looked as peaceful as babies lying down to sleep. He closed that drawer and opened another of blue macaws. Then another of red ones.

My inner six-year-old was in bliss, my spine tingling after each room. This was the world in boxes. I was traveling from country to country with every step, every glance in every direction. Tropical ferns. Arctic foxes. Tiny birds from East Africa. Rocks excavated from so deep in the earth that the name of the country seemed too far away, as if saying it was from Mongolia were akin to calling muscle skin. We kept on through rooms full of scrolls and the tools of long past civilizations.

While my inner child was floating in bliss, my inner gay was full of questions. Was Erikson taking me on this tour because he thought I was cute? Why did this feel unlikely to me? How could I know? Would I wonder this about every gay man I ever wanted to be friends with? Could I be friends at all with gay men? Would it always be a case of will he/won't he?

Or maybe, Erikson simply saw in me something of kinship. Two gay men who put themselves out into the world to try and do something good with their lives. And perhaps, and I thought, most likely, he was simply honoring that kinship with this gift of showing me the world as he saw it every day. And the view took my breath away.

While I traced the edges of a sarcophagus with my eyes, Erikson tapped me on the shoulder and then guided me through another hidden door. On the other side, we joined a crowd of people gathered around the Hope Diamond. Then just as quickly we were back into the white hallways, turning into a room that I knew immediately I'd be thinking about for the rest of my life.

The room was not large, perhaps the size of a high school chemistry class. Packed inch-to-inch on metal shelves were rows and rows of dinosaur bones.

My mouth dropped open. I looked to the bones and back to Erikson and back to the bones and back to Erikson.

He smiled back and nodded.

I couldn't close my mouth.

"This is too much," I signed. "I don't know what to think."

He smiled again and gestured an invitation to walk down the aisles together. I walked ahead of him past fully reconstructed skeletons of tiny dinosaurs. One shelf held only one massive diplodocus femur. Next to it, as if on a grocery store endcap meant to impress shoppers, a triceratops skull looked out over Erikson and me as I passed with my mouth still agape. And at the end of the room, an entire shelving unit had been removed to make room for the reconstructed skeleton of a small stegosaurus.

While I traced the stegosaurus spine plates with my eyes, I signed to Erikson without looking, "I will... N-E-V-E-R... see something this... C-O-O-L... again. Thank you."

Erikson nodded, smiled, and walked me out onto an open, second-story atrium where we looked out over a great hall. I said goodbye there and left, walking past tourists who gazed at what the Smithsonian kept outside closed doors.

34

Weeks went by in DC. I'd stopped calling my family much
and instead mostly emailed them. I caught Chase a few days
a week on the phone, and he quit asking about the plane
ticket or my plans, settling into the fact that I'd have to make
a decision right at the end of my forty-five days. He mailed
a care package to my hotel with snacks he loved, a few pairs
of cute underwear and sexy pictures on a flash drive he made
me promise to protect with my life.

My leg had atrophied, and I still needed my brace. But
I felt stronger and more confident going out into the city. I
could spend the morning slowly touring more Smithsonians
and come back for the afternoon to ice my knee and go find
takeout in the evening. It was a soft schedule, but it became
comforting with repetition. I went to bookstores and even
a sex shop where, nervous and tantalized, I found toys I'd
never seen, buying them as a surprise for Chase. Honestly,
using them would be a surprise for me, too.

I visited a high school friend in a suburb and then a
college friend, who picked me up for coffee. I came out
to both of them, which worked like medicine, a rush of
healing. It became easier each time, and each time my friends
were simply curious, lavishing me with a nurturing kind
of attention, letting me tell them whatever I wanted to tell

them, and providing each of my details and stories with a soft place to land.

Zoe had emailed a college friend of hers who was married and gay. He took me to dinner and on another night to a musical, and I felt just a twinge of happiness at the idea that I could have friends who easily accepted a part of me I hadn't accepted for so many, many years. That they could hold that truth as if it were no more significant a fact than knowing where I grew up. Interesting, always a source of conversation, but no more exceptional or unexceptional than a rose.

John joined me for dinner a few times, and at one dinner I told him I wanted to go to a gay bar. My days in DC were dwindling. I'd never been to a gay bar in the US. I'd only ever been to Cocoon in Yerevan.

"Come with me to Secrets," John said. "You'll love it."

To get to Ziegfeld's Secrets we took a taxi beyond city neighborhoods to the edge of somewhere where the streets started sloping downhill to a waterway. I lost sense of cardinal directions and began to see only tall, grey, unremarkable warehouse buildings. And then, in a spot you would never have imagined a club to be, a neon sign lit the night over a small crowd waiting to show a bouncer their IDs.

At the door, John pulled a wallet from the pocket of taut blue jeans that wrapped around his butt. I followed, trying to be as casual as possible about the leg brace around my jeans and my accompanying limp. Inside the door, I forced myself into a casual posture, sticking my hands in the pockets of Chase's grey hoodie. I followed John to where he leaned on his thick arms over the bar and ordered both of us drinks.

Walking to the center of the large open room that took up most of the bar, I sipped my vodka soda. Both of us looked out over the crowd gathered near a stage, cheering for a drag queen who twirled, leaped, and lip-synced to a Tina Turner song. We stayed for one song before John asked me if I wanted to go upstairs.

"You'll need singles," he said, not acknowledging any surprise he might have read on my face while men and then more men passed by us on their way up to the stairs.

"I only have a twenty," I told him. He took my twenty to the first-floor bar and had it changed into ones.

Men sailed past me while I took the stairs one at a time with both feet. I emerged to the second floor with a view of my first of many, many penises.

How do you name the emotional whirlwind of what feels like transgression, exhilaration, fear and promise all at the same time? I limped straight to the bar for a drink.

"Vodka soda," I told the bartender.

An army boot moved up next to me on the wooden bar surface. I followed the boot to a calf up a leg to the man who owned it. His curly hair waved while he pivoted and bobbed to the music as if he were casually dancing on the floor instead of on the surface of the bar. My heart pounded. The nakedness of him, his tan skin, his muscular legs, felt like looking up a redwood.

This was a view of a man I'd never had. I could count on one hand the men I'd seen fully naked in my life. And to be fair, this man was wearing something—black boots and what looked like a rubber ring at the base of his junk that, I assumed, kept it plump and extended to its full length without it standing at attention. The man moved in time to the music, making his sausage bounce way off the beat as if the tool itself had no rhythm but tons of confidence.

I hardly noticed when my drink was placed next to me.

I can stare, I told myself. *That's why he's up there dancing.* I let my eyes wander across his body. He caught me looking and smiled down at me. In a millisecond I fought with myself, unsure of whether to run to John, run out of the bar, or stay staring.

I can't run at all with a bum leg, I reasoned. And then I nodded warmly back at the naked man with the kind of look you'd give if you were tipping your hat to someone. Then I walked over to John.

"I have no idea what to do," I said.

"Dance," he replied, starting to sway.

"But like, am I supposed to… I don't know … have some exchange with these dancers?"

John laughed. "If you appreciate someone, give him a dollar. Watch."

John walked up to a naked man in sneakers whose smile seemed somehow extra kind coming from inside his full beard. Unlike most of the men in the room, he hadn't shaved his body, and he was fully grown out from head to hips to toes. John approached and started to dance, and the man joined him, grinning, the two of them bobbing and weaving together. They kept their eyes locked, and then John dropped low enough to reach the top of the man's socks, pulling the top of the sock away from his leg so he could press a dollar into it.

"So, like that?" I asked when John returned to me. He nodded, his eyes half-closed in a sense of sweet satisfaction.

As I walked up to the same dancer in sneakers, I felt at once repelled and captivated. When I bent down to put a dollar in the man's sock, my proximity to his naked body made goosebumps travel over my skin. Blood rushed through me everywhere, and the rush felt uncontrollable to me, heightened in waves when I felt the elastic of his sock pull my fingers toward his skin. Another rushing wave of blood and electricity when I stood up, my face now so close to his smile. Another rush when he squeezed my shoulder before I walked away.

As the music bounced and men crisscrossed the hall, John and I left each other and came back together and left each other again, both of us moving around as if window shopping. I walked up to more naked men who smiled when I approached, let my eyes travel their body, pressed their hand to my arm and squeezed to acknowledge the dollar I'd put in their sock.

Was it just hormones, or was it the kind of freedom you feel when you freefall? I was intoxicated by this feeling of looking at men so obviously lusty. It was a way of looking I'd never done in public before. Certainly, never to strangers.

I moved through the dance floor full of men. Some danced in groups. Some, like me, strolled through the space from naked dancer to naked dancer. Some leaned back on the bar and nursed drinks. No one burst into flames. No one was hurt. While I imagined, like any room of people anywhere, there were people hurting in human ways, what I could see was a room full of smiles and swagger and heat.

I had never been invited to look. I can remember the first time I'd seen a man exuding a sensuality that I found intoxicating. I'd grown up fantasizing about boys in secret but never knowing those fantasies meant anything. I couldn't have defined the word "sexuality." I hadn't even connected those fantasies to the bullying that happened at school. I'd been sensitive, sweet even. And seeing sensitivity as vulnerability, other schoolboys and then girls began calling me words they'd sharpened like knives.

"Faggot."

"Queer."

Every day of school was a day when my books might be slapped out of my hands, when I might be shoved against the lockers by kids running by and jeering.

I'd been cornered by two boys, both named Nathan, day after day at the back of the junior high band hall where we played percussion.

"Do I make you horny, baby?" one Nathan asked me, coming close to me as if coming in for a kiss, projecting his Austin Powers accent so that our classmates would hear. "Do I?"

And they laughed. They laughed every day.

The truth I can admit now is that my body reacted to their proximity the way it reacted to these men in Secrets. The smell of their breath. Their broad shoulders, their swagger. But in middle school it created a terrible mixture of hormone-induced heart-beating blended with fear and rage and horror.

I was taunted and tortured in this way, mocked in front of groups of kids who laughed with the Nathans or with other bullies or looked away in embarrassment.

At some point during these middle school days, my dad, a computer programmer, had brought home a Hewlett Packard—a massive, grey box that smelled of electrically warmed plastic.

Dad showed me how to play a game where I would type in a code, like coordinates, and a gorilla would throw a banana into the air, arcing until it landed on another gorilla and exploded.

On one night, when I was playing the gorilla game alone, the thought occurred to me that I could use the thing my mom used when she helped me with school papers—Internet Explorer. You typed in a word, and it would show you something called websites with information about that word.

I'd been called "gay" so many times, and I wasn't actually sure if I was or wasn't. So, on a weeknight in the middle of a junior high school year, my trembling hand moved the mouse and clicked on the icon for Internet Explorer. I found the long box for typing in words. With a heartbeat audible in my ears, I typed so slowly that you couldn't hear the keys compress. G. A. Y.

The screen reloaded slowly, and then I clicked on the first line of words. My search results disappeared to a grey screen. Then, at a rate that felt agonizing, the screen filled from top to bottom, as if unrolling a scroll. The image of a man covered in muscles began to appear. Set like tiles, the image repeated over and over in a grid across the screen. The same man stood posing in each tile, both of his hands on his chest and six-pack as if he were rubbing lotion down the front of him. Wind tousled his golden-brown mullet. His pecs appeared like they'd be larger than my head. And from his waist to the tops of his tanned, muscular thighs, a pink, silky fabric pressed against him, extending from one side of the image to the other like it was falling. Where it pressed against him, the fabric formed an imprint of his manhood, fully erect, leaving only the mystery of color, not size or shape.

My heart rushed, filling each end of me with oxygen-rich blood. I had no name for what I felt until I realized that this part of me that rushed was now conscious to me in a way it had never been before.

Then, a jolt of realization. Anyone in my family could walk in at any second. Terror spiked.

I clicked the window closed, my hand shaking over the mouse. I closed Internet Explorer and the gorilla game and ran to the bathroom. I stood at the sink wanting both to cry and to press my whole body into something, a desperate yearning to weep and to have sex, both of those feelings becoming unfathomably tangled.

For the rest of my life, I was afraid to look at men. I would calculate all eye contact. I would resist any urge to look at any male body. I feared so deeply some lingering of my eyes could be caught by someone who wanted to use even a single glance to taunt me or torment me or ask me questions I knew I'd be terrible at lying through.

From the moment I saw that man with the pink fabric over his body, I had a word for how I felt. Gay. And because of the way I'd been treated and what I heard about gay people burning in hell, I also believed that gay meant torture. Torturous taunting from church kids and from the kids at school. Torturous negligence as I watched parents and teachers say nothing of how those kids treated me.

And in the fall of my eighth-grade year, when a young man was dragged and beaten to death and left tied to a post in the middle of nowhere when stories of his murder were on every channel, gay meant a kind of torture that no one in my house or church or school would speak of no matter how many times the story appeared on the news.

And finally, according to what adults said at church, gay meant an eternity of having Satan burn you and burn you and burn you and burn you and burn you and burn you and burn you and burn you.

I knew all this terror before I knew what complete and simple joy there could be in holding your lover's hand.

In Secrets, with these dancers, naked, their eyes warmly affectionate as I looked at their bodies, as I looked right at their softest parts, they simply smiled and allowed me to put a dollar in their sock. Then they squeezed my shoulder in appreciation or at least in confirmation that my staring, my smiling, my heart beating, my enjoyment of this night of looking was okay. I could look. I could let go of my calculations. I could let go of my fears that someone would see me, see my curiosity, see my want, see my hope that such a man might one day love me. No one here cared. This was, in fact, a place to stare, to look, to let go of fear.

In this, my first American gay bar, I ordered more drinks. I danced with John, and when he was walking around, I danced alone. I watched John connect so deeply with his eyes that a dancer leaned down to make out with him. I walked alone to a side of a room where a man who looked like a Greek sculpture with a much, much larger phallus than any statue, danced in a shower, soap suds careening in the grooves of his six-pack. I slipped him a dollar through a thin crack in the plexiglass, which he took and rubbed down his body, covering it in water, before he slapped it on the edge of the glass where other patrons' dollars had been slapped into a sort of soapy display of wet cash.

I returned a few times to a thick-muscled cowboy who danced from his hips, pivoting on the toes and heels of his boots, often holding the top of his hat when he looked down to find the music and feel it. I would look back to him. He'd smile at me across the room. I'd walk over, watch him dance, and put a dollar in his boot. On maybe the third or fourth time I walked up to him, he extended an upturned hand, gesturing with his fingers for me to walk closer.

I limped until we stood face to face. With a soft and intentional touch, he held the back of my arms and pulled me into him. With our chests touching, our faces inches apart, he suddenly bent to the side, grabbed onto my torso, and spun me around upside down. My face pressed against his naked inner thigh, and my legs waved slowly in the air, my leg brace holding firm. I felt his body against me through my own clothes, and then my eyes nearly jumped out of my head when he slapped my ass once and then again and again. Then he flipped me back around, smiled at me, touched my face, and then patted my shoulder.

My wide eyes stayed wide. I put all the rest of my dollars into his boot.

35

In my surgeon's wood-paneled office, he gave me a choice. I hadn't healed back completely, but I'd healed enough. He offered to tell Peace Corps I needed to early terminate and go straight to Texas to finish healing.

"Or," he proposed in a kind voice, "if you want to go back to Armenia, I can send you back with exercises and your leg brace, and you can take it from here."

Chase nearly yelled with joy through the phone when I told him I'd be going back to Armenia to catch my flight to California.

"I wish you could just come here now," he told me.

And I did, too. But the policies on the lowest fare available on Aeroflot, the one Chase had booked for me, said that my ticket was nonrefundable and there was no possibility of changing the departure and arrival cities, meaning I had to return to Armenia to board the first part of the flight. Otherwise, the entire ticket would be forfeited. And as much as I wanted to go to Santa Barbara, I also wanted to return for my last few months in Armenia. I wasn't ready to say goodbye.

I decided to return to Armenia for a week. I'd spend a couple of nights in Yerevan staying at Phillip's with Margaux, who was coming to the capital just to see me when I returned. Then I'd go to Stepanavan for a few days. Then back to Yerevan for my flight.

At the DC airport, I asked for a wheelchair, which I didn't know meant I'd have an attendant at each airport and first boarding on all the flights back to Yerevan. Attendants wheeled me to holding areas and went to food courts to buy me meals. While I waited, I journaled and worried.

My Peace Corps service was ending in a way I knew must be atypical. I felt like I'd been gone from Stepanavan so much since December between my trip through Armenia with Margaux and Chase, two weeks of Nor Tari, the time I'd spent in Yerevan doing tests for my knee, and a month and a half medevacked to DC.

Now, in the middle of April, I was headed back to Armenia so I could catch a flight to California where I'd stay for almost a month. I'd, of course, submitted all my travel plans as required by the Peace Corps. I was within Peace Corps rules, using my accrued time off to fly to California, returning within the threshold Peace Corps set. They required all volunteers to be in-country for the last ten weeks of their service. All the appropriate managers were aware. No one ever questioned my plans or suggested an alternate path. Why did I feel like I was doing something wrong?

I balanced a personal pan pizza in my lap and ate it among other strangers sitting in wheelchairs in this tucked-away corner of the airport terminal. It felt, in some way, wrong to choose time with Chase over time in Armenia. I thought of Naira, Vazgen, Nazeli, and Ani. I thought of my World Vision friends. I felt disconnected from them. None, but Liana had the internet at home. I hadn't been able to call any of them. None of them had Facebook, where

I occasionally posted updates. I was going back to them, but I'd turn around a week later and leave again for my trip to Santa Barbara.

In every other time in my life, I would have called my mom to ask her advice. But when it came to this, she wouldn't be objective. I couldn't tell her how lucky I felt to have fallen in love with a man who was now flying me to spend a month with him to see how deeply we could keep falling together.

I wanted Chase. I wanted to feel his arms around me like the night he'd invited me to sleep next to him in my freezing cottage. I wanted to kiss him with the reckless abandon I'd felt running into alleyways and empty stairwells in the dark night in Yerevan. I wanted to try for more between us, whatever that meant. And I knew a chance like this wouldn't come again.

Yet neither would the opportunity to really say goodbye to the people and places I'd come to love in Armenia. At this point, with all the travel, I'd already missed so many evenings at Naira's table, so many afternoons on my side of Vazgen's nardi board. I'd missed opportunities to keep working with friends in villages I'd come to know. There were projects I'd wanted to start and couldn't because I'd been gone.

I flew from DC to Paris. I limped onto my flight from Paris to Yerevan, thinking that by the time I got back from this trip, I'd have just a couple of months left before I officially left my Peace Corps service and returned to what Peace Corps understood as my home of record. I'd make the most of that. And in the meantime, still unsettled, I'd complete this slingshot trip back to Armenia and then to Santa Barbara, where I'd give everything I could to building on the love I'd found with Chase.

From the Yerevan airport, I took a taxi to Phillip's apartment, where Margaux soon arrived from her six-hour journey on the Friday marshutni from Kapan.

After Margaux showered and dressed for the cool spring evening, we went out to dinner.

Before I left for DC, I'd become friends with Imogen and Claire in Yerevan. They wanted to celebrate my return, and they joined Margaux and me at Lagonid. We all dipped into fatteh, telling each other stories of the last forty-five days. Margaux was having her own knee trouble. Claire and a Peace Corps volunteer had fallen in and out of a romantic entanglement. Imogen was tutoring a new English student at the university.

"We're going out after this. Right?" I asked them.

"Duh," Margaux said. "I mean, you can go out. Right?" She looked at my leg brace.

"Yeah," I returned, navigating a pita chip full of hummus and chickpeas into my mouth. "I've been walking a bit with my knee brace. And as long as I take breaks and keep icing it, it doesn't swell too much."

We went out, stopping at cafés so I could put my leg up on a chair while we ate fries, drank beer and people watched. We danced at That Place with Yervantsis and Armenian diasporans to songs like "Give It To Me" and "Just Dance."

Margaux, Imogen, and Claire were friends I could be completely myself with, and I hadn't been completely myself since I left Armenia. I plunged into celebrating my return to Yerevan, making it out of DC and back into Peace Corps. I made toasts with vodka soda after vodka soda. I ordered all of us shots and drank the ones my friends rejected. But after all that alcoholic celebration, I felt my ability to concentrate, to link my thoughts together, diminishing.

We made it to the bar that used to be Cocoon, and I still had the wherewithal to slowly take the stairs into the basement club, keeping my left leg straight and extended. Unsurprisingly, we stumbled into an empty room. "Who cares!" I yelled in a slurred voice. I spun with my arms out wide. I ordered everyone shots again before Margaux and I twirled toward each other. Claire and Imogen started into a syncopated freestyle, their hands on their foreheads swaying. I left them and leaned up against the wall, my hips out and waving to a beat of a song that felt so far away from my spinning mind.

When I lifted my eyes, a hazy figure of a man close to me left me wincing with confused surprise. He'd started dancing with me without my knowing, the gold chain on his chest flashing in the open triangle of his black button-up. He maintained an unsmiling, serious face when he looked at me, seemingly lost in his moment only inches away. I looked at the top of his head, which only rose as high as my shoulders. His hair gel caught the faint, blue light from the bar. His hands jutted out to the side, dancing.

I reached my arms over his shoulders, letting my hands find the air behind him, an acceptance of his advance.

We danced like this for a few minutes before he beckoned me to bend down so he could whisper in my ear. "*Come with me,*" he said in Armenian.

I stood up straighter to make space and tried to look at him with more focus. I grinned a mask of a grin, let my eyes loose, and feigned being lost in the music. Beneath the facade I weighed my circumstances within a whirling mind.

I'd fantasized my entire life about being picked up, about attracting the sexual attention of a man.

I'd put myself in this very room on so many weekends, formerly the only gay bar in Armenia, hoping a man would look at me the way this short man in a white suit was looking at me now.

Yes, he was short. Yes, he wasn't anything like any man I'd fantasized about. But he was here. If the universe wanted me to have a torrid, one-night stand, wasn't this it? Wasn't a free gay spirit meant to fly on the wind wherever it blew?

And Chase. He came to me like the smell of a candle just blown out. So pleasant and so far away.

With my boozed brain, I negotiated with myself. We'd never talked about being exclusive. What did I know about being exclusive? Practically nothing. But I knew it was something modern couples ought to discuss, I told myself. And we hadn't. As far as I knew, he could be having sex with other people right now.

I leaned down to this short man's ear. "Ayo," I whispered. *Yes*.

He looked at another, taller man dressed completely in black at the bar. I registered then that I was drunk enough not to have noticed when the man in the white suit and his friend in black entered the room, which previously only held the bartender, my friends, and me.

I walked lazily to Margaux. Before I could tell her, she spoke. "We're thinking we want to go home."

"Okay," I said. "That guy wants to take me home." I smiled a drunken smile in an attempt to be cute, though even then, I felt cartoonish with my limpy, unsure legs and my eyes half-closed.

"Do you want to do that?" Margaux asked.

I felt my stomach turn, confusing thrill and fear, unable to tell them apart.

I was right in feeling like this was an utterly unique experience. This was the one, singular moment of my life in which a man saw me, approached me, and without speaking any other words, asked to spend the night with me. It would, in fact, up to the writing of these pages, never happen again.

Margaux, Imogen, and Claire climbed the bar stairs outside into the moonlight while the man in the white suit, his friend, and I took another round of shots.

I hadn't expected his friend to get into the taxi with us.

I also hadn't expected the man in the white suit to help me out of the cab and into a building where he approached an older woman, speaking quickly in words I couldn't follow. Booze swirled my heart and brain into a hormonal stupor. I watched the man in the white suit take off his jacket and put it on a couch in what seemed like an apartment. My eyes slowly took in the couch, a chair, a TV mounted on the wall. And off that central room, I saw a large bathroom with a shower, a massage table, and a bathtub. The man, now without his white jacket, filled the tub with hot water.

I kicked off my Doc Marten boots, and we kissed. Our mouths moved like two dying moths trying to find a place to land. I felt lost in the kisses, not from ecstasy but simply from my mind trying so desperately to find a place to land.

The man removed Chase's grey sweatshirt from my shoulders. Then my T-shirt. I unstrapped my leg brace before he removed my jeans, then my underwear.

Instinctively, I walked to the bathtub. I stepped in and then let out a guffaw.

"My socks!" I shouted in English. I could tell he didn't understand my words. I stepped out and pointed at the long, white tube socks, the drenched length of them stretching up past my calves. I laughed more as I sat down on the black massage table, struggling with the wet fabric and then throwing them to the ground.

He walked up between my legs and tried reaching up from his short frame to kiss me. Then he leaned me backward on the table and lay down on top of me.

When I felt him try to initiate sex, I pushed his hips back from mine.

"*Condom?*" I said.

"*No,*" he said in Armenian. "*I don't have one.*"

"*No condom, no sex,*" I replied.

He tried again, and I playfully pushed him back. "*Really. No sex.*"

He raised himself onto his knees and humphed, so I sat up and kissed him again. I could tell he was disappointed, and I still drunkenly tried to keep the hope of my romantic fantasy alive in the haze of alcohol and hormones and jet lag.

He stood on the table and was short enough that he was the perfect height for a blowjob. After I'd finished, I lay back and smiled at him. Without looking at me, he got down from the massage table and stepped into the living room, a place my drunken mind had simply forgotten existed.

Don't fall asleep, I told myself, lying there on the black table, the light from the living room illuminating my feet. *Don't fall asleep.* I repeated it like a mantra, a faint far away panic starting to peek over the horizon of my consciousness.

And then, after minutes of me talking to myself, a switch flipped. I'd been waiting for some romantic man to return, and suddenly realized I had no idea where this short, hairy man was, wondering, in fact, what could take a man so long to return to me and give me the pleasure I imagined I was entitled to. I lifted my pants from the floor and took my phone from my pocket to check the time. Three a.m.

The panic that had crept toward my mind surfaced more clearly and then for some reason morphed into anger. I stood up naked. Still wet from the bathtub, I walked into the bright light of the living area. There he was, fastening his belt buckle over white suit pants. His friend in black looked up at me from the couch, away from the TV he'd set to an Armenian soap opera.

They were leaving, I registered. I felt a tidal wave of disgust, of filth. They were about to leave me here. I'd been trying to keep myself awake. They probably would have been happier if I'd passed out.

With my naked body lit up in the threshold of the bathroom door, I spoke in full-voiced Armenian. *"What are you doing?"*

The friend in black held his gaze, suddenly tense. The white-suited man lifted his eyes and stopped tying his shoes.

"Where are you going?" My voice started to raise. *"Where are you going? Why are you not talking?"*

Silence. They didn't say a single word. The friend turned off the TV.

"Are you leaving?" The anger in my voice started to bubble.

The man in white clumsily sped up his fingers to tie his other shoes, throwing glances up as if watching a feral cat.

I considered for a moment that he was dressing, and I was naked. And I was suddenly and stupidly unafraid. I let them both see me, a me I'd never been. Naked and white in the fluorescent light. Used. Violently mad.

I began then to truly yell. Water still caught in the soft hair on the softest parts of my body. My soft belly hardening with each breath that left me, carrying words I didn't know I could string together without a single ounce of worry that I wasn't speaking Armenian correctly or that I might be misunderstood.

I yelled at the man in white in Armenian. I told him that only an evil man would bring me here, use my body, and leave me naked and drunk in another room. I grabbed my leg brace and swung it wildly in the air. I screamed at him that I was injured. That I was alone. That I was not here to serve him and let him leave me. That I deserved to feel good, to be touched by someone who respects me.

"*I am not on this earth for you,*" I screamed like a wild man. "*I am on this earth for me and for people who love me and to treat other people well. You are on this earth to hurt people. To take from them. To use them. To make yourself feel good and leave other people in the dust.*"

Both of the men hurried then to the door, and as they opened it, I found some deep voice and projected it as if on a storm wind. I yelled, "*What life can you live after this, you rat?*"

They didn't even bother to slam the door.

In the threshold with the bright living room in front of me and the dark bathroom behind, I heaved deep breaths, my leg brace falling in my hand to my side.

I turned around and set the leg brace on the massage table.

I got back into the tub. The man in the white suit hadn't entered the water, and I began to slowly lift it, splashing it onto my body. I looked for soap and found none. I stepped out, looked for a towel, and found only one on a table next to the tub, half wet from my splashing.

I put on my pants, my mind still spinning with booze. I'd forgotten to put on my underwear and picked them off the wet floor, stuffing the soggy pair into my pocket next to my wallet. I put my hand on my other pocket to make sure my Nokia was still there.

I put on my T-shirt. I grabbed my wet socks and resolved to simply carry them loose in one hand, my leg brace in the other.

Outside, the moonlight still shone brightly between high-rises, creating harsh lines where building shadows cut across sidewalks and streets. I breathed in cool air and gripped my leg brace like a weapon, committing to swinging it like an axe at any other person who tried to come at me. When I was a couple of blocks away from the building, I realized it must have been a kind of nondescript sex hotel. I began to see streets I recognized, realizing I needed to walk north to get to Phillip's apartment.

I decided not to take a taxi. My disheveled appearance and the soaking socks that dangled from my hand could invite questions I still could only answer with spits of rage fueled by a swirl of emotions I couldn't yet name.

I laughed to myself about the fact that I was in a T-shirt in April weather that was still nearer to winter than summer. But I had the comfort of what Peace Corps volunteers called the "Russian Blanket"—vodka, which helped you forget about the cold.

And then, in a shock of realization, I remembered Chase's grey sweatshirt. My shoes scuffed to a halt on the sidewalk. My whole body churned. I braced myself against the cement building next to me and pressed my wet-sock hand into my stomach, flexing it harder than I'd ever flexed it to keep me from shouting a barbaric wail into the night.

What had just happened? Why had these men done that? And why had I so blindly put my fate into the hands of strangers? Had I been lucky? The man in the white suit simply came and left. He could have done more. He could have made me disappear into the night. Gay men had been killed this way in this city, though these stories I'd learn well after this was over.

Instead, I was thinking of Chase and his grey sweatshirt he'd left for me as a love token.

I rushed back two blocks, heaving gasps with every uneven step, careful to keep my leg straight. *Please be there,* I whispered over and over to myself. *Please be there.*

Inside the door of the unmarked building, the same woman who'd let us into the room watched from the top of the stairs, her arms folded. I smiled to her, a smile that meant that nothing was wrong, though seeing her had only taken the slightest edge off my fear.

"*Please excuse me,*" I said in Armenian, my wet socks and leg brace still dangling at my sides. "*I left my sweater in the apartment.*"

"Lav," she said, nodding with understanding. She recognized me, looked at me with a sort of gentleness, the way a mother looks at someone else's troubled child. She took out a large ring of keys from the sagging pocket of her long, brown sweater vest and led me up three flights of stairs.

In the apartment again, I found the sweater on the couch. Inside me, relief and shame smashed so hard into each other that I nearly went to the bathroom to throw up.

"*They are evil men,*" I told the woman.

She nodded lightly and said, "*Go home now. Stay well.*"

36

On the flights to Los Angeles, I decided not to tell Chase about the man in the white suit and the sex apartment.

Zoe helped talk me off the ledge while I packed in Stepanavan, stuffing everything I'd need for a month in Santa Barbara into my hiking backpack. She gave me cautious reassurance when I rationalized that Chase didn't need to know, that we hadn't said we were exclusive. I didn't worry about how unsafe that actually had been and focused all requests for advice on what this episode might mean for my relationship with Chase.

I felt like I'd entered a world of sex and relationships I didn't know anything about. I'd been listening to gay dating advice podcasts, and the rule book I conjured from all that listening made me feel okay with this secret. Chase lived in California, and I thought he must know what I had assumed were modern guidelines for gay relationships. Gay people had sex with who they wanted to. Right? We weren't bound by heteronormative rules of monogamy. Right? It was fine. Right? I felt cautiously optimistic that Chase would be okay with it if he found out, and I also felt like he would never find out.

Outside the terminal in LA, I found Chase immediately. He was impossible to miss, wearing a cream-colored hoodie, jumping up and down, and clapping. He took me into his arms and kissed me hard. His hands moved slowly, pulling me against him. His lips moved in a kiss that fit perfectly into the pocket of my long-held hope that the love we'd had in Armenia was real. When we pulled back from our long kiss, I could see his eyes were filled with tears.

"I'm taking you up Highway One," he told me, and he held my hand in his Honda Civic while we passed the cliffs of Malibu and then beach after beach.

He'd asked his friends to pull together a potluck picnic at a beach in Santa Barbara. When we arrived, they flooded me with hugs. First, his roommate Rafael and then Sophie, her blonde bob waving as she approached. On the ride, Chase had mentioned how annoyed he was that Rafael and Sophie were dating, but when Sophie let go of me and backed away, she slid her hand into Rafael's in a way I found incredibly charming. Before I could mimic her by putting my hand into Chase's, more friends walked up, hugging me, asking about my flight, my leg brace, and what I would do with a whole month in Santa Barbara.

Well into the picnic, while Chase was gabbing with two of the group, Sophie leaned over to me and said, "I want you to know, I've never seen him happier. You're good for him." I savored her words.

Rafael opened the door for me at his and Chase's apartment before Chase gave me a tour of the two bedrooms, the living room, the closet-sized kitchen, and the balcony where a sliver of ocean was visible between buildings. Chase lounged on the bed and told me more about his friends, his school, and his family while I unpacked my clothes into the drawer he'd cleared out for me in his dresser.

I spent the afternoon on the couch, where Chase brought me an ice pack for my knee, which had swollen in flight. That night, Chase's friends came to the apartment with new friends I hadn't yet met. We ate from party platters. Chase made cocktails. I brought out two bottles of house-made mulberry vodka I'd bought at the market in Yerevan and packed in the center of my hiking backpack hoping they wouldn't explode, which they didn't.

The house-made vodka was so strong it produced an instant buzz, and I passed it around and around until an entire two-liter bottle had been consumed one shot at a time. After snacking and chatting, they all gathered around a dancing game on their Wii. They took turns waving the controllers and their bodies until finally settling into rounds of "Rasputin" by Boney M., the disco fable of the titular Russian mystic of the early 1900s. Sweat poured down Chase's face as he took turn after turn, leaving me to settle into the couch and watch his friends. As the room heated up, Rafael swung open the balcony doors, and ocean air blew softly over our warm skin and then out through the open front door.

Chase and I made love a few times a day that weekend and crawled into bed together at night, our bodies wrapped up in each other. Each night, pressed up against him like a spoon, I thought of that first night together, his body as warm as the sun. Each night, I lay there long after he fell asleep, remembering.

By Monday, my tonsils had swollen to the size of golf balls, so large it altered my voice. No one I was spending time with really knew me and could barely register the change of my voice, though for me it felt like talking to them through water.

When weekdays started, Chase left for work early while I stayed home, mastering level after level of *Super Mario Brothers*. I took off my knee brace sometimes, opting to wear it when I felt in pain or particularly stumbly. I'd cut a pair of slacks into cut-offs, so when I really looked at my left leg for the first time without pants on, I was shocked at the sight of it. I'd depended on my right leg for close to two months, and now my left leg was half its normal size and looked pale and absurdly shrimpy to me in the light of the West Coast sun.

And then there was the rash. It had started in DC at the site of my surgery incision. The surgeon prescribed a cream, which helped the itching but not the spread. Once the dermatitis took hold, it slowly spread around my knee. I didn't know anything about skin care and couldn't have predicted how the temperature-controlled air would dry my skin out and cause itching all over my body.

In Santa Barbara, the rash spread like a blaze over dry grass. Thick red hive patches took over everything from my neck to the small of my back, around my hips to my thighs. I tried powders and lotions. I stood in the shower and turned it up hotter and hotter, my pores seeming to open and close in panic that felt like euphoric relief. I didn't even realize how high I was going until I'd increased the heat to the point that the hot water faucet wouldn't turn any further.

My skin was rashed and bumpy. My tonsils were so big I sounded funny. I had a shrimpy left leg. I felt like a gollum.

Chase never said a word about any of it, making love night after night for the first few days. But falling asleep began to take me hours, the itching of the rash crawling over me like an army of bugs. One night I took the comforter from the bed and slept on the floor, the relief so instant that I fell into a deep sleep and woke up on the carpet after

Chase had already left for school. Rafael later came home and told me the same thing had happened to him. When he and Chase decided to wash sheets in Rafael's free and clear detergent, I finally started sleeping through the night.

Chase didn't adjust his life when I arrived. He kept his plans with friends. Sometimes he invited me to join them. Sometimes he didn't. Sometimes, he came home and went straight to his room to bed. He told me his roller derby practice schedule but never asked me to come watch. And he never suggested what I might do while he was away.

On one of Chase's roller derby practice nights, Sophie picked me up and drove the two of us to a Maundy Thursday service at an Episcopal church. I'd craved the kind of ritual I'd experienced at the Episcopal Church I attended in my last year of college in West Texas. I'd expected my first church service in years to be traditional, but instead, this Episcopal Church in Santa Barbara conducted their Maundy Thursday in a large room with tables and a meal.

Sophie and I sat together at a table where a woman in a loose-knit blue sweater explained that this wasn't a traditional service. We were served simple food—potatoes, green beans, and chicken. While we ate, a priest used her soft, gentle voice to guide us in prompts, questions we all asked each other about what it meant to die to some things and live for others. Did we believe in a purpose for our lives? What made us happiest? What made us the most grateful?

"Oh, I miss this," I told Sophie. I shared just a hint of my religious background and my nonreligious present. Thinking of my mom and the church at the end of the street where I grew up, I told Sophie, "I don't miss trying to believe things that didn't make sense to me. But I really miss talking to people, being with people who are really trying to be good, wanting to be good so bad that they gather in pursuit of goodness and belonging. Do you know what I mean?"

On my birthday, Chase took me to dinner at a small café and then dancing at a bar called Wildcat. I'd studied percussion for ten years in school and depended on the beat to sync with a dance partner. I couldn't tell if Chase had a beat in mind at all. We couldn't sync, but this didn't seem like a concern to Chase. When the two of us became awkward, he simply spun out on his own, leaving me alone to step side to side, watching him, waiting to see if he came back to me, which he never did.

"I have a surprise for you," Chase told me when we got home. "Sit on the bed. Close your eyes, and hold out your hands."

While I was in DC, Chase had listened to me on Skype talk about how much I'd been inspired by the drag queens from *RuPaul's Drag Race*. He'd watched the show online, too, and we shared our favorite moments, the catch phrases, our favorite runway walks.

"They're making a whole life out of being all these sides of themselves," I had told him. "It just makes me believe that I can."

"Open your eyes," he told me, and there in my hands were tickets to a showcase of drag queens from the show's first two seasons.

The next night, in an auditorium on the UC Santa Barbara campus, we watched queens I knew from the show dance and twirl on stage.

"Slay!" Chase shouted from our seats in the crowd. I knew their names and put on my most genuine smile. Something that said, "I don't know what to do, but I'm glad you're here."

One queen, Miss Tammie Brown, sang an original song called "Clam Happy" that made Chase put his hand on my shoulder and double over giggling. Another queen, Morgan McMichaels, danced to "So What" dressed as P!nk and got so close to me she tousled my hair, sending a tingle up my spine. At the end of the show, outside on the sidewalk, the queens posed with fans for pictures.

"Thank you for this," I told Chase. I put my hand in his, feeling grounded for the first time in this place with him doing something I knew we both loved. We waited under the sidewalk lights and took a picture with Kylie Sonique Love and Ongina.

After the drag show, we didn't do much together, and toward the middle of my trip, I wasn't sure what we'd do on any given day. He went to his job at the middle school, and I sat on the couch playing his Wii or borrowed his bike and pink helmet to whiz around town.

I biked around town, telling myself to hold tight, to not read into anything while the ocean air swept bare skin, exposed by my short shorts and tank top. I focused on the thrill of exertion, the first real exercise outside of sex with Chase. Biking made me feel hopeful that I really would heal. But I shrank when a stranger passing in a car yelled, "Stupid faggot," from their window.

I spent my days this way—eating cereal in Chase's apartment, then biking to a coffee shop or a bookstore, and then heading to the beach where I'd unpack a picnic lunch I made for myself and watch people biking or walking or lounging in the sand. I passed a man every day who roller skated over the beachside sidewalk, his Walkman headphones more classic than outdated, his smooth moves, hips swaying, legs pumping, and I thought if I ever actually lived here, I wanted to be him, skating in the sun.

Still, when I was alone, I tried hard to tamp down the fear I felt as days went by with so little interaction with Chase.

"I feel distant from you," I confessed one night, sitting on the edge of his bed while he picked work clothes for the next day. "You know, you keep making plans without talking to me. Sometimes I have no idea what you're going to be doing. I feel like I'm just waiting around to talk to you."

He didn't look back at me at first, unbuttoning a shirt just enough to pull it from the hanger. He laid it out on an ironing board, plugged in the iron, and then sat down next to me.

"This time with you is really precious to me," I said.

He waited and then let his finger lightly move against my thigh. "It's precious to me, too."

I sensed more was coming. He kept his eyes on the floor. "I'm sorry," he finally said. "This is kinda different than I thought it would be. I don't always know what to do, so I've just been living my life like I normally would."

I felt my heart cringe, reading into his words that if we stayed together, that if I moved to where he was, he wouldn't want to change much about his life, that we couldn't become something new together, that instead I would simply be grafted onto his life like an acquired branch. I wasn't sure about this, but dread creeped in.

"Maybe we could go on a date or something this week? Maybe a picnic?"

"Okay," he said. "There's actually a restaurant I want to take you to."

So on that Wednesday, I showered before he came home from work. I rubbed lotion on my fading rash. I took an extra dose of Dayquil to fight what I felt sure was a cold living in my tonsils. I ironed my clothes and blow-dried my hair. I had music on, borrowing joy and confidence from pop stars singing about love. I tried to put on clothes that made me feel proud and sexy. I sat on the couch waiting for Chase to come home. When I heard him honk from the driveway, I rushed on my imperfect legs to the car.

On the way to the restaurant, he told me he needed to borrow a tool from his dad's workshop where his father worked as a cabinet builder. Inside the shop, surrounded by wood, I told him it was sexy, thinking of Chase as a carpenter. The sawdust. The sweat. I kissed him, and he kissed me back, pushing me against the shop wall. I thought of splinters.

As we drove, Chase told me that we were in Oprah's neighborhood. Beautiful, wide-spreading trees covered the streets and sidewalks. Large, midcentury homes sat back in massive lawns and gardens

So this is where money went to live, I thought. And here Chase is, a teacher, the son of a carpenter, living here in the crevices between the very rich and the even richer. I felt proud of him for that, for choosing this place and for making it. The flood of images from the past nearly two weeks—the dancing with friends in his living room, the quiet apartment, his opening the windows to let the ocean breeze through, the expensive bicycle, the plane ticket he bought for a man he loves to come near to him. I felt proud of him and sank into love and watched him eat a salad.

After dinner, he took me to a side of a mountain that overlooked the ocean. He parked his car just off the road, and the two of us found a bench to sit on and hold hands. I'd brought a film camera, an old vintage thing I'd bought at the Vernissage, the huge outdoor market in Yerevan. I took pictures of Chase looking at the ocean. I took a picture of my hand holding his.

Back in his apartment, we made love in his room, and I climaxed so hard that I couldn't stop laughing.

That Friday, I finally went to an urgent care clinic. My huge tonsils wouldn't shrink.

Sitting on the tissue paper over the clinic room bed, I told the doctor about every bodily thing that had happened to me. My knee. The atrophy of my leg. The rash that spread and tortured me at night until Chase started using Rafael's detergent. The swelling tonsils. The likelihood of airborne viruses caught on so many cross-the-globe flights.

"You have a respiratory virus," she told me in an accent I couldn't place but that seemed Persian. She looked down at papers on a clipboard. She handwrote notes in a manila folder. I hadn't seen a doctor write a note in years. It all went into computers, I thought. Even at the Peace Corps medical office in Yerevan

"Ah. Okay," I said, accepting the doctor's diagnosis.

I thought of my mom. In any doctor's appointment, she pushed her mind to think of every question she could possibly ask. When Mom knew she had ten minutes with a physician, she wanted that ten minutes packed. She could rattle off questions the average person would only think of when they left the clinic and were sitting in their car in the parking lot.

"Is there any chance of an STD?" I asked.

"What?" she said. She looked up from the clipboard.

"An STD?" I said again.

"Are you sexually active?"

"Yes." I cringed inside, a habitual reaction to the thought of myself having a sex life. I had been so trained to have a single view of my own sexual self—one female sex partner to whom I was married and monogamous for life. I had a

Pavlovian distaste still at the sound of myself admitting I had a sex life that looked any different from the one I was told as a child that a god wanted me to have.

"Do you need me to examine you? Is there anything happening below your waist you are concerned about?"

"No," I said.

She looked at her notes for a second and then looked up. "Have you been tested recently for STDs?"

"Yes." Which was true. I'd gotten tested after Chase left. I wanted to be sure. And I thought that's what good gays did. Test regularly and often, a paraphrase of advice I'd absorbed from podcasts and conversations on TV. I hadn't gotten tested in DC. I thought about the Yerevan troll and nearly asked this doctor to test me then.

Then she said, "This doesn't look like an STD to me."

"Well, that's good news." I tried to joke, "My boyfriend would probably be really upset about that."

She looked up from her clipboard more quickly than before. "You are gay?" she said

Her response triggered a panic, and I watched her more carefully. "Yes," I said.

She stood up from her desk and looked at me with her head cocked to the side. "Have you been tested for HIV?"

And the next few seconds stretched out to hours in my mind. HIV. No. Surely not. I'd had sex with one person. I fooled around with three other men. Until very recently, I'd been the most chaste person I knew. I felt the doctor's question ignite an instant whirl of emotions. I felt fear, panic, shame but also rage, dread, and even laughter at the idea of it.

Why hadn't she thought it could be HIV when she thought I was straight? Why, at the mention of my boyfriend, his mere existence next to my cold, did she feel I needed to be concerned about HIV?

I knew the answer, of course.

I remembered my mom on the night I came out. "What about AIDS?" she'd said. "I lived through the eighties. I saw what it can do."

And here I was, my first doctor's appointment in the US since coming out.

"I don't think I have HIV," I told the doctor. "I've only had sex with one person."

Her eyes hadn't left my face since she asked if I was gay. "Only one person recently. Or one person ever."

"Ever."

She studied me. "There is little I can do." And she sent me home. She told me I had a respiratory illness. "Drink lots of water," she said. "Take Dayquil and Nyquil. Come back if you still have symptoms in a week."

I wouldn't come back. The swelling would be nearly gone by the time I returned home.

At the apartment, Chase said he was relieved when I told him it was just a cold.

And for a while, we settled into a sweet zone. On my last weekend in Santa Barbara, Chase took me to lunch at his parents' house, and though they didn't say more than hello to me, though they never asked me a question about my family or my work in Peace Corps or my plans after Peace Corps, I was happy to be there with Chase. I smiled brightly to both his parents, trying to exude the honor I felt in meeting them. I asked about Chase's school photos on their wall and asked questions about their dog. After lunch was over, Chase and I took the dog on a walk on the beach near their home.

When we came back, his parents left for errands. We made love in his childhood bedroom, and when he wouldn't kiss me afterward, I chalked it up to the fact that we had just gone down on each other.

Chase broke up with me the next day. A Sunday.

Sitting on the edge of his bed, I looked up to where he stood near the doorway, listening as he said, "After the last few weeks, I don't see us living together. I don't think we can make it work." I searched for anything in his face that might make this untrue and saw nothing but conviction.

I stared at his tan comforter and scratched at the fuzz where it was pilling. "I never said I wanted that, to live together," I told him. "I just love you. I just wanted to try, whatever it looks like." I looked up at him again when I said that. I thought of how, in Armenia, Chase would find my eyes from across the room and smile at me with a smile meant only for me, one meant to tell me how happy he was to be looking at me. I thought of the way he looked at me when I told him I loved him. I thought of how he looked at me, tears filling his eyes, when he jumped up and down seeing me walk through the exit doors when I arrived at the LA airport. I knew I would never see him look at me that way again.

Chase was quiet. I kept trying to find his eyes, but he wouldn't look at me. A minute passed in silence.

"Is this it?" I asked.

"Yeah," he said. He lifted his keys from the dresser. "I made plans. Stay in the apartment as long as you want. I won't come back until after six tonight."

And with that, he walked out his bedroom door and out of the apartment.

A few more days passed while I waited on my flight back to Armenia. Chase stayed with a friend and let me have his room, letting me know when he needed to come back for clothes or food or other things. He let me keep using his bicycle, so I tried to simply stay out of the apartment until after dinner.

On my last day in Santa Barbara, I biked to the beach. I touched the ocean with my toes and wrote in my journal.

I wanted to feel the saltwater. The sand. I wanted to bike through the damp air to the now familiar coffee shop that I knew would become unfamiliar to me soon.

I wanted to wear Chase's pink helmet and my short little shorts and be out and gay and happy and free, so I spent the day alone letting all that California freedom wash over my skin.

The next morning, Chase dropped me off at a local bus stop to wait for a bus that would take me back to the airport in LA. From my seat, I looked out the window, but Chase had already driven away. I never saw him again.

37

After so many weeks away and nearly two years of Peace Corps service, walking through Vazgen and Naira's gate felt like coming home.

Even though my mid-May homecoming was well past the Christian holiday, I ran up to Naira and Vazgen's house, hugging them and the girls with bags full of Easter knick-knacks and candies I'd bought on clearance at Target in California.

In the warm sun, with the garden's green grass underfoot and new leaves overhead, I threw an Easter party for Vazgen, Naira, and the girls in the way my parents had done for my siblings and me growing up. I packed pastel-colored baskets with green shredded paper and piled on chocolates and candies. I topped two baskets with stuffed rabbits for the girls. In Naira's I put a hand mixer. In Vazgen's, a fancy screwdriver with a variety of attachments. I hid eggs around the garden, at the edge of potato rows, at the base of cherry trees, resting on the cellar door knob. I passed out bunny ear headbands to everyone, even Vazgen, who smirked in the selfie I tried to take of us all under the arbor of grape vines. After the egg hunt, I made chocolate chip cookies with Naira in her kitchen. Afterward she, Vazgen, and I sat down with cookies and coffee while Nazeli and Ani bounced down the garden path on bright green hopper balls I'd brought them, their rabbit ears nearly wagging off their heads with every bound.

When Vazgen asked me how my trip to California was, I said simply, *"It was not what I thought it would be."*

I hadn't told them about Chase or about falling in love in December. So, I didn't need to tell them about Santa Barbara. I didn't tell them that I'd cried on both long-haul flights across the planet. I didn't tell them how I had to keep telling myself that I had to try with Chase, even though, ultimately, we failed to stay in love.

"I'm happy to be in my home in Stepanavan," I told Vazgen and Naira.

"Of course," Naira said. "Brent jan, du hay es." *You are Armenian*, she told me. Vazgen smiled, always so much quieter than his wife.

I sipped coffee while looking with pride at my friends. And then a thought caught my breath. I turned that thought into words and said, *"And it feels like the end of my time in Stepanavan will come too quickly."*

Naira pursed her lips. "Akhbers, *don't say it. You have the whole summer."*

I didn't. We all knew it.

I had considered for months, actually, staying in Armenia. Peace Corps offered a year extension. And I knew other volunteers who stayed after service and found jobs at the US embassy or in nonprofits. I knew the language now. And much more importantly, I'd found a sense of belonging. In Vazgen and Naira's cottage. In their kitchen. At their table at every celebration. I found belonging in the World Vision office and with the people we worked with in surrounding villages. Even in Yerevan where I knew I could dance, could find queer friends, could meet new people to come out to.

But I'd decided not to extend my service because I knew also that my sense of belonging could never be complete. Liana had, as a protective friend, warned me about coming out in Stepanavan. In Texas I'd already lived a life in which I could never be completely myself, where I had to walk around with a secret and tell no one. I'd left that life behind on the night I came out to my parents. And now I knew that even though part of me longed to stay in Armenia, I'd have to face the pain of leaving it, knowing I'd never come back, never get the life back I was living right now. I needed to leave, to go back to the US, to be fully and more safely myself.

So, no, I didn't have the whole summer. I would be leaving in July. Naira, Vazgen and I put my leaving out of our minds, sipped coffee, and watched the girls bounce after the chickens in the yard.

As my last days in Armenia went on, I still felt under the weather, my body weak which I chalked up to travel and the leg which still seemed a few sizes too thin. Still, I hardly wore the leg brace at all unless I went hiking up the field behind Stepanavan. On the first hike after my return, I sat among millions of daisies. I looked out over the tops of buildings in Stepanavan and wandered the streets between them, using memory and imagination.

Before I walked back to town, I took a picture of my hand touching the ground.

I'll put this photo up, I thought. *I'll frame it and look at it and remind myself I was there.*

Chase emailed me one more time. In his message, he told me he had chlamydia, that I might want to get tested. I went for a weekend to Yerevan, and when my test at the

Peace Corps doctor's office came back positive, I called Zoe to curse everything.

"I never had anything going on below the belt. I never thought chlamydia had been in my swollen tonsils the whole time. That fucking troll," I grumbled to Zoe into my Nokia, my memory of the man in the white suit burning in my mind.

Dr. Torosyan, the Peace Corps doctor, told me my tonsils had carried the disease across the ocean to my ex-boyfriend's bedroom.

"And that damn doctor in Santa Barbara. I told her I was sexually active. I should have just asked her to test me then. I didn't know, but shouldn't she have?"

"It's a fucked-up world, sometimes," Zoe told me. I kept on then about guilt and how I was trying to keep it at bay, how maybe someday I would process my regrets, but that right now, I just wanted to be here in Armenia and enjoy it. We both talked about how much we wanted to date when we got home.

Zoe called me again when she got her email about her Close of Service dates. When she told me we would be leaving on the same day, we looked up flights, finding that we could fly all the way from Yerevan to Boston together, touching US soil hand-in-hand before she left from there to Maine and me to Texas. I nearly jumped from my desk at the World Vision office and yelled with joy into the foyer. I stopped myself, though maybe I could have gotten away with it since Liana and Yeraz's desks were still empty.

When Seda heard I was back in Armenia, she came from Privolnoye, and together, we planned my last project in Armenia, an environmentally-themed day camp at Seda's youth center.

To round out our project team, we invited Kristine, who I hadn't seen since the night that triggered my medical evacuation, the night when my leg busted in her apartment. Kristine and I stayed with Seda and her parents again. Each day I stood in front of some thirty kids talking to them about garbage and trees and ecosystems and the impact of being alive in a world of plastic bags, industrial farming, and global shipping. We talked about these ideas in the most bite-sized way we could. We talked about how, even though things can feel so incredibly complicated, you just keep doing the next right thing.

"*That's how you make change,*" I told them.

In planning for this camp, I thought about my own childhood summers in my grandmother's craft room, her quilting or embroidering something, me on the floor exploring every kind of craft. My own needlework would eventually turn into bookbinding in college, and I led these thirty or so Armenian kids through the craft of binding a book with needle and thread. We then used their books as journals, taking breaks to write down their thoughts about trash and the treasures of nature. They shared their writing and their thoughts with each other, talking about the places in Privolnoye where the trees grew tallest or the roadsides filled flush with flowers in spring.

When we came together as a group, one young girl shared her love of a hilltop at the edge of the village where you could climb and watch the sunset. Seda suggested we all climb to the spot that evening.

There, on dirt and gravel, fingering almost hair-thin strands of grass, I sat next to Kristine, both of us painted in the orange and pinks of sunset light. I said to her, "This I will miss. This nearly breaks my heart."

Overcome with a pain I was grateful for, I went on, "This feels special to me, you know, because it's exceptional. It's different. I'll probably never sit here again. And I wouldn't be here except that these kids know... they know about the amazing parts of their lives... like their whole, everyday lives lived out right here, you know, and they share them with us.

"And then we get celebrate that together."

Kristine smiled and nodded before turning to a group of young boys rolling themselves like logs down the slope.

While we watched the kids play after our camp, I told Kristine that this was the job I signed up for. I got to do this for two years—ask and ask and ask about what people love about their lives and what they don't, and to offer a direction for their gaze and tools to build. And celebrate everything about this place and this time together. To love what they love. And what they don't love, to help find a way to move around it or even change it.

And then, feeling the pain of my break with Chase leave me, feeling the fear of losing my family calm to small tremor, I said with clarity, "This has been the greatest honor of my life. Just to be here."

I watched the youngest child at our camp take a stand on a rock ahead of us, her body blocking the sun creating the most beautiful silhouette, beams of light shooting from the sides of her and through her curly hair.

In the last month, I tried to do everything I loved about living in Armenia. I stayed in Naira's kitchen as long as she would let me. I played as many games of nardi with Vazgen as I could. I played with Ani and Nazeli in the garden, and when I couldn't do any of those things, I lay under the garden fruit trees, reading, or just staring through branches to blue sky. In Yerevan, I danced with Imogen and Claire and Margaux and Zoe. I restaurant-hopped to every favorite spot with them and sat around talking at packed tables at Calumet until the bar closed. I hitchhiked with Margaux to Tatev and then to Kapan, where we watched movies together, did puzzles, and learned the choreography to Lady Gaga's new video for "Judas."

On another weekend, Zoe even initiated a final night in Yerevan to hang out with Ana, who brought Vartan. We walked the city together, listening to Ana's plans to pursue violin work in Europe. Vartan kept his distance but was kind. We ended the night at a new alternative bar called DIY, where the bartender let Ana make drinks. I joined her, chopping citrus and shaking a cocktail mixer any time she asked. As that night went on, Vartan wandered to the back of DIY, where I noticed him getting close to and finally kissing an Armenian woman I didn't recognize.

Ana saw me watch him while she sliced a lemon. "You are egoist," she said.

"Egoist?" I said, sour vapor from the fruit lifting to my nose. Ana's accent made words hard to hear sometimes, but this time, I wasn't sure I heard the right word at all.

"Yes," she said. "Egoist. Vartan doesn't have things easy. He likes you then, but then you didn't give him time. He is Iranian. He is Armenian. You don't know. Egoist."

I accepted her word. I'd keep the image of him in my mind, silhouetted by the back bar light, the neon spray paint on black walls framing Vartan and the woman he kissed. I thought then that I missed something, like a train I could have boarded but didn't. And years from now, I would worry for him, wondering if he stayed in Armenia or went home to Iran or found a way somewhere else to be free.

I passed more days in Stepanavan, walking with World Vision friends through the mountains collecting wild thyme, thistle, and mint, making jingalov hats with Karine and her parents, savoring the thin bread filled with wild leaves. I counted days.

On my last day at the World Vision office, I made tacos for my friends.

In my final toast to them, I choked back tears, lifting a shot glass of vodka into the air. I looked at their faces, some with tears, all with smiles, knowing I'd likely never stand before them like this again.

"*Barekamutsyan hamar*," I said and drank. *To friendship.*

Before my final walk home, I said goodbye to the TDFs, to Karine, Aram, and Hermine. And Ayda held a tissue to her eyes as she waved goodbye from the World Vision door. I stopped in the haraparak by the statue of Stepan to cry, trying to stifle my heaving sobs, my face in my palms.

I walked on, stopping to hug the man at my vegetable stand who had greeted me on nearly every walk home from the office. Next, I hugged the woman at the grocery store who sold me M&Ms and Coca-Cola for two years. She wouldn't let me pay for the final bag of M&Ms she put in my hands.

At the bakery, one of the bakers put down her lavash dough to come put an arm around me while I sat and tearfully watched them stretch the lavash dough over their pillows, slapping them on the surface of the hot brick oven.

I didn't know how to say in Armenian, "Oh, I'm such a sappy person at times like these." So, instead, I told them, "*I have to leave, or I will become like a lake on the floor.*" They each came to hug me before gifting me an extra bag of lavash and then ushering me out the door.

I needed the lavash for Ani's party. On my last night in Stepanavan, Naira planned a party for Ani's fifth birthday. When I arrived, Naira and her mother were making salads in the kitchen. I threw my bags into my cottage and joined Vazgen and Naira's father where Vazgen skewered lamb and chicken before laying them over the fire pit. I stood there listening to the two of them talk, zoning out as the speed of their chatter became too much effort to follow with an aching in my chest that was starting to grow.

Instead, I watched them, two men brought together by love, standing together to make khorovats, a meal they'd been eating and making their whole lives for nearly every celebration. I listened to them laugh, Vazgen's familiar escalating chuckles bouncing into the air. The long point at each end of Naira's father's mustache lifted with his wide smile.

I listened to the Nazeli and Ani play in the softening sunlight, their squeals of glee moving through the small orchard of trees by my cottage. The two of them barely stopped to look up when Vazgen scolded them for running too close to the fire.

When Vazgen deemed the khorovats ready, we joined Naira and her mother to eat on the porch, the family's laundry behind us waving in the light breeze.

"*Are you going back to Texas?*" Naira's father asked me in between bites of lamb.

"*At first,*" I told him. "*I'm not sure where I will live after I visit home. I will apply to jobs, and I will probably move to wherever the job is.*" Then I followed with a phrase that I'd heard nearly every Armenian friend say at some point. "Astvats giti." *God knows.*

Everyone nodded. Naira turned to her plate, facing it, focusing on each bite. She seemed unwilling to participate in the conversation.

"Will you live with family?" Naira's father continued.

"At least for a little while," I said.

I'd sent my parents my return flight information, and they told me they'd be there in Austin with all my siblings to pick me up. My mom had been calling and sending texts multiple times a day about how excited she was. She told me to keep my head up, to know that any pain I felt in leaving the home I'd made in Armenia was just a sign of how wonderful and rich my life had been.

She'd cried on the phone, talking about Naira and Vazgen and the girls. She said that in her way she would miss them, too, miss having them in her life through their connection to me.

I loved how much she loved them. I felt loved by how much she tried to comfort me as I had gone through weeks and weeks of saying goodbye.

And I hated how much this journey home felt like something altogether new. Mom called me often as my service came to an end. But she never asked about what happened with Chase. She never asked me how I felt about coming home gay. Never mind that my dad didn't call at all. No one from home who knew about my being gay asked me any questions.

I didn't need them to now, but I wished that they would. I knew now I could live somewhere else. I could make a beautiful life with adventure and love and hope, and I could experience pain that I could care for on my own. My leg could malfunction, and my heart could break, and I could still get up and go on and keep building a life I loved.

After everyone ate, Naira, her mother, and the girls took dishes to the kitchen to wash. Vazgen went down the porch steps to clean the ash and coals from the fire pit. And Naira's father came to where I sat on the porch and sat down next to me, smiling beneath his grey mustache. He patted my knee with his large, rough hand.

"Naira is being quiet because she will miss you," he said. And his eyes caught the porch light and sparkled with tears that welled but didn't quite fall.

And to that, I could barely respond. *"I know,"* I said.

"We will all miss you," he said.

It moved me then, a thought I hadn't had yet. That I was important enough to them that they'd all talked together about my leaving. And that Naira's father wanted to say this to me now.

"Yes," I said quietly, unable to speak a full sentence in Armenian and still keep myself together. *"Me..."* I said. "Nuiny." *The same.*

Later, alone in my cottage, as I packed my final things into my bags, I wished to go back to their house but knew I couldn't. I thought about how I'd wanted to stay, how I didn't want to leave them or my friends in Armenia or the life I'd built here.

But I wanted to be out now, to be free, or at least free enough, to find love and to not just make new friends but to be fully known by them. I wanted a family—a husband who might throw birthday parties with me for our own kids. Someday, maybe.

I looked out my cottage windows watching the silhouettes of the girls in their window, jumping on their beds, knowing they'd all be there in that window long after I left.

In the morning, with my bags in Artavan's World Vision Lada outside the gate, I stood at the steps of the porch, crying, looking at Naira and Vazgen, my hand on my heart.

"*Saying goodbye is terrible,*" I said to them. They didn't move. Vazgen held Naira. Nazeli and Ani hugged their mother's legs. I huffed at the air, caught my breath, and said, "*I will miss all of you so much. I think you will not know how much. I will miss you the way I miss my family. I will miss seeing you every day. And I will wish to come back. I love you. I love you very much.*"

And for the rest of my life, I will remember them there on the stairs looking at me, all of us in tears over this love we had hoped for but had never expected to grow, knowing we'd planted the seeds and watched the seasons pass and, like a miracle, seen all of it come and go like raspberries in the summer.

EPILOGUE

I heard the click-thud of the door to the gas cap open as my mother turned to put the gas station's nozzle into her RAV4. The sounds were muffled inside the car where I sat and watched my mother fill her SUV with gas.

I could have gotten out to fill the gas myself and felt some pull toward the Southern version of chivalry I grew up in. But I didn't. Because she was a grown woman who'd driven herself across Texas alone, who had filled up her own gas for decades, who had driven the car the last few hours and needed a break from me and from the air we were breathing together in the small SUV's cab.

"I know you just got home," she told me the day before we left. "But I've been putting off going out there. And your Grammi would love to see you. It would mean the world to her. Really, Brent. She would love it."

My mother's parents, my grandparents, lived on the edge of Louisiana in a little blip of a town called Merryville.

"You don't have to convince me," I told her. "I have no job. Nowhere to be. I don't even remember the last time I was there. Gosh... maybe a summer in college?"

And so, though I'd just arrived on Wednesday from Armenia, on Friday we packed.

We drove for a while, and I ate snacks and listened as my mom told me the changes she'd made since I left. She and Dad kept their early morning workout routine, which they'd been doing for nearly two years now. They watched their diet. She told me about new recipes they loved and how they never knew they could enjoy food this way.

When we exhausted that topic, she updated me on everything she could remember from the last two years of *The Young and the Restless*.

At some point during the drive, we both became silent except for my munching on snacks from the gas station. She'd changed beyond her diet and how much she worked out now. In Armenia, her approach to me had an edge, a sharpness. Since I'd come home, I noticed something that seemed softer. More of a dull knife maybe.

"Okay, Mom, do you want to talk about it?" I asked between Cheetos Puffs. We hadn't said a word about my being gay since I got home. Not about any of it. Not my trip to California. Not Chase. Not Vartan or Ana. Not Zoe or John.

"I don't think so," she said. "I mean, we can if you want to."

"I don't really," I said.

"Okay." She kept both hands on the wheel.

With hours ahead of us, we talked instead about everyone else in the family.

Her sisters weren't talking to her again.

My dad's youngest brother and Aunt Susan were busy with my cousins and their show pigs.

"And Uncle Robert?"

"Nope. No one has heard from him."

My brother had a new teaching job and started missionary school. He wasn't talking much to my oldest sister and disapproved of her moving in with her boyfriend, something my sister had told me when I called her before my surgery in DC.

And then Macey, my youngest sister.

"Mom, she's grown," I said of her. "I feel like I missed it."

"Yeah. You kinda did."

When the conversation trailed off into silence, I stared out the window, sipping occasionally on a Dr. Pepper that became progressively more tepid and flat. I replayed words in my head, my mom said the night I came out, "If you choose this lifestyle, we won't let you be around Macey." I replayed myself telling Zoe in her host family's house in Teghenik. "I don't know what I would do. I couldn't stand it if Macey thought I left her behind to go be gay."

And I thought about Macey, who was fourteen now, and still no one told her.

My mom asked about Naira and Vazgen.

"We had a party before I left," I said. "Not particularly for me. It was for Ani's birthday. But it felt so special to me."

"I bet you miss them," she said softly.

"I do." I turned to watch houses pass by in my window.

"I think about them most days," Mom told me. "Partly because I thought of you every day, and then I'd think about being there with you. I'd wonder what you were doing and think about you in the garden playing with the girls or you and Vazgen playing that game on the porch. And then I'd think about all of us having coffee in the kitchen. They made me feel so special."

"They loved you."

"I felt that. And I especially felt that they treated me that way because they loved you."

I said nothing to this but looked to her and saw her crying.

"Oh, Mama," I said and reached out. Mom removed her hand from the steering wheel and held mine.

Pulling up to my grandparents' house felt like a step into memory. The crepe myrtles tall as the house, bending over the gravel driveway that led to the carport. The carport where the cool cement under my bare feet always reminded me of my much younger self, who would run outside to see my parents come back up the driveway from a trip to town for treats or sandwich fixings.

Unlike most of my childhood visits, there were no aunts and uncles and cousins already playing in the yard. I looked out over the yard that had seemed endless to a child hunting for Easter eggs around every bush and bird bath, in the birdhouse and the creek that ran through the side yard.

With the screen door propped open by her shoulder, Mom knocked and then opened the back door softly yelling, "Hello!" in a greeting I knew as an announcement of entry and a request to enter in one word.

Paw Paw's armchair creaked upright, and as he turned to get up, he shouted a familiar, "Well, hi, kiddo!"

I dropped some of our bags inside and went to the car for the rest. When I came back in Paw Paw told my mom, "She's in there taking a nap. It's been an hour or so, so I bet she'll be up soon."

"All right, Dad," my mom said.

I went to the bathroom and then found a seat in the rocking chair next to Paw Paw's recliner.

He turned to me and said, "What d'you know, Sport?"

"Not much," I said back. And he asked if I was happy to be home.

"For the most part. I miss the people I lived with, my friends, and my Armenian family." I'd repeat this to everyone who asked for weeks. I would tell almost none of them, including my grandparents, about being gay, about navigating life at home with parents who seemed like they might never be ready to talk seriously about how they intended to live life with their gay son.

When Grammi woke up, she called for my grandfather, but my mom asked to go help her from bed. Mom walked with her from the bed to the bathroom, waited outside, and then helped her walk from the bathroom to the couch.

After Grammi sat down, I walked to her and joined her on the couch, which was sunk in now from years of her sleeping on it.

"Brent." She said my name with bright eyes, looking up to me in a way that caught the overhead light. "Oh, Brent. They didn't tell me you were coming."

I hugged her thin frame and pulled her into me. "I'm here," I told her.

"How long have you been here?"

"A couple of hours," I said.

"You shouldn't have let me sleep so long, Ron," she said to my grandfather.

"You needed to sleep, Wanda." He lit a cigarette.

Grammi turned back to me. "How long are you staying?"

"A couple of days," I said.

She paused, considered, and then leaned in for another hug.

"You need to put your oxygen on," Paw Paw said. He held out the thin tube connected to a rolling tank of oxygen. I reached for the tube with outstretched fingers and then passed it from Paw Paw to Grammi, who pulled the cannula up to her nose and draped the clear tube behind her ears.

She coughed into a handkerchief she held in one hand and squeezed my hand with the other. I smiled at her and then felt my bare toe hit the edge of singed floor. Mom had already told me that Grammi had caught the oxygen tube on fire with her cigarette and burned a looping track into the thin carpet.

Silently, I said to myself, *Thank god the flame didn't make it to the oxygen tank.*

I thought of us all exploding.

My grandmother soon fell asleep again on the couch. While my grandfather watched more TV, my mom and I wandered around and looked at my grandmother's tchotchkes and pictures. Displayed on shelves were small statues, ornate boxes, and bowls she'd picked up when, in her fifties, she finally decided to travel on her own for the first time. We walked to the back of the living room, which my grandmother had filled with framed pictures of her children, her grandchildren, and her great grandchildren.

I asked my mom to tell me the names of people I didn't recognize. After she did, I looked at my own school photo, one from fifth grade, and said, "I'm just so touched that she has all these up."

"Yeah," my mom said, her voice going quiet.

Then Mom looked down, her eyes wet. She whispered, "This chest here…" And she pointed to the chest we stood in front of, the lid of which was covered in framed photos and more tchotchkes. "I looked in here on my last visit. It used to have all our childhood photos. Mom threw them out. All our childhood photos. All of them."

Stunned, I watched her trace her finger around the edge of it, leaving a line in dust, tears pooling in her eyes.

The next morning, my mother took me to the track at Merryville High School. The June sun hadn't yet crested over the tall pine trees, but the swampy heat had already glued our T-shirts to our bodies.

Mom set a fast-walking speed on the cracking black rubber track, stepping over the grass that grew in the openings.

"It's not easy to be here sometimes," she said. I found myself breathing heavily and felt a wave of admiration that she had gotten herself in such good shape that she could outpace me.

"What do you mean?" I asked.

"I just feel like I should come here more. Thank you for coming. It's not always easy to visit. I'm glad you're here."

I asked more questions, mostly to let her know I was listening and interested until she said, "I intentionally forget things. You know that."

"No," I said, confused. "I don't. What do you forget?"

"The hard stuff," she said, the words coming out in a huff. "It's not even like I store it away. I just don't have it in my mind anymore."

I hadn't heard her talk about anything that hard. She'd told me about how much work she'd done as a kid in her house. I'd heard some of this before, how as a young child she'd worked hard, cleaning everything in the house so that when her parents came home from work, they'd be happy.

"Do you remember any of the other hard stuff?"

And out it came like rain from a thunderstorm. Mom suddenly told stories I'd never heard, stories I knew came from somewhere deep.

She told stories about her parents and their fights and the episodes of childhood fear and noises of things shattering that rang through the house. She told me of the pain she tried to forget. She told me of things that wounded her, that had drawn her to the god she'd grown up with, one that she was told could save you from your pain and the harm of generations.

Lap after lap she told me stories, and in that moment, I knew she didn't yet have room for mine. She'd focused so hard on following the rules of the community she'd grown up in because they were supposed to keep her free of fear and lead her into a worthy life.

When those same rules had terrified me so badly, and after years of prayer and zealous Christian living hadn't changed a thing about being gay, I left those rules behind. But on the night I came out, my mom hadn't yet considered that perhaps her son would be fine. Perhaps he would even be better than before. No, on that night she still believed what everyone her whole life had told her—that God would send me to hell.

I was born into a world that has been, for the most part, awful to queer people. And on that day, walking circles around that broken high school track with my mom, I realized she was born into that world, too. She had learned its rules from her parents and from preachers and churches and the communities where she grew up and where she lived now.

I wished then that she could love me exactly the way I needed to be loved. She couldn't. Maybe one day she would. But she'd been born into the same world I had. It would take many more trips around the sun before she could see the world, me, and maybe even herself in a new way.

~ ~ ~

We spent my last night in Merryville with my grandmother, telling stories when she was awake. When her pain meds put her to sleep, we played cribbage while Paw Paw stayed in his chair watching war documentaries.

As the night grew darker, my mom took a shower, and when she looked for a blow dryer, she found a set of pink hot rollers she remembered my Great Granny Ella using when my mom would visit her as a child. I'd known my great granny before she died and knew my mom had a special connection with her.

My mom plugged the hot rollers in, and when, after all those decades, they still warmed, Mom wrapped her own hair in them. Adorned in pink rollers, my mom looked in the mirror for a connection to the grandmother she knew, her own grandmother who always made time to talk with her, to look into her eyes and listen and love her with her attention. I wondered if my mom saw in her own face the face of her mother, of her grandmothers, and perhaps even bits of every generation of grandparent she'd never known.

She'd know the next generation, though. True, it would be years before Mom apologized and before we could talk about everything that happened. But we did, and she and my father danced at my wedding with my queer friends and ally friends. They took pictures with them, cutting up and hugging and posing together in our wedding photobooth. And after everyone left, my mom and Zoe stayed behind, washing the wedding dishes together in our tiny kitchen after my husband and I took off for a hotel downtown.

Years later still, my husband would lift our daughter, on the night she was born, into my mother's arms. I'd kneel beside Mom, wrap my arm around her, and watch my mother admire the face of the newest part of our family.

After Grammi died, when a small urn of her ashes rested in the cabinet of the same dining room where I came out to my parents, my mom brought a picture of Grammi to me.

There Grammi sat at her kitchen table in Merryville studying a piece of paper she held up before her.

"This was when she was working on our family tree," my mom said. And in the picture, spread out on the table, I saw papers and photo albums, Grammi surrounded by clues, the typed and handwritten names of our ancestors like drops of water making a wave that delivered my grandmother and my mother, and me, all of us, to this shore, to this moment where we could all live under the sun.

ACKNOWLEDGMENTS

If you have read this far, I'd like to thank you first. Sharing my story with you is a dream. Now, go read another queer person's story as soon as you can! There are so many beautiful ones, and bearing witness to queer lives is more powerful than you can imagine.

To my Armenian friends, some of whom I'm so honored have read this book, and many of whom I know never will, you cannot know how much living with you in Teghenik, Stepanavan, and Yerevan changed my life. I am immeasurably grateful to you.

To my mom—Our love has grown bigger and stronger while writing this book. We've come so far together, and I know that looking back at our past was deeply painful. And still, as you have done since your kindergarten son said he wanted to be a writer, you cheered for me, even when my first book put our hardest days on the page. We belong together, damn the torpedoes.

To both my parents—When a world of people told us we shouldn't still be together, we chose love. I love you.

To my husband, Charlie, who never complained, not one single time, through four years of late nights and crying nights and nights when I came up enraged at pages that wouldn't come together—still never a word other than, "I believe in you, honey." I love you. I love you. I love you.

To my kids, thank you in advance because I know one day you'll ask me why I wrote this and why I gave up so much to do it. And I know you'll let me tell you.

To my sisters who have never wavered. I love you forever.

To the many women who have made this world safer for me, many of whom are my very best friends. I wouldn't have been able to come out and live proudly without you.

To my chosen family who have cheered on this opus for all the years while I lived it and then wrote it. I wouldn't have survived to write this without you.

To Kristina McNulty. Together, we survived the early parent years, which were also the pandemic years, which were also the years when I wrote this book. I would be buried in tears and snow without you.

To Nicole Helget whose brilliance and belief in my work saved this book twice.

To the teachers who nurtured my work long before I did, including Cherie Broadway, Julie Griggs, Lori McLaughlin, Sandra Nix, Scott Dudley, Jan Doke, Peggy Hughes, Caron Gentry, Steven Moore and so many others, including you, Mom.

To my early readers whose generous attention to my text breathed new life into it including Al Haley, JP DerBoghossian, Liana Sargsyan, Christine Hurley, Lily Diamond, Mich Nicole, and Camari Carter.

To my editors Asa Lowenstein and Anne Kelley and my entire publishing team, especially Susan Bies.

And to the early supporters of this book. You rolled out the red carpet for *Leap*. In addition to those listed above, thank you to everyone who made this book possible including

Laura Dunn, Laura Murphy, Macey DeZee, Tanner DeZee, Nancy Crowe, Hayley Brandt, Erikson Young, Kyle Lagunas, Brittney Costello, Heidi Dickson, Molly McNeil, Sarah Schoolcraft, Beckett Love, Kimberly Parker-Lewis, Aisha Formanski, Lisa Edwards, Susanne Lubanga, Jehvana Cook, John Clinton, Jessica Phinney, Cherie Peterson, Amy Kothe, Carla Burger, Hannah Grassie, Kristin Wood, Alissa Jordan, Carly Lunden, Barbara Palmer, Jill Pridemore, Rachel Kurtz, Tara Osterberg, Lara Morgan, Maddie McElhenny, Paula Doroff, Chad Zellner, Corinne Todd, Emily White, Nicole Moore-Kriel, Raneve West-Singh, Kathryn Sisa, Lauren Beattie, Jennifer Motz, Kisha Knight Phillips, Claire Townsend, Ronald Hand, Robin Peeples, Mary Helen Conroy, Sue Groveunder, Eric Johnson, Rachel Subasic, Margaux Granat, Katie Haag, Mary Murphey, Talene Ghazarian, Amelia Bierschbach, Ashley Klein, Janet Moore, Jean Magarian, Zoe Armstrong, Jessica Arnold, Natalie Hansen, Grace McSoley, Jill Laing, Maria Taylor, Sarah Rake, Ritu Bhatt, Nancy Miller, Emily Hobbs, Katherine Ware, Katie Maxwell, Allison Broeren, Eric Koester, Damon Kalar, Quyen Tang, Susan Prentice, Thang Holt, Philip Park, Maia Tarrell, Ruth Rosengren, Jessica Strobel, Aundrea Phillips, Vanessa Lucius, Kari Martin, Katlyn Abbott, Jane Marie Ford, Leanna Young, Angela & Ashley Harness-Jimenez, Jasna Burza, Amanda Woodall, Alix McAlpine, Tanna Thomas, Lisa Quick, Sarah Callinan, Beth O'Neil, Megan Atkinson, Stela Center, Danielle Douglas, Jenny Robinson, Cindy Blackstock, Susan Hines, Holly Hines, Mason Hines, Taleen Voskuni, Rachel Sklar, Angela Eifert, Ashli Tinnin-Trinh, Anna Love, Joanna Douglas, Emily Fishman, Romik Danial, Rita Mehta, Justin Vance, Sam Hines, Travis Fraser, Cara Skowronski, Brandon

Kinder, Leslie Plesser, Marian, Megan and Evie Brackney-Helms, Ashley Sherwood, cindal heart, Claire Garmirian, Elise Estrada, Anthony Mielke, Jennifer Reed, Betty Jäger, Anita Smithson, Zee Warholm-Wohlenhaus, Cris Gomes, Laura Brown, Beverly DeBolt, Danelle Wassink, Caroline Munro, Katrina Kubeczko, Erin Collins, Matthew Ruten, Valerie Garcia, Mike Anderson, Jason Bryan, Carrie Rietti, Liz Allen, Sheila Frankfurt, Christine Wells, Kathryn Defilippo, Mark Leech, Debbie Riggs, Vanessa Rankin, Milo Cumaranatunge, Brian Zaleski, Penny Sartin, Joshua Perrizo, Julie Peterson, Sharon Keld, Katy Davies, Sarah Schultheis, Heath and Joey Bryant-Huppert, Maya Akpowowon, Hilary Lund, Lauren Rigby, Haley Sutherland, Amanda Wilson, Kristine Trautmane, Janine Morgan, Kady Hexum, Carla Burger, Matt Worthington, Meghan Clair, Yi Shun Lai, Sunny Han, Fiona McAlpine, Jordan Mesenbourg, Kate Madden-Raja, Donnis Smith, Katy Perry, Sarah Perron, David McAlpine, Cassie Scott, and Catherine Lleras.

AUTHOR BIO

Brent Love is an American memoirist and returned Peace Corps volunteer. During his work as roving correspondent for the American Refugee Committee, Love covered stories across the Horn of Africa, the Middle East, and Southeast Asia. Love studied political science and international relations at Abilene Christian University and began his career in refugee resettlement in West Texas. He is the host of the surrogacy podcast *Hope Works*. After living and working abroad for most of his adult life, Love settled down to raise two gorgeous kids with his gorgeous husband. When he isn't playing outside with his family, you'll probably find Love cooking, cleaning, or, if he's lucky, cuddled up with a book and his dog, Cricket.